Praise For

"*Poetic Song Verse* by Mike Mattison and Ernest Suarez exposes and critiques how and why time runs the bloodline of American music—blues, folk, rock 'n' roll, R&B, pop, funk, rap, and hip-hop—as it travels the world. And race and racism are not sidestepped in this heartfelt query. The authors not only know and show, but also feel the music; they cinch up all connections, detailing the cross-pollination, as well as venture behind the scenes existentially. *Poetic Song Verse* reveals the artist reckoning with music in language, whether seeking atonement or praise."
—Yusef Komunyakaa, Pulitzer Prize–winning poet

"*Poetic Song Verse* secures the blues and rock 'n' roll lyrics' signature place in history as a *literary* genre. Mattison and Suarez unravel the threads linking Orpheus, Rimbaud, Walt Whitman, Emily Dickinson, Bessie Smith, Robert Johnson, Charlie Parker, Bob Dylan, Mick Jagger, John Lennon, Jimi Hendrix, Nina Simone, Bruce Springsteen, Joe Strummer, Lucinda Williams, Grandmaster Flash, and many other artists. During the twentieth century the United States' oral history was sung, not spoken; it was written in code and camouflaged by melody and rebellious rhythms that influenced artists around the world. This book translates the people's story as told by artists. Symbolism in work songs of the enslaved, ties between Bebop and Beatnik jive, between '50s' rock 'n' roll and segregation, between poetry and psychedelic imagery, and between soul, street funk, and rap battles are peeled back and situated in their cultural contexts. The quest for freedom is never-ending—and artists' efforts to break down barriers and influence the world has never stopped adapting and evolving."
—Luther Dickinson, the North Mississippi Allstars

"A deep delve into the influence of blues on poetry and songwriters, *Poetic Song Verse* makes a meaningful contribution to both music and poetry. Mike Mattison and Ernest Suarez explain the roots of poetic song verse and connect the past and future, outlining how poets and songwriters have influenced each other over the years. A must-read."
—Charlotte Pence, editor of *The Poetics of American Song Lyrics*

Poetic Song Verse

POETIC SONG VERSE

BLUES-BASED POPULAR MUSIC AND POETRY

MIKE MATTISON AND ERNEST SUAREZ

University Press of Mississippi / Jackson

The University Press of Mississippi is the scholarly publishing agency of
the Mississippi Institutions of Higher Learning: Alcorn State University,
Delta State University, Jackson State University, Mississippi State University,
Mississippi University for Women, Mississippi Valley State University,
University of Mississippi, and University of Southern Mississippi.

www.upress.state.ms.us

The University Press of Mississippi is a member
of the Association of University Presses.

Any discriminatory or derogatory language or hate speech regarding race,
ethnicity, religion, sex, gender, class, national origin, age, or disability that
have been retained or appear in elided form is in no way an endorsement
of the use of such language outside a scholarly context.

Copyright © 2021 by University Press of Mississippi
All rights reserved

First printing 2021
∞

Library of Congress Cataloging-in-Publication Data

Names: Mattison, Mike, author. | Suarez, Ernest, author.
Title: Poetic song verse: blues-based popular music and poetry / Mike
    Mattison and Ernest Suarez.
Description: Jackson: University Press of Mississippi, 2021. | Includes
    bibliographical references and index.
Identifiers: LCCN 2021026156 (print) | LCCN 2021026157 (ebook) | ISBN
    978-1-4968-3727-1 (hardback) | ISBN 978-1-4968-3728-8 (trade paperback) | ISBN
    978-1-4968-3729-5 (epub) | ISBN 978-1-4968-3730-1 (epub) | ISBN 978-1-4968-3731-8
    (pdf) | ISBN 978-1-4968-3732-5 (pdf)
Subjects: LCSH: Popular music—History and criticism. |
    Songs—Texts—History and criticism. | Blues (Music)—History and
    criticism. | Music and literature.
Classification: LCC ML3470 .M364 2021 (print) | LCC ML3470 (ebook) | DDC
    781.64—dc23
LC record available at https://lccn.loc.gov/2021026156
LC ebook record available at https://lccn.loc.gov/2021026157

British Library Cataloging-in-Publication Data available

published with a grant
Figure Foundation
sanging the blues

To Alison and Maggie, with love.
Despite my untold miles of roaming,
you always kept the home fires lit.
—Mike Mattison

For Diana, who is my everything
—Ernest Suarez

Elvis and Eliot were driving by the sea,
Elvis said, "Eliot, ain't nothing on TV."
Eliot said, "Elvis, you ain't alone.
Let's go to Rat's Alley,
Hear the Dead and the Stones."

—**AmeriCamera,** *Highminded,* vol. 1

Contents

Acknowledgments xv
Introduction 3

1 ★ The Origins of Poetic Song Verse 15

2 ★ Bob Dylan, Chuck Berry, and the
Evolution of Poetic Song Verse 45

3 ★ Myth-Making, Personae, and Poetic Song Verse:
The Beatles, the Rolling Stones, and the Doors 85

4 ★ The Fantastic: Beyond Surrealism and Psychedelia 119

5 ★ A New Era of Verse Composition 145

Appendix of Songs and Poems Discussed 197

Notes 201

Works Cited and Consulted 209

Credits 217

Index 219

Acknowledgments

Ernest Suarez: This book percolated in my mind for many years, but I wanted to coauthor it with a professional musician, someone who knew songwriting and the music business from the inside. Derek Trucks suggested I speak with Mike Mattison, who was the lead singer and songwriter for the Derek Trucks Band at the time. After first speaking with Mike, I realized he was the right person. He knew literature and poetry like a professor of literature (I discovered he had graduated from Harvard University with a degree in English and American literature, and that his wife, Alison Umminger, was an English professor). After several more conversations, I approached him about the possibility while we were having dinner at Derek's dad's camp at the Wanee Music Festival. It's the best professional decision I've made. We launched into the book and other endeavors as full partners and quickly became close friends.

I've enjoyed the great fortune of having generous and brilliant mentors. Some of them have left us, but I continue to feel a deep gratitude to them. William Andrews, Lawrence Broer, Sargent Bush, and especially Thomas Schaub were my teachers and became good friends. Harold Bloom, Matthew J. Bruccoli, William Bedford Clark, John Hollander, Victor Strandberg, and most of all R. W. B. Lewis ushered me into the wider world of literary and academic life. My graduate school buddies—William Demastes, Kevin Donovan, Philip Gould, Jonathan Little, Lawrence Rodgers, and especially Michael Vanden Heuvel—and I have discussed literature and music seamlessly for years. My colleagues at Catholic University—Tobias Gregory, Michael Kimmage, Virgil Nemoianu, Taryn Okuma, Rebecca Rainof, and Chris Wheatley—read early versions of the manuscript and provided valuable advice. My friends and former students—Joan Romano Shifflett and Ryan Wilson—did the same. Kate Daniels, Yusef Komunyakaa, Garrett Hongo, Philip Levine, Dave Smith, Ellen Bryant Voigt, Rosanna Warren, Joshua Weiner, Charles Wright, and most of all David Bottoms and T. R. Hummer are among the many poets who influenced my thinking. Billy Cioffi, Willie DE, Luther Dickinson, Tyler "Falcon" Greenwell, Warren Haynes, Paul Olsen, Butch Trucks, Derek Trucks, and Dave Yoke are among the music-makers who did the same. I also would like to thank friends at the Association of Literary Scholars, Critics, and Writers for seminars and conversations that have helped shape my thoughts: Marco Antolin, David Bromwich, John Burt, Steve Cushman, Mark Edmundson, Walt Hunter, Major Jackson, Robert Levine, David Mikics, Lee Oser, Marjorie Perloff, Brian Richardson, Richard Russell, Mary Jo Salter, Meg Tyler, and Noah Warren. Chuck Dasey, Mary Lindsay Dickinson, Mia Ferris-Artiga, Emily Noel, David Walsh, and Bishop David O'Connell deserve thanks, too. And thanks to the Catholic University of America for providing valuable financial support that allowed us to purchase permissions to reprint lyrics.

Finally, I'd like to thank my wife, Diana, who is my happiness, and my children, Amy and Chris, who have spent decades listening to music, attending concerts, and discussing literature with me. Chris read our manuscript as it developed and offered terrific advice at every stage.

Mike Mattison: I would like to like Ernest Suarez for taking me on board over eight years ago to tackle this project. His knowledge, patience, editorial instincts, and steady hand have been invaluable in helping me transition from yelling the blues to academic writing, reigniting the deep pleasures of collaboration. Making the acquaintance of his many colleagues and peers—especially at Catholic University and the ALSCW—has played no small part in sustaining my musical imagination. I'd like to thank Gregory Fraser of the University of West Georgia for pointing me in the right direction on "The Fantastic."

I'd like to acknowledge my fellow working musicians in Scrapomatic, the Derek Trucks Band, and the Tedeschi Trucks Band—especially Paul Olsen, Dave Yoke, Tyler "Falcon" Greenwell, Ted Pecchio, and of course, Derek Trucks and Susan Tedeschi—who have battled valiantly in the trenches these many years in the service of live performance and the blues.

I'd also like to thank my teachers and mentors in literature and music—Michael Martone, Susan Dodd, John Snyder, and Ann Young—who said yes.

We both would like to thank David Bottoms and Megan Sexton at *Five Points* for giving "Hot Rocks" a home for many years, Ryan Wilson at *Literary Matters* for providing the feature with a new home, the University Press of Mississippi for giving our book a home, and the two anonymous readers who provided valuable insights and suggestions.

Bob Dylan at piano. Image 86204288. Elliot Landy/Redferns photographer, permissions supplied via Getty Images.

Poetic Song Verse

Chuck Berry/Keith Richards. Image #1088202125. Terry O'Neill photographer, Iconic Images Collection, permissions supplied via Getty Images.

Introduction

This book discusses the relationship between blues-based popular music and poetry in the twentieth and twenty-first centuries, but it is anchored in the 1960s. We synthesize a wide range of writing about blues and rock and examine the development of a relatively new literary genre that we call *poetic song verse*. Poetic song verse was nurtured in the fifties and early sixties by the blues and in Beat coffeehouses, and it matured in the mid to late sixties in the art of Bob Dylan, the Beatles, the Rolling Stones, the Doors, Jimi Hendrix, Joni Mitchell, Leonard Cohen, Gil Scott-Heron, Van Morrison, and others who used voice, instrumentation, arrangement, and production to foreground semantically textured, often allusive, and evocative lyrics that resembled and engaged poetry, a phenomenon discussed in sundry books and articles about individual artists or bands. We draw on these materials—biographies, histories, popular magazines, personal reminiscences, and a selective smattering of academic studies—to detail how a range of artists ushered in new forms of verse composition that have gradually—and often grudgingly—become recognized as possessing literary value, leading to Dylan's Nobel Prize in Literature in 2016.

A primary reason for the controversy surrounding Dylan's award is that his songs don't belong to a recognized literary genre. Other works containing song verse have drawn sustained attention as literature, but all are associated with established literary genres. For instance, medieval Provençal poetry and Robert Burns's ballads are treated as archaic forms of poetry, and John Gay's *The Beggar's Opera* and the adaptation of it by Bertolt Brecht and Kurt Weill are plays.[1] While Dylan's Nobel Prize eventually may help encourage larger considerations of song verse as literature—songs from many periods and in different styles contain compelling verse—it's clear that something happened within blues-based popular music in the sixties that resulted in a concentration of songwriters who transformed it from entertainment to art-that-entertains. As we discuss, Dylan almost indisputably played the central role in poetic song verse's development, but he didn't spring out of nowhere and he wasn't alone. By examining the confluence of blues and poetry, and by considering the creative practices of various seminal artists and the cultural conditions and landscapes in which they worked, we identify a relatively specific subgenre of song that's also a form of literature.

In discussing this phenomenon we are entering a conversation that already has started, but that's at a fairly early stage—and that too often centers on the question of whether or not song lyrics can be poetry. Our assumption is that song lyrics can be poetic and poetry can be musical, but that songs and poems are different things, and one form doesn't need to be justified by the other. We use "poetic" to describe lyrics that have literary intent and that consciously strive for aesthetic impact. We do not mean "literary" in the clichéd sense of high-minded, or heaven forbid, willfully opaque, but to denote linguistically rich compositions that operate on many levels simultaneously, incorporating image, metaphor, narrative, linguistic nuance, and play in ways that often deliberately correlate to broader cultural conversations. Lyrics that seek to transcend the grasp-and-release mechanism of pure entertainment. Lyrics that prick our curiosity and invite repeated visits and renewed scrutiny (which, in itself, is a fine step toward a definition of "literary"). Are some lyrics more consummately literary than others? Yes, of course. And the author's intent is one of the main drivers of their success. What we call poetic song verse isn't poetry set to music, like the Beats' poetry with jazz accompaniment, but it sometimes takes a hybrid form in recordings like Gil Scott-Heron's or Leonard Cohen's. The distinction we draw, while acknowledging room for ambiguity and debate, rests on the symbiotic relationship that most often occurs when potent lyrics and sonics are developed together. By "sonics" we mean every aural dimension of song, including voice, instrumentation, arrangement, and production. Simply put, how a song is sung, performed instrumentally, arranged, and recorded affects how the lyrics are experienced emotionally and intellectually. Hence, different arrangements, productions, and performances of the same lyrics are experienced differently. In poetic song verse sonics combine with verbal techniques often associated with poetry—imagery, line breaks, wordplay, point of view, character, story, tone, and other qualities—to create a semantically and emotionally textured dynamic, resulting in songs that, in T. R. Hummer's formulation, "tap into the fundamental power of the subterranean unity of music and language, of tone and word" (Hummer and Cioffi 2013, 185).

Among the questions we seek to answer are the following: What, exactly, is this new genre? What were its origins? And how has it developed? How do we study and assess it? To address these matters we engage a long line of works that discuss song lyrics and the many relationships between songwriters and poets. In 1969 Richard Goldstein, a journalist who worked closely with the Doors, assembled *The Poetry of Rock*, a collection that presents lyrics in a way that resembles a poetry anthology. Many books, of varied quality, that address rock, country, punk, rap, and hip-hop lyrics have followed. In *The Beat Generation: The Tumultuous '50s and Its Impact on Today* (1971) Bruce Cook claimed that without Beat poetry, "what many are now calling the rock poetry movement might never have happened" (225–26), and a slew of subsequent books that discuss the Beats' and other poets' relationships with musicians have been published.

The three books that perhaps speak to our project most immediately are Charlotte Pence's collection *The Poetics of American Song Lyrics* (2012), Simon Warner's *Text and Drugs and Rock 'n' Roll: The Beat and Rock Subculture* (2013), and Adam Bradley's *The Poetry of Pop* (2017). Pence's volume stakes its claim as the "first collection of academic essays that treats song as literature by bringing to song lyrics a level of artistic and critical appreciation that has been too often reserved for other art forms such as the novel, poetry, and drama" (Pence 2012, xii). The book features excellent essays on Dylan, Johnny Cash, Leonard Cohen, Bruce Springsteen, Michael Stipe, and others, as well as ten essays under the heading "Poetic History and Techniques within Poems and Songs." Bradley's book is the work of a gifted New Critic: he systematically examines how attention to rhythm, rhyme, figurative language, voice, style, and story helps listeners understand the poetry of popular song. Warner's study is an amalgam of essays, profiles, reviews, and interviews that elaborately details the Beats' influence on and interactions with rock musicians during the period on which our book primarily focuses.

Our study takes another step. Like most of the essays in Pence's collection and Bradley's study, our project is aesthetically oriented, and like Warner's book, our work is historically centered, but we engage in an extended discussion of the roots of the relationship between blues-based music and poetry and address how it developed into a distinct literary genre. Much of the material we discuss will be familiar to different kinds of readers—specialists in the blues and jazz, or experts in twentieth-century poetry, or connoisseurs of rock 'n' roll and folk music. We recombine and recast this material to tell the tale of poetic song verse. In chapter 1—"The Origins of Poetic Song Verse"—we consider the relationship between blues, jazz, and poetry and discuss how it contributed to poetic song verse's development. Chapter 2—"Bob Dylan, Chuck Berry, and the Evolution of Poetic Song Verse"—focuses on how a synergy between the blues, fifties rock 'n' roll, folk, and poetry contributed to Dylan's and others' creative practices. In chapter 3—"Myth-Making, Personae, and Poetic Song Verse: The Beatles, the Rolling Stones, and the Doors"—and in chapter 4—"The Fantastic: Beyond Surrealism and Psychedelia"—we extend our discussion of the then-nascent genre's characteristics by examining how an emphasis on personae and the fantastic helped release songwriting from assumptions that ranged from the length of individual songs to how albums were conceptualized, recorded, and produced. In chapter 5—"A New Era of Verse Composition"—we discuss poetic song verse in the seventies and beyond, primarily by looking at artists—including Bruce Springsteen, Marvin Gaye, and Stevie Wonder—who did not draw on poetry as a source for their lyric practices; these artists had been exposed to the work of Dylan and others, and they *assumed* that semantically sophisticated lyrics were vital to their craft, a development that helps affirm the genre's growth and vitality.

Throughout the manuscript we refrain from making claims about poetic song verse's importance as a literary form—it's too soon to know, and much more work needs to be done. We also realize there are more songwriters who fit within our paradigm than we could cover, a fact that suggests the genre's dynamism. Many readers will, inevitably, frown at our omissions, but we are confident that all of the artists we include are central to the topic we're exploring. We also want to stress that what "qualifies" as poetic song verse isn't an exact science any more than what is, or is not, poetry (consider discussions surrounding prose poetry, found poetry, chance poetry, and spoken word verse). Nonetheless, people who are reluctant to recognize poetic song verse as a type of literature may want to consider two moments we evoke again later in the book: Allen Tate's response to the manuscript of Robert Lowell's *Life Studies* (1959)—"But Cal, it isn't poetry!"—and novelist Michael Chabon's 2013 plenary address, "Rock 'n' Roll," to the American Academy of

Arts and Letters on the occasion of Dylan's induction. Chabon notes that "the question of whether or not Dylan's lyrics are poetry feels irrelevant" and goes on to assert that

> song lyrics are part of my literary firmware, programmed permanently into my read-only memory. . . . Not just words: writing. Tropes and devices, rhetorical strategies, writerly techniques, entire structures of allusion and imagery: entire skeins of the synapses in my cerebral cortex by now are made up entirely of all this unforgettable literature. (Chabon 2013, 26–27)

Tate's remark reminds us that it's sometimes difficult to alter people's conception of what characterizes an existing genre. We would add that it's even more difficult for people to conceive of a new genre, but as Chabon asserts, Dylan's and other songwriters' lyrics possess distinct literary qualities and are a form of literature.

Again, the term *poetic song verse* reflects our emphasis on a *literary* genre: "poetic" is intended as a descriptor, not as a superlative. We use it to convey song lyrics' relationship to poetry, and not in the idiomatic sense of "lovely" or "outstanding." This distinction also speaks to our study's relatively specific focus: we detail how properties embedded in the blues came to underpin rock and contributed to a convergence of song and poetry. Our focus is on a literary form that developed—or, perhaps, developed more fully and widely—after blues-based popular music came into sustained contact with poetry. Poetic song verse grew out of the blues much like the blues grew out of nineteenth-century spirituals and work songs, and much like those styles grew out of various African musical traditions. For over fifty years discussions of song lyrics and poetry primarily have centered on singer-songwriters of the sixties and the seventies—from Bob Dylan to Joni Mitchell to Paul Simon—who wrote lyrics that resemble poetry on the page. We focus on this phenomenon but don't assert that artists writing in this mode are superior songwriters or musicians to those who work in other styles; there are powerful songs, including instrumentals, in many modes. We also don't confine poetic song verse to lyrics that poetry influenced directly. After the mid to late sixties, poetry influenced many songwriters indirectly. As we discuss in chapter 5, many songwriters of the seventies and after who wrote semantically resonant lyrics—including Gaye and Springsteen—were not directly influenced by poetry, but they were influenced by Dylan, Jagger, Lennon,

McCartney, Mitchell, Scott-Heron, and others who had been. As a starting point to discuss poetic song verse as a literary genre, we primarily stress the moment—the mid to late sixties—that blues-based popular music and poetry intertwined.

We hope our examination of the origins and development of poetic song verse will lead to further explorations of the genre, and we would like to stress that our book is not a work of ethnomusicology, nor is it conventionally academic. Ours is not a scholarly study of race, sound, or performance, and the studies we draw upon tend to focus on verse practices or biography. In our discussions we hew closer to artists' understanding of poetic song verse than to many recent academics' interest in blues and rock as cultural phenomenon (one of this book's authors is a professional singer-songwriter who has worked in the blues idiom for over three decades). As with any art form, understanding song verse benefits from discussions of marketing, consumption, representation, and other sociological contexts, and these topics are treated at length in many highly specialized studies.[2] We aim at a broader audience, including a general readership that is increasingly looking for ways to approach the music they love with greater attention and discernment. The blues/poetry/rock path we follow moves primarily, but not exclusively, from emphasizing songs African American men composed and recorded during the first half of the twentieth century to songs Anglo-American and British men wrote and recorded in the 1960s. Our rationale is that Black men wrote and recorded the majority, though certainly not all, of the blues songs that came to influence the most visible singer-songwriters of the sixties, the white men who primarily formed the rock canon. This history is fraught with overt and covert forms of racism, sexism, and almost every conceivable type of exploitation. For many musicians such matters long were part of everyday life, and most current professional blues or rock musicians are well aware of them, whether they experienced them directly or heard of them from older counterparts. Our discussions of business practices often are informed by artists' or music industry professionals' perspectives and subordinated to discussions of creative practice. In our final chapter we discuss rock songwriters of the seventies and then touch on more recent forms of lyrically ambitious music. Adam Bradley, in his seminal studies *Book of Rhymes: The Poetics of Hip Hop* (2009) and *The Poetry of Pop* (2017), and other critics have stressed the lyrical and stylistic intricacies of rap, hip-hop, and pop, as well as of the more "uncomplicated" lyrics of dance-oriented genres, where the play of language often works through techniques based in sound (like rhyme patterns and using language as a percussive rhythm).[3] In *Book of Rhymes* Bradley asserts that rap and hip-hop are poetry and examines how the forms contain metered verse that employs rhythm, rhyme, and wordplay. He claims that the "best MCs—like Rakim, Jay-Z, Tupac, and many others—deserve consideration alongside the giants of American poetry" (Bradley 2009, xiii). Our premise is that poetic song verse is a literary genre related to but distinct from poetry. Near the end of our manuscript we discuss how rap, hip-hop, punk, and country challenged and extended the poetic song verse of the sixties and the seventies, a phenomenon that could be a robust topic for future critics.

We also should note that by "rock" we refer to a wide range of blues-based popular music of the sixties and seventies, when Dylan, the Beatles, the Rolling Stones, Smokey Robinson, Diana Ross, the Doors, the Who, Sam Cooke, Gordon Lightfoot, Aretha Franklin, Cream, Otis Redding, Van Morrison, the Band, Rod Stewart, Marvin Gaye, Stevie Wonder, Neil Young, the Allman Brothers Band, the Grateful Dead, Joan Baez, Janis Joplin, Joni Mitchell, Dr. John, Led Zeppelin, Al Green, the Staple Singers, the Moody Blues, the Byrds, the Flying Burrito Brothers, Judy Collins, Lou Reed, King Crimson, Pink Floyd, the Marshall Tucker Band, Leonard Cohen, Gladys Knight & the Pips, Bruce Springsteen, Carole King, Laura Nyro, Nina Simone, Sly and the Family Stone, Parliament, the Charlie Daniels Band, Elvis Costello, Patti LaBelle, Bill Withers, Curtis Mayfield, Waylon Jennings, Willie Nelson, Rita Coolidge, Bobbie Gentry, Warren Zevon, Jackson Browne, and many others who might be partitioned into categories including rock, soul, funk, Americana, and country were played on the same radio stations. Their hits were spun over and over on AM "Top 40" stations, and their music became familiar in more comprehensive ways to people who tuned in to FM "album rock" stations and bought LPs (which often included lyrics and elaborate liner notes). All of these artists and the progeny they inspired, including artists ranging from the Sex Pistols to Prince to the Red Hot Chili Peppers to Run DMC to Snoop Dogg to Phish to Amy Winehouse to the Foo Fighters to Kendrick Lamar, are indebted to the rural and urban blues that developed during the first half of the twentieth century. But, again, only some of these artists (e.g., Dylan, McCartney, Lennon, Mitchell, Jagger, Cohen, Scott-Heron, Jim Morrison, Van Morrison) were directly influenced by poetry. Bands like the Allman Brothers were virtuosos but were not practitioners of poetic song verse, or at least not very often, because such bands almost always foregrounded instrumentation. Poetic song verse can, and often does, contain potent instrumentation—as well as sophisticated arrangements and production techniques—but these things are used to enhance compelling lyrics, as in many of Jimi Hendrix's songs. And all practitioners of poetic song verse have songs that are less than lyrically gripping. As with poems, songs' lyrical powers come down to individual works or closely associated sequences of individual works, though some artists consistently aim at creating more richly textured lyrics than others.

That said, it's worth noting that evaluating any art form involves subjectivity. What constitutes "richly textured," "semantically resonant," or "compelling" (we use these phrases and similar ones throughout our manuscript) song lyrics can be matters of taste and critical discernment—and what particular critics stress inevitably will guide their interpretations. However, there's a general approach that we suggest, and our close readings of songs throughout the book are, among other things, provided as examples of it. A detailed examination of how a song's various elements conspire to enhance lyrical content is the best way to assess and communicate its power as poetic song verse.

The first step in analyzing poetic song verse is acquiring lyrics. There are many sites on the internet that provide convenient sources for song lyrics, but most are crowdsourced and often unreliable (our favorite malapropisms include a transcription of Manfred Mann singing "wrapped up like a douche" in the Springsteen-penned "Blinded by the Light"). More reliable sources include lyrics on musicians' or bands' official websites, and an even better source, albeit more costly, is printed sheet music. One of the hurdles in writing a book like ours is that obtaining permission to reprint lyrics is often burdensome and prohibitively expensive. We quote extensively from a substantial handful of songs but sometimes don't quote lyrics (or poems) as fully as we would prefer. In the appendix we include a list of songs and poems that are vital for a full understanding of each chapter (and that could accompany this book for courses on poetic song verse). We also have created a playlist of those songs on Spotify (https://open.spotify.com/playlist/4em RCtg3eCWDdp36aFtf6m?si=NuWr-VrLQoqOLN46FXHuoQ). We strongly urge readers to listen to the songs and to become familiar with the language in the songs and the poems before or while reading specific chapters.

We've found that the most effective way of acquainting ourselves with lyrics is to transcribe directly from the recording. Songs happen quickly, and to have to start and stop a recording and write down what you hear is an excellent, if sometimes cumbersome way to incrementally inhabit a musical performance. If you are reading this, you might be familiar with how to write expositorily about poetry. However, when considering poetic song verse, it's important to remember that while song lyrics can be poetic, they are not poems. Lyrics adhere to the criteria of the music to which they are wedded, so some of the techniques and nomenclature used in analyzing poetry must be replaced or massaged. Lyrics are presented in verses, rather than stanzas. Verses usually are followed by or interspersed with choruses: recurring, smaller verses that generally contain the main thrust of the lyric, often incorporating the title of the song and underpinned by a different harmonic progression. Any content that falls outside of the verse/chorus framework might be considered a bridge or something like a pre-chorus. The idea is that the rules are loose and that it's up to the listener/critic to create his or her own architectural understanding of the song.

Let's consider two songs by the Beatles for the sake of differentiation. "She Loves You" is catchy but less than ambitious lyrically. The song begins with a chorus ("She loves you, yeah, yeah, yeah!"), continues into a verse ("You think you lost your love . . ."), moves into a pre-chorus ("She said she loves you . . ."), then back to a verse ("She said you hurt her so . . ."), followed by another pre-chorus that gives way to the actual chorus. The form's simplicity belies the lyrics' simplicity; its aesthetic ambition lyrically is nothing more than pop sugar. We wouldn't call it poetic song verse. "Norwegian Wood (This Bird Has Flown)" is more experimental. It begins with an introductory sitar melody (an "intro"). There is a verse mimicking the intro melody, then a shift in chord structure resembling a chorus ("She asked me to stay . . ."), followed by another verse. Next, instead of the expected chorus, the sitar intro is repeated, followed by another chorus harmonically compatible with the first, but with different lyrics ("She told me she worked in the morning . . ."). The song concludes with a verse and that persistent, perhaps even pesky, intro (now an outro?). Uncharacteristically, the chorus of "Norwegian Wood" is not the locus of the song's impact. What could the song's complicated architecture reveal about its lyrical suggestiveness?

With these structural concepts in mind, we transcribe the lyrics, matching them to the song's form, identifying verses, choruses, bridges, and other formal elements. The lyrics then can be discussed in terms of meter, rhyme, language, narrative, imagery, or whatever is appropriate for a particular song, with the understanding that nothing is set in stone and that a song's building blocks may be repeated, altered, or discarded (which may or may not have an effect on a critic's analysis).

Next we consider the music itself. With the lyrics in hand, we usually have a solid sense of the song's composition, which consists of its *form, harmonic progression,* and *melody.* Starting with its form: Is there anything familiar about it? Does it conform to any specific genre, like a strict blues with an AAB format? Does it match the classic AABA American popular song form, which also is the benchmark for jazz standards? Is it a form unique unto itself? If so, what does this mean for our analysis?

Harmonic progression—the chords that underpin and propel the melody—is the musical bedrock of song. One might consider the frequency of chords or lack thereof. Are the chords generally major or minor? It's important to remember that, for the most part, harmonic progression is at the service of the melody and should be considered more of a framework than an edifice. But how to describe melody? Lilting, wistful, or singsong? Dissonant, complex, or inscrutable? Catchy or unremarkable? Does it sound like other melodies you might have heard? Is this significant?

Once we have considered the elements of composition, we encounter one of the most gratifying and highly subjective joys of interpreting poetic song verse: determining what it sounds like. To do so, one must consider a song's *performance* and its *production.* Performance involves how a song is played and sung. We start by identifying how instrumentation affects performance. Which instruments are used and to what effect? Is it a solo performance, is there accompaniment, or is it a group's work? Next, what is the tempo: Is it fast, slow, in between, lethargic, or energetic? (The more musically advanced listener-scholar might even consider a song's meter: Is it a waltz in 3/4 time? A basic 4/4 time signature?) More broadly, is the overall performance executed tentatively, confidently, delicately, or sloppily? Is it brash, plaintive, minimal, or baroque? Collect your impressions and be prepared to ground them in specific heard elements in order to begin analyzing the song's effect and intent.

Next, how does your understanding of the performance inform the lyrics? Take Chuck Berry's vocal performance on "Brown Eyed Handsome Man." The lyric—as we detail in chapter 2—is a comment on racial injustice and a coded nod to interracial sexual relations in mid-twentieth-century America. Berry sings that for "three thousand years / In fact, ever since the world began" white women have been "shedding tears" over men of color.

It's pretty heady stuff—revolutionary when taken in historical context. Yet Berry's vocal delivery is nonchalant. His singing is off the cuff, presenting the lyric in an almost perfunctory manner that's nowhere near many of his blues peers' righteous indignation or heart-on-the-sleeve yearning. How do we interpret this? Does Berry fear his own lyrics? Or is he so confident in his message that he feels it needs no augmentation? Can he simply not sing as passionately as, say, Howlin' Wolf? Or is his nonchalance an ironic nod to the fact that society's mores are not what they seem? Or is it part of how he codes and masks the lyrics?

Finally, a song's production is the recording's cumulative aural qualities. Unless it is a live album or track, most recordings of poetic song verse take place in a studio. Even if one isn't familiar with studio techniques, it's possible to generally surmise the production's intent. Is the overall sound intimate, like Bob Dylan's "Blowin' in the Wind"? Or is the sound epic and orchestral like Bruce Springsteen's "Born to Run"? Always provide aural evidence for your conclusions: What do you hear that makes it feel and mean that way? In the case of "Blowin' in the Wind," we hear Dylan accompanying himself on guitar and harmonica. There is no band. The overall effect is intimate and perhaps wistful. The lyrics are clear and unadulterated. The production is "dry": there are no added effects like reverb or echo. It is, simply, what it is, sounding very much like sitting on a porch with the artist as he performs for us. "Born to Run," however, boasts layers of production. The initial raucous drumroll gives way to a wall of horns, tremolo-laden electric guitars, and even a glockenspiel that lends a martial feel that would have made John Philip Sousa proud. The entire production aims at evoking an epic, larger-than-life quality, which certainly is realized by the time we get to the last verse with its sweeping, symphonic strings. It is obvious that this piece has layer upon layer added to it; it is intentionally constructed, not merely the product of an afternoon porch-sit. Again, how do these production choices buoy or hinder the lyrical content? And it's worth repeating that different productions or performances of the same song may result in the sonics and the lyrics conveying different thoughts and emotions.

Poetic song verse has the advantage of actually being music, which is, as the great Sufi mystic Hazrat Inayat Khan wrote, "the finest of the fine arts." Unlocking the combination of richly textured lyrics wedded to recorded music reveals a dynamism that often can go undetected or unrealized in what's frequently considered popular entertainment. This dynamism is at the core of poetic song verse, and it helps us determine not only what the genre *is*, but what it could be.

One of this book's authors is a literary historian who writes about music in the mainstream press; the other is a professional songwriter, singer, and musician who pens essays on music and poetry (often on the tour bus). Together, we've edited a feature on music and poetry since 2013. We each wrote distinct sections of the manuscript, but all of the chapters contain material by both of us, and we carefully collaborated on the entire book. Our goal was to balance historical details and analysis of particular songs with accessibility, and to create a lively, intelligent, and cohesive narrative that provides readers with an overarching perspective on the development of an exciting, relatively new literary genre: poetic song verse.

The Origins of Poetic Song Verse

"The *On the Road*, *Howl*, and *Gasoline* street ideologies that were signaling a new type of human existence weren't there, but how could you expect it to be? 45 records were incapable of it."

—**Bob Dylan,** Chronicles, vol. 1

The relationship between blues and poetry, or jazz and poetry, has drawn a good deal of scholarly attention, but this attention largely focuses on how music influenced poetry.[1] There's a good reason for this. Since the 1920s many poets have been influenced by blues and jazz, and have written blues or jazz poetry, but poetry had little effect on popular music until the 1960s, when it began to influence rock, a phenomenon that has drawn a good deal of scattered attention. While there are hundreds of books on Bob Dylan, the Beatles, the Rolling Stones, Joni Mitchell, Van Morrison, the Who, the Kinks, the Doors, Gil Scott-Heron, Leonard Cohen, Marvin Gaye, Carole King, and others that discuss individual lyricists' practices, and though these books sometimes mention how particular poets influenced an artist, almost all of these books are written for a general audience and the analysis is scant. Exceptions include Wallace Fowlie's *Rimbaud and Jim Morrison: The Rebel as Poet* (1994), Michael Gray's *Song and Dance Man III: The Art of Bob Dylan* (2000), Christopher Ricks's *Dylan's Visions of Sin* (2004), and David Yaffe's *Bob Dylan: Like a Complete Unknown* (2011) and *Reckless Daughter: A Portrait of Joni Mitchell* (2017), as well as the books discussed in our introduction.

There also are collections of essays on songwriters, such as Lisa and John Sornberger's *Gathered Light: The Poetry of Joni Mitchell's Songs* (2013), but again, these studies focus on individual songwriters or a band. Our study is more akin to books that tread the line between scholarly and popular approaches, like Alan Lomax's *The Land Where the Blues Began* (1970), Robert Palmer's *Deep Blues* (1981), and subsequent books that discuss the blues' origins, structure, and content. In this chapter we'll consider how verse practices associated with blues-based poetry and music during the first half of the twentieth century helped set the stage for understanding the larger synergy between poetry and rock.

The influence of blues and jazz (two terms often used interchangeably in the 1920s and 1930s) on poetry was unintentionally initiated in 1903, when W. C. Handy declined the opportunity to direct a white municipal band in Michigan that offered "more money, more prestige." Instead, he took over the Knights of Pythias band in Clarksville, Mississippi, a fateful choice "down the road that led inevitably to the blues." On a day familiar to blues aficionados, he was napping while waiting for a train in Tutwiler when he heard a "lean, loose-jointed Negro . . . plunking a guitar beside him" and singing the line "goin' where the Southern cross' the Dog" three times and playing the "weirdest music" Handy had "ever heard." Handy immediately became attuned to the Delta country blues, the sound Robert Palmer calls the "deep blues" and that widely is considered a cornerstone of American rock 'n' roll.

> I leaned over and asked him what the words meant. He rolled his eyes, showing a trace of mild amusement. Perhaps I should have known, but he didn't mind explaining. At Moorhead the eastbound and the westbound met and crossed the north and southbound trains four times a day. This fellow was going where the Southern cross' the Dog, and he didn't care who knew it. He was simply singing about Moorhead as he waited. (Handy 1969, 72–74)

Handy had discovered a style of music that was based on the human voice and that placed an emphasis on the local and the immediate, traits that would help bring music and poetry into closer proximity as the century unfolded. In 1912 Handy copyrighted and published the instrumental "The Memphis Blues," a twelve-bar blues embedded in a larger sixteen-bar structure. Discouraged by sales, he sold the song to a Memphis record store owner, who hired a professional lyricist to put words to it and convinced the popular minstrel Honeyboy Evans to perform it in New York City during the spring of 1914. Handy felt he had been cheated out of the song's profits—though nothing illegal was done—and at age forty he helped establish the Pace & Handy Music Company in Memphis and composed and copyrighted "St. Louis Blues" and a succession of other blues and pseudo-blues songs. In 1918 he moved his business to New York City, where a host of Black and white artists sang and recorded his songs.

The blues soon influenced poetry. In 1917 the poet James Weldon Johnson mentioned "Handy, who is a negro musician of Memphis," and "The Memphis Blues" in the *New York Evening Post*.[2] Five years later, in his preface to *The Book of American Negro Poetry*, Johnson cited the power of blues that originated in "Memphis, and the towns along the Mississippi." He felt that blues lyrics tended to be "crude, but they contain something of real poetry," and that the blues might inspire poetry "expressing the imagery, the idioms, the peculiar turns of thought, and the distinctive humor and pathos, too, of the Negro, but which will also be capable of voicing the deepest and highest emotions and aspirations, and allow of the widest range of subjects and the widest scope of treatment" (1922, xii–xiii, xli). Johnson was right, of course, though the blues' influence on poets would extend well beyond African American bards. As David Yaffe observes, "White modernists and black populists did not always run in the same literary circles, but that did not stop Crane, Hughes, and Stevens from writing their own versions of jazz poems" (2006, 102).

In the twenties and thirties Hart Crane, Langston Hughes, Wallace Stevens, Sterling Brown, Carl Sandburg, Claude McKay, E. E. Cummings, Jean Toomer, DuBose Heyward, Mina Loy, Kenneth Rexroth, T. S. Eliot, William Carlos Williams, and others wrote poems influenced by or about blues and jazz.[3] Handy and Abbe Niles's *Blues: An Anthology* (1926) featured essays on "The Blues as Folk Verse," "The Folk Blues as Music," "The Modern Blues," and the "Adoption and Influence of the Blues." Niles draws parallels between the verse of Handy and Hughes, whose first book of poetry, *The Weary Blues*, also was published in 1926. By the time of the anthology's publication, Handy, who was born in a log cabin in Florence, Alabama, perhaps was the best-known blues musician in the world, and the association between blues and poetry had been established. Handy and Hughes would form an enduring friendship and would work together on various projects, including musical dramas.

Handy's ability to popularize the blues largely can be attributed to his capacity to take rural country blues and blend it with other styles, a maneuver that helped him appeal to white audiences and increased his revenues. For instance, he noticed that when his band played the "Habanera rhythm, containing the beat of the tango," white people "took the rhythm in stride" as they danced. Handy then incorporated it into several songs, including "St. Louis Blues" (Handy 1969, 72).[4] This tendency to combine one form with other styles follows a well-established pattern that has given birth to new genres and art forms throughout history, one that is readily apparent in the relationship between music and poetry in the twentieth century.

Like Handy, Hughes experimented with blues forms. Steven C. Tracy points out that while Hughes sometimes used traditional blues structures, including the dominant twelve-bar blues format, he also "used varied stanzas, line placement, and typography" (2001, 144). In several poems he combines traditional blues structures with syllabic verse and rhyming free verse. "The Weary Blues," which Hughes called "a poem about a working man who sang the blues all night and then went to bed and slept like a rock," "included the first blues verse" he "ever heard way back in Kansas when I was a kid" (Hughes 1940, 215). The poem's narrator describes a song he heard a Black man play in a bar on Lenox Avenue. At the end of the poem the narrator enters the blues singer's consciousness, and the blues become a metaphor for a Black man's life: "the singer stopped playing and went to bed / While the Weary Blues echoed through his head. / He slept like a rock or a man that's dead."

In "Jazzonia" Hughes uses rhyming free verse to invoke the emotional connections between dance and music. The poem is about jazz, but its power emanates from its use of figurative language, rather than from a blues or a jazz structure. Hughes describes a "whirling cabaret" where "Six long-headed jazzers play," an image that invokes the fluidity of music and dance, and that fuses the musicians with their horns. The shimmering instruments become "shining rivers of the soul," and "A dancing girl whose eyes are bold / Lifts high a dress of silken gold," creating a series of associations between jazz, the human spirit, dance, and sensuality.

In contrast, his much anthologized "Negro Dancers" captures the rhythms of a twenties dance craze, the Charleston. The speaker's clipped diction and use of "m," "b," "t," and "d" sounds mimic the song's beat.

"Me an' ma baby's
Got two mo' ways,

Two mo' ways to do de Charleston!"
Da, da

Tracy calls "Dream Boogie" a "twelve line, twelve bar, boogie-woogie poem, annexing an exclamatory 'tag' ending like that occasionally employed in music" (2001, 229). The poem's Vaudevillian conclusion creates an ironic tension between the pain that inspired the music and the sense of celebration the music inspires:

Sure,
I'm happy!
Take it away!
Hey, pop!

In an early study of Afro-American poetics, Stephen Henderson asserted that Black poetry "derives its form from two basic sources, Black speech and Black music" (1973, 30–31). An emphasis on African American rural vernacular and music helped blues poets anticipate the larger turn among mid-century American poets toward free verse and sometimes shocking confessional narration. However, with the possible exception of Hughes's poetry, the blues and jazz poetry of the twenties and thirties has not commanded the artistic cachet ascribed to the high modernist poetry of T. S. Eliot, Ezra Pound, Wallace Stevens, and Marianne Moore—but it would influence future blues and jazz poets, including the Beats, Bob Kaufman, Amiri Baraka, Jayne Cortez, Sonia Sanchez, William Matthews, David Jauss, Yusef Komunyakaa, and many others. Yet, as Arnold Rampersad points out, even Hughes's reputation remains "controversial": for a "substantial number and, especially, scholar-critics, Hughes's approach to poetry was far too simple and unlearned" (1995, 3).

The relative anonymity of blues poetry—especially among white readers—before the 1960s is suggested by the fact that despite the quality and ingenuity of Sterling Brown's *Southern Road* (1932) and Margaret Walker's *For My People* (1942), neither artist was able to secure a publisher for another book of poetry for decades. *Southern Road* contains sonnets and poems that draw on spirituals and folk songs, but its use of blues makes it a landmark in verse composition. In his preface to the book James Weldon Johnson noted that Brown had "taken this raw material and worked it into original and authentic poetry," a phase that recalls Johnson's hope (expressed a decade earlier) that the blues would stimulate rich forms of poetry" (Johnson 1932, 17). Fifty-five years after the publication of Johnson's preface, Houston A. Baker Jr. noted that the "indisputably modern moment in Afro-American discourse arrives . . . when the *intellectual* poet Brown, masterfully mantled in the wisdom of his Williams College Phi Beta Kappa education, gives forth the deformative sounds of Ma Rainey" in his poem "Ma Rainey," which according to Baker, blends "class and mass—*poetic* mastery discovered as a function of deformative *folk* sound" (Baker 1987, 92–93). In "Southern Road," "Riverbank Blues," "Tin Roof Blues," and other poems Brown uses blues verse's dominant form (AAB) to create the types of accessible internal dialogues that anticipate poetry's more widespread shift away from traditional Anglo-European forms and modernist poetics after World War II. The title of Brown's "New St. Louis Blues" recalls Handy's famous "St. Louis Blues" (1914), which Bessie Smith and Louis Armstrong popularized in 1925. The poem divides into three sections—"Market Street Woman," "Tornado Blues," and "Low Down"—consisting of five stanzas cast as three-line blues. In "Low Down" the second stanza's first two lines present the speaker's battered state through images of bodily decay and psychological aggravation, and the third line conveys the cause—relentless work—and potential consequence—"Death"—of his misery:

> Bone's gittin' brittle, an' my brain won't low no rest,
> Bone's gittin' brittle, an' my brain won't let me rest,
> Death drivin' rivets overtime in my scooped out chest.

Walker's *For My People* took the Yale Younger Poets prize, the first major award given to a book of blues poetry. Like Brown's book, her volume contains poems cast in variety of forms, particularly the sonnet, but part 2 draws on African American folk songs and legends to create ten character portraits. In the foreword Stephen Vincent Benét points out that these poems "are set for voice and the blues" and "could be sung as easily as spoken" (1942, 6). Seven of the portraits are based on original characters and set in quatrains with a variety of rhyme schemes. Three poems—"Molly Means," "Bad-Man Stagolee," and "Big John Henry"—draw on folk legends and are cast in irregular, swinging couplets. The legend of Stagolee, a notorious pimp and murderer, already had been popularized in recordings by Ma Rainey, Furry Lewis, Mississippi John Hurt, and Woody Guthrie. Walker describes him as fearless trickster who killed a policeman and evaded punishment, an action that probably would elicit sympathy from an oppressed population:

> But the funniest thing about that job
> Was he never got caught by no mob
> And he missed the lynching meant for his hide
> 'Cause nobody know how Stagolee died.

By the time Bob Dylan moved to New York City in January of 1961, a new blues and jazz poetry movement had been thriving for over a decade. Guthrie P. Ramsey Jr. observes that by "privileging improvisation" over written arrangements as the "source of jazz composition," Dizzy Gillespie "turns on its ear one of the 'truths' of the Western music tradition and modernism" (2003, 96). Unwittingly, Gillespie and Charlie Parker also changed the relationship between jazz and poetry in the midforties when they jettisoned the harmonics and meters of jazz dance music. In the twenties and thirties Hughes and others had modeled their poetry on rural blues and modern jazz, but in the forties and fifties a new generation of poets turned toward bebop for inspiration. The saxophone—played with previously unmatched rapidity and range—became the iconic instrument, and many jazz musicians' unconventional lifestyles became the stuff of legend, prefiguring rock guitarists' cult hero status in the sixties. Poets who became associated with the San Francisco Renaissance and the Beats in the fifties embraced a bohemian lifestyle, and bebop's stress on improvisation prompted them to develop new free verse techniques.

Robert Creeley's use of bebop as a catalyst for his poetics provides a good example. He observes that "Charlie Parker and Miles Davis and Thelonious Monk and those people were extraordinarily interesting to me . . . they seemed to have only the nature of the activity as a limit" (Feinstein 1997, 94). In a letter of July 24, 1950, to his mentor, Black Mountain poet Charles Olson, he cited bebop's emphasis on velocity and timing.

> Miles Davis: Boplicity & reverse side.
>   "   " :Move.
> The Bird   :Chasing the Bird   i got
>   :Cheryl   rythmethe, . . .

Creeley didn't want "to write like jazz," but he drew on bebop's sense of timing to structure his poetry. In his letter to Olson he uses song titles ("Boplicity," "Move," "Chasing the Bird," "Cheryl"), breaks within and between lines, and the phrase "reverse side" (literally of the LP) to suggest bebop's tendency to abruptly alter the music's pace.[5] The empty quotation marks signal a space filled with improvisations, and the conflation of words indicates the speed with which the music is played at moments within the song, signaling techniques he would modify and employ in his poetry.

Like much of his poetry, "I Know a Man"—perhaps Creeley's signature poem—manipulates lines and grammatical units to capture bebop's emphasis on the tension between staccato phrasing and improvisation.

> As I sd to my
> friend, because I am
> always talking,—John, I
>
> sd, which was not his
> name, the darkness sur-
> rounds us, what
>
> can we do against it, or else, shall we &
> why not, buy a goddamn big car,
>
> drive, he sd, for
> christ's sake, look
> out where yr going.

The poem consists of a single sentence paced by line breaks, commas, and dashes. Like bebop, which punctuates melody with pauses and improvisational flights that alter the music's pace, Creeley's sense of timing modifies the narrative's direction and creates the impression of spontaneity. His use of spare lines and abbreviated words quickens the poem, but the first two stanzas contain interjections—"because I am / always talking" and "which was not his / name"—that delay its primary thrust. The poem begins with five lines consisting of five or six syllables; however, the second stanza's last line consists of three syllables and is self-consciously shortened. Dividing "sur- / round" between two lines causes a slight halt, and the comma between "us" and "what" creates a pause before "what" pours into the longer lines of the penultimate stanza, extending the question—"the darkness sur- / rounds us, what / can we do against it"—that expresses the poem's theme. The phrase "or else, shall we & / why not" stops and starts, conveying sentiments that range from conviction to whimsy and that point to the premise the poem poses: whether to continue "talking" and contemplating the possibility of existential "darkness," or focus on the concrete and act—"drive . . . / . . . look / out where yr going."

The associations between poetry and music were strengthened in the fifties as poetry readings with jazz accompaniment became a larger phenomenon. Hughes, Kenneth Rexroth, Vachel Lindsay, and others had read their poetry to jazz since the 1920s, but their efforts garnered brief attention compared to the sustained publicity the Beat and the San Francisco Renaissance writers enjoyed in the mid to late fifties and after. In the midfifties articles on the Beats appeared in *Esquire*, the *New Yorker*, and other popular venues, and *Time* reported that "when Rexroth first read . . . 500 fans stormed The Cellar (seating capacity: 43) to hear him."[6] In 1958 San Francisco gossip columnist Herb Caen famously played off the term *Sputnik* and condescendingly dubbed these writers "beatniks," a word that quickly was applied in the press from coast to coast.[7] In the late fifties and the sixties Beat coffee shops, bookstores, and nightclubs sprang up across the United States and spread to Western Europe.

Rexroth—who initially served as a father figure to the younger writers—and Lawrence Ferlinghetti, accompanied by the Cellar Jazz Quintet, released *Poetry Readings in the Cellar* in 1957, and a wave of similar recordings by Kerouac, Kenneth Patchen, and others ensued. But the readings on these recordings are mediocre and the music is uninspired; the combination of the two often borders on parody. After the session for his second album, *Blues and Haiku* (1959), Kerouac wept and went on a drunken binge because the accompanying players—Al Corn and Zoot Sims—left the studio before listening to the tapes (Amburn 1999, 295–96). Corn's and Sims's actions, and Kerouac's reaction, point to an important component in the relationship between poetry and music before the sixties. Many poets were influenced by music and detected strong links between their poems and jazz or blues, but musicians tended to see little or no relationship between the two forms, though they were glad to get a paying gig.

Hughes—who regarded the Beats with contempt and amusement—would prove an exception. His recording of *The Weary Blues* (1958) with Charles

Mingus, Leonard Feather, and other jazz musicians was much more successful, largely because many of his poems were based on twelve-bar blues and set to original music. But despite their recordings' uneven quality, the Beats and the San Francisco Renaissance poets played a pivotal role in creating an atmosphere where the two forms were viewed as complementary, and they helped lead Dylan and others toward innovations that balanced the scales: whereas blues and jazz influenced poetry into the fifties (and beyond), poetry influenced rock in the sixties. But before discussing the rise of rock and poetic song verse, a number of distinctions need to be made.

After the midforties the terms *blues* and *jazz* no longer were used as interchangeably as in previous decades, primarily due to the emergence of bebop and modal jazz, instrumentally centered musical forms that *tended* (there are exceptions to almost everything) to contain scant or no lyrics. While jazz influenced the Beats and other poets, Dylan and his musical counterparts tended to be much more interested in the blues, though contemporary poets' jazzlike wordplay and verse rhythms captivated them.

But what are the blues?

Three prominent African American literary artists who also were musicians offered responses that remain among the most well known. In 1945 Ralph Ellison asserted that the "blues is an impulse to keep the painful details and episodes of a brutal experience alive in one's aching consciousness, to finger its jagged grain, and to transcend it, not by the consolation of philosophy but by squeezing from it a near-tragic, near-comic lyricism" (Ellison 1945, 199). Eighteen years later Amiri Baraka—then LeRoi Jones—distinguished older, largely rural blues and what he calls "classic" blues from music created by "Negroes, jazz musicians and otherwise, who have moved successfully into the featureless syndrome of that (American) culture." Baraka felt that the former are related "directly to Negro experience" and that the latter is by Black musicians "who can no longer realize the basic social and emotional philosophy that has *traditionally* informed Afro-American music" (Baraka 1963, 94, 235). In 1976 Albert Murray offered a description closer to Ellison's. He insisted that while the term *the blues* is "synonymous with low spirits," "blues music is not," and he associated it with the heroic: "André Malraux might well have been referring to the blues and the function of blues musicians when he described the human condition in terms of ever-impending chaos and declared that each victory of the artist represents a triumph of man over his fate" (Murray 2017, 42, 45).[8]

Ellison's assertion predates electric blues and rock 'n' roll, Baraka's formulation is shaped by the Black Arts Movement and the cultural politics of the early to mid sixties, and Murray's focus is on Black rural blues and jazz musicians from W. C. Handy to Miles Davis.[9] All are of interest and many other formulations are available, but we'll present a conception of the blues—historically, sonically, thematically, and formally—from a professional musician's perspective, a view we feel is similar to the one that primarily influenced the songwriters of the midsixties and after, and that will help readers (particularly nonspecialists) comprehend how and why the blues and poetry came to influence each other.

Much scholarly attention has been paid to the etymology, anthropology, metaphysics, marketing, and appropriation of the blues—and for many people today "the blues" means music ranging from Robert Johnson to Billie Holiday to B. B. King to Cream to Led Zeppelin to Robert Cray to Keb' Mo'. However, for our immediate purposes, we will focus on four basic elements in blues music across all strata—from the humblest solo acoustic country blues to the most grandiose arena blues-rock—in order to understand how they combine to make the blues an effective mechanism for poetic expression.

1. Rhythm

The blues' roots are in African musical forms that slaves brought to the Americas. As with most African music, the cornerstone of the blues is steady, insistent rhythm. Much effort has been spent tracing American music's syncopated rhythms—in blues, jazz, and rock—to African and slave sources. And musicologists are correct in noting that the "clave" beat is essential to pre-blues music and evolved into the foundation of modern American musical forms. Essentially, a clave beat is a syncopated pattern that allows other beat patterns to be layered over it. Syncopation means placing and extending beats over a set time signature. A classic example of a clave beat in a more contemporary context is the beat for Bo Diddley's eponymous song "Bo Diddley": boom, boom, boom, *boom-boom*. The rhythm falls between and carries over the regular beats in the time signature to create a propulsive, chugging sensation. (As the saying goes, "It's got a good beat; you can dance to it.") Hence the usefulness of the clave beat in African societies and among American slaves. It is *compelling* in the literal sense of the word: it invites the listener to participate. Rhythm becomes a powerful social force, utilized in ritual, celebration, and even daily work life. Rhythm builds and maintains community.

Count M'Butu is an Atlanta-based percussion player. Born Harold Jones in 1941 in Sandersville, Georgia, the Count began playing percussion in his midthirties and eventually traveled to Nigeria, where he lived for two years, immersing himself in the study of African rhythms and drum making. On his return, the Count parlayed his skills into a decades-long career encompassing Broadway shows, stints with George Clinton's Parliament-Funkadelic and soul singer Nancy Wilson, and dozens of recordings with artists ranging from blues-woman Francine Reed to alternative rockers the Stone Temple Pilots. The late southern absurdist rock icon Colonel Bruce Hampton gave him the nickname "Count M'Butu" while touring. Why? "Bruce said it sounded good," says M'Butu.

With his deep-seated knowledge of African drumming, rhythm, and culture, M'Butu's account of their use in American slaves' communal life is enlightening:

> See, you'd have the griot. And he'd be sitting there with a stick beating out clave rhythm on the ground: "boom *boom* boom, boom *boom* boom..." And the slaves would be coming in from the fields, and he's telling them what happened that day. It was like the six o'clock news: "Boom *boom* boom, boom *boom* boom... A mule died today... Boom *boom* boom... Susie was out behind the barn with Nate... Booom *boom* boom..., etc."[10]

Drumming's effectiveness as a form of coded communication among the enslaved led to Black Codes that strictly limited or curtailed it in many Southern states. However, outside of its social and recreational uses, rhythm continued to have a very practical application in day-to-day work. Even after the abolition of slavery, work teams of southern Blacks—whether conscripted inmates or hired laborers—used rhythm and song to organize their work.

Take, for example, the song "Lining Track" (also known as "Lining Song"), which can be found on an array of sources, from Alan Lomax's anthology of Negro work songs, collected for the Library of Congress in 1939, to Lead Belly's folk-blues recordings. The song originates from railroad work teams who were "lining" or setting up long sections of steel track. The song basically is a rhythmic cadence sung by a leader with a refrain that allows for three "beats" of response. In the space those response beats create, the team would move the steel beam. The remainder of the verse would allow the team to reset and prepare for the next movement. Here's a version introduced and sung by Allan Prothero from Lomax's *Negro Work Songs*:

> Oh, what'd I hear about a lining track?
> Send ahead then join it back
> Oh, boys can't you lining? [*beat*]
> Oh, boys can't you lining? [*beat*]
> Oh, boys over yonder? [*beat*]
> Oh, ho, that'll do.

The song describes the work of lining the rails and organizes the actual work with its rhythm. This type of song was used in rail yards, by stevedores off-loading ships, by farm workers in songs called "field hollers," and anywhere there was dangerous, difficult, backbreaking work for groups of Blacks to do. Through its varied and limitless forms, African rhythm established itself in the African American musical tradition and gave birth to the blues' irresistibly *inviting* and *insistent* beat. As we'll discuss, in poetic song verse blues-based rhythms often play a role similar to that of traditional metrics in metered poetry.

2. Blue Notes

To Mississippi Fred McDowell, who played the "straight, natural blues," the blues were a direct musical manifestation of a feeling. McDowell was so adamant about his brand of blues that he even named one of his albums *I Do Not Play No Rock 'n' Roll Y'all* (1969). On the record, McDowell intersperses spoken-word tutorials among his songs. On "Everybody's Down on Me," he explains how a misunderstanding with a best friend could elicit what might be termed the blues, and even goes so far as to take his slide (in this case a dulled knife blade, although he contends he was trained on a beef bone) and attempts to approximate on his guitar how betrayal might "sound." And sure enough, the resulting musical figure is a concerned, sad moan. "It's a worrisome thing," McDowell says. "You had that confidence in him that he wouldn't have did you like that." And yet there it is.

Blue notes help make the blues expressive. Like many students of the blues, we find it most helpful to define blue notes as "notes that fall between the notes." Consider a piano's keyboard. It's the perfect manifestation of the Western harmonic concept. The piano consists of a series of twelve notes (seven white keys, five black) ascending in half steps and repeated along the keyboard in progressively higher octaves. Each key represents one discrete tone. Technically, blue notes can be made by "flattening" the third, fifth, or seventh interval on a Western scale, which creates a tone slightly lower than the third but higher than the sharp second, for instance. Hence, it is technically impossible to play a blue note on the piano; the key simply doesn't exist. To elicit a blue note on the piano, one must play two adjacent keys, which produces a dissonance that approximates a blue note. (We should note that the blue notes in American blues are African in origin, but blue notes occur in ancient folk music from Europe and Asia as well.)

What, then, is blue notes' purpose? In a word: expressiveness. Blue notes approximate the human voice, which—as the original instrument—perhaps is the most expressive. Blue notes most easily are achieved on wind instruments by overblowing a note, and on stringed instruments by bending a string up or down. It's no coincidence that reed pipes and simple stringed instruments such as a diddley bow are among the most ancient and accessible instruments. They could be assembled relatively easily and used by American slaves, or anyone lacking financial resources for mass-produced instruments.

In essence, blue notes add resonance and humanity to an instrument's tone, making it another *voice*, as it were. Before many instrumental passages he plays, the great country blues guitarist and "Harlem Street Singer" Reverend Gary Davis can be heard on his recordings commanding his guitar to "*talk* to me," as if he and the instrument were telling a story together. As we'll discuss, in poetic song verse blue notes often serve as crucial sonic elements that lend expressiveness and impart complexity to lyrics.

3. Blues Form

The typical blues form—a twelve-bar blues—is so ingrained in the American listener's consciousness that many of us aren't aware that we understand it innately. It's the cornerstone of rock 'n' roll. Bill Haley and the Comets' "Rock Around the Clock," Elvis Presley's "Hound Dog," and Chuck Berry's "Johnny B. Goode" all are composed using the twelve-bar blues form.[11] Even country classics, including Hank Williams's "Move It On Over," or jazz standards like "Fine and Mellow," popularized by Billie Holiday, are twelve-bar blues.

So what is this form, where did it come from, and why is its use so widespread?

The twelve-bar blues' origins most likely are rooted in the call and response of African American field hollers, work songs, and church hymns. Simply put, the twelve-bar blues is a song form consisting of twelve measures or "bars." Each bar typically contains four beats. The progression goes like this: A musical or lyrical statement is made in the tonic key (the basic key in which a song is written) over the first four bars. We'll call this "A." The key shifts up a fourth step and the statement is repeated over the next four bars ("A" again). Finally, a closing statement is made ("B")—usually in response to the first lyrical or musical statement ("A")—over the last four bars, which descend from the fifth step to the fourth step and back to the tonic. Then the process starts all over again. A single verse of the form could be described as "AAB."

Take, for example, Bessie Smith's seminal 1923 recording of the Alberta Hunter composition "Down Hearted Blues." After a lengthy—some might say redundant—introduction in a Tin Pan Alley style, the song's proper blues part begins. In four verses, Smith sings a tale of loss, probable revenge, and heavy drinking, all in twelve-bar AAB form:

Trouble, trouble, I've had it all my days
Trouble, trouble, I've had it all my days
It seems like trouble's going to follow me to my grave

I ain't never loved but three men in my life
I ain't never loved but three men in my life
My father, my brother, the man that wrecked my life

It may be a week, it may be a month or two
It may be a week, it may be a month or two
But the day you quit me, honey, is coming home to you

I've got the world in a jar, the stopper's in my hand
I've got the world in a jar, the stopper's in my hand
I'm going to hold it until you come under my command

If we equate a verse of this twelve-bar blues to a poetic stanza, the song itself is not terribly different from, say, the Elizabethan sonnet form. Fourteen lines, often divided into two or more stanzas, the sonnet comes in classic flavors—Italian, Spenserian—as well as in variations, and still is a staple in contemporary poetry. Why? What's the usefulness of this form? Or of verse form in general?

Let's look at the first verse—or stanza—of "Downhearted Blues." The first line—or A— is, "Trouble, trouble, I've had it all my days." A fairly broad statement, with significant ramifications for the speaker: "My life is nothing but trouble." The statement is so significant, in fact, that it bears repeating: "Trouble, trouble, I've had it all my days." The repetition at once focuses, deepens, and emboldens the initial statement. It lets the listener know the singer means business, confirming that, yes, "My life is nothing but trouble. You heard me correctly. Did I *stutter*?" A palpable sense of tension has been built, and the verse/stanza's third line acts as a complicated sort of release: "It seems like trouble's going to follow me to my grave." The narrator/singer now is looking toward the future, and the prediction is grim: her assessment of her past might very well *be* her future. By this time the listener—who has been drawn in by the story's repetition and release—begins to ask all kinds of questions: Where did all of this trouble come from? Who is responsible? How will the story end?

As we discussed earlier, a major facet of the blues is communality, a compulsion toward inclusion. If the performer and the audience agree on how to tell a story, if the story comes in discrete, agreed-upon packets that we call "form"—in this case a twelve-bar blues—then the mutual participation is richer, and an audience can be relied upon to respond knowledgeably, and perhaps enthusiastically. It is no small coincidence blues audiences—like African American church congregations—traditionally participate loudly and vocally in the narrative, encouraging and agreeing with the performer: "Tell your story!" "Yes!" "I *hear* you!" There's no need to reserve one's approval (or disapproval) until the end, when applause traditionally is invited. The response is instantaneous and becomes part of the story. Although they are works of righteous beauty, one does not observe this during performances of Strauss's *lieder*.

The twelve-bar blues also is a road map for musicians. A musician can walk into a performance, out of the cold as it were, and immediately recognize and participate in a twelve-bar blues. And yet, the twelve-bar blues isn't the only blues form. Much like in jazz, wherein the American popular song form (AABA) is utilized widely, we realize there is more than one way to skin a cat. Consider Muddy Waters's "Mannish Boy," one of the most popular and recognized songs in the American blues repertoire. It begins with an iconic statement, one of unfettered self-assurance: "Oh yeah, oh yeah. Everything gonna be alright this morning!" This is followed by a classic riff—"duh-*da*-duh-da-*dum*!"—repeated over a 4/4 pulse. The lyrics rhyme, but they aren't repeated, and they don't follow an AAB pattern.

> I made twenty-one
> I want you to believe me honey,
> We'll have lots of fun
> I'm a man

Waters then spells the word *man* to stress his point. The rest of the song consists of Waters describing and/or literally spelling exactly what type of man he is, accompanied by young women's responsive screams. The key never changes. This is not a twelve-bar blues. Yet it has an innate form, a repeated musical figure, a riff, a call and response with an actual studio audience, blue notes, and an insistent beat. It wouldn't take much for a listener or musician to fall right in line. Waters's confidence, his *brio*, compels the listener to hear his story to the finish.

If the twelve-bar blues truly is the standard, ideal blues form, why do musicians change it? Yes, the blues require a blues audience to achieve communal emotional expiation, but the musician still is in the driver's seat. It's his or her story, after all. The musician, like the poet, sometimes uses form and the audience's familiarity with it to tamper with expectations—to make sure the audience pays attention and to make sure that, in the end, the creator maintains ownership of his or her creation.

When first experiencing the early twentieth-century recordings of solo country blues players, the listener is surprised to hear supposed masters of the genre—including Robert Johnson, Bukka White, and Skip James—routinely drop beats, skip whole sections of songs, and change keys, seemingly at a whim. On the one hand, this could be attributed to stream-of-consciousness, automatic creation, a process sometimes ascribed to the primitive, "outsider" artist. On the other hand, a much more obvious and practical reason is that musicians didn't want rival musicians to—if you'll forgive the vernacular—*steal their shit*. Artists fiddle with form to announce and maintain their originality.

4. Authenticity of Feeling

Let's be clear: the blues are not, by definition, "sad" or "depressing." But for many musicians and aficionados, including this book's authors, the blues often convey a sense of emotional authenticity. "Authenticity" is, of course, a complex concept that, among other things, has been used as a marketing device by performers and music industry executives, and as a cultural signifier by people ranging from right-wing politicians to academic Marxists. The literary critic Scott Romine and others have questioned whether "authenticity," in its conventional sense, exists at all; they see it as contested terrain for cultural authority (Romine 2008). But many people, including many musicians, of different races, nationalities, and generations who are well aware of these dynamics have and continue to experience the blues as authentic. In 2020 Henry Louis Gates claimed that at a "time when many in our country are deeply divided and distrustful of institutions across the board, we would do well to listen to (Albert) Murray, who, produced by another century, spent a career *believing* in things, like the gospel according to Ma Rainey and Jimmy Rushing and Duke Ellington. More broadly, he believed in the sublimity of art, and he was never afraid of risking bathos to get it" (Murray 2020, xxii). As we discuss in subsequent chapters, the sense of authenticity the blues convey helped attract Bob Dylan, John Lennon, Paul McCartney, Mick Jagger, Keith Richards, Jimi Hendrix, Joni Mitchell, Gil Scott-Heron, Eric Clapton, and other rock artists to it. At a performance at the Iridium Jazz Club in New York City in March of 2003, Hank Crawford—the legendary alto saxophonist who played with Bobby "Blue" Bland and B. B. King and served as musical director for Ray Charles—succinctly described the emotional authenticity many artists, connoisseurs, and even casual fans associate with the blues: "The blues ain't nothin' but a soul explosion." Similarly, musician and blues scholar Steven C. Tracy notes that a person once asked him if the blues express or produce emotion. Tracy replied, "Yes . . . As a musician, the best way I can describe how I feel when I play is that it is as if something from very deep within me wells up, and at the best times takes over and tilts me towards some kind of heaven" (2015, 5).

In effect, the blues begin as thoughts, emotions, even intuitions, that demand expression, regardless of the bearer's will to conceal them; small eruptions, like solar flares, from the very core. They may be positive or negative, agreeable or torrid, violent or benign, humorous or deadly serious, but they will not be ignored. It's the blues musician's job to convey these "explosions" as accurately as possible. Great talent and technique are helpful, but shepherding *authenticity of feeling* is the musician's top priority. And as we'll see, summoning a sense of authenticity was essential in the creation of poetic song verse and manifested itself in ever-evolving ways that remain underpinned by the blues.

But who is to say whose feelings are more or less authentic? The audience for the blues—and for poetic song verse—is not necessarily a collection of scholars, specialists, or experts. The audience consists of initiates who, understanding and/or feeling the necessity of *insistent rhythm*, the meaning and placement of *blue notes*, and the use or appropriation of *blues forms*, deign to judge the *authenticity of feeling* present in songwriters and musicians who are "telling their story." In simpler language, the blues audience consists of music fans from any strata of life who at some root level—intellectual, spiritual, emotional, musicological—want to *get with* musicians telling soul-stories, because the soul-stories somehow reflect their own. This is something that any practicing blues musician knows and feels when he or she performs. With this in mind, it's important to remember that in the blues, technique takes a back seat to emotional expression. On many occasions, we have witnessed legendary musicians referring to less technically adept playing as "broke dick" with awe, humility, and tears in their eyes.

Take the example of Hound Dog Taylor (1915–1975), a twelve-fingered (literally) guitarist originally from Natchez, Mississippi. In a story similar to many blues greats', Taylor made his way from the Deep South to Chicago after World War II and started playing on the scene in the early 1960s. For some reason, Taylor's career didn't take off as many of his contemporaries' did. Could it have been the extra fingers? Or the nontraditional instrumentation—slide guitar, baritone guitar, and drums, sans bass—of his band, the HouseRockers? Or even the HouseRockers' reputation for being maniacal boozers in a field that rarely, if ever, batted an eyelash at overindulgence?

Taylor's approach to blues was loose, at best. Captured live on the posthumous collection *Have Some Fun* (1995) Taylor, obviously intoxicated, banters between songs about Chinese food and . . . it's hard to tell exactly what else. The band's intonation is atrocious, and the beat can veer dangerously toward obfuscation; yet the twinned guitars weave a hypnotic logic of their own. After a few numbers, one doesn't miss the bass at all. In fact, Taylor's karate-derived yelps of "Hyeah!" are an invitation to dance. The crowd obviously loves the HouseRockers because they *feel* authentic and are, for lack of a better word, fun.

We might say that the HouseRockers were to the Chicago blues of the 1960s what punk music became to rock in the late seventies, an upstart younger sibling, technically less talented, nontraditional in approach, but supplied with enough energy, enthusiasm, and serious-dash-of-crazy to get over. Bruce Iglauer, an employee of Chicago's stalwart blues label Delmark Records, became a true believer in Hound Dog Taylor. In 1970 he left Delmark, and with $2,500 of his own money started Alligator Records to record, produce, and promote the HouseRockers. Alligator Records went on to add countless legendary artists to its roster, including Buddy Guy, Clarence "Gatemouth" Brown, and Koko Taylor. Authenticity of feeling found the HouseRockers a steward and a home, and it launched one of the most successful contemporary blues labels.

As any casual listener knows, authenticity of feeling in the blues often manifests itself as frank, brutal language. Words that could be construed as libelous, threatening, even prosecutable, are *de rigueur* in the blues. Upon hearing Bentonia, Mississippi, bluesman Skip James's sweet, keening voice on "22–20," one might not realize until the third or fourth playback that he is singing about cutting a woman in half with a shotgun. Almost any topic is allowed on the sacred patch of the blues, as long as the narrator says it from the heart. We'll note, as anyone familiar with the famous country blues ballad "Frankie and Johnny" can attest, that in the blues desperate lovers' unspeakable acts cut both ways across the gender line. Striking a balance between shepherding authenticity and walking the path of Christian righteousness has burdened many blues musicians who jumped (or were forced) on or off the "gospel highway."

The blues also can serve as a mask. Again, taking Skip James as an example, his "Crow Jane" seems like just another violence-fulfillment fantasy, a murder ballad starring his ex-lover:

> I want to buy me a pistol
> Want me forty rounds of ball

Shoot Crow Jane just to see her fall
She got to fall

On close scrutiny, we come to understand that James is embracing the first precept of blues language: frankness in saying what's considered unsayable. Crow Jane isn't a mixed race Native American; she isn't a woman, or even a person. But the blues audience knows what the noninitiated would miss: Crow Jane is Jim Crow, and James intends to use arms and violence to end this unjust system of social confinement. This is the most robustly transgressive statement a Black man in the American South could make in the first half of the twentieth century, one that could lead to his lynching if the wrong people comprehended his meaning.

Blues lyrics also are sexually frank. The bawdiness of the great female blues pioneers—Bessie Smith, Ma Rainey, Lucille Bogan—is part and parcel of their legend. Later, explicit tropes from the blues idiom crossed over into rock via blues-based acts like Led Zeppelin. It's not surprising that Zeppelin's "Lemon Song," for example, lifts its suggestive metaphor verbatim from Robert Johnson's 1937 recording "Traveling Riverside Blues": "Squeeze my lemon, baby / 'Til the juice run down my leg."

Johnson was one of many artists to use this specific sexual innuendo. "Squeezing lemons" was firmly entrenched in the blues vernacular by the time Johnson wrote "Traveling Riverside Blues." We might be forgiven if our most vivid memory of its use is captured in a salacious snapshot of Robert Plant—golden-locked with a python packed into his denims—screeching about his fruit onstage at Madison Square Garden circa 1973.

Yet the blues long have been a reliable incubator of the power, exhilaration, and humor contained in human sexuality. We are reminded of a performance by Nappy Brown—author of the great Ray Charles hit "Night Time Is the Right Time"—at the Variety Playhouse in Atlanta in October of 2002. Brown was seventy-one years old. He was performing with "Steady Rollin'" Bob Margolin, a former guitarist in Muddy Waters's band, as part of a revue that featured other Waters alumnae, including Willie "Big Eyes" Smith on drums and Pinetop Perkins on piano. There probably were one hundred people in the audience, mostly blues fans under forty, in the 1200-capacity venue. Nappy Brown came onstage in a banana-yellow zoot suit. He began a slow-burning blues, ably backed by Margolin and the revue. As Brown sang about an "itch" he could not scratch, he became more agitated. He sang about his "lemon" and whom he'd like to "squeeze" it. What followed were three minutes of the filthiest blues exhibitionism one is likely to see outside of pre-WWII Detroit, Chicago, or Memphis. Brown screamed in pain, holding his crotch and rolling on the ground as if experiencing a monumental, once-in-a-lifetime attack of *tinea cruris*. Continuing to sing, he stuck his hand down his trousers, and with his fist pantomimed an assault on his person by some pulsating monster come to inhabit and persecute his nether-self. It literally was a sexual horror story, told by a rambunctious senior citizen, that had fifty people laughing in the aisles and the other fifty heading to the exits and demanding their money back. It's difficult to say if this was a good thing or a bad thing, but it was a blues thing. Perhaps such experiences are what Black-identified white jazzman Mezz Mezzrow meant when he called his autobiography *Really the Blues* (1946). The blues creates its own community by calling to those within earshot and by amplifying its aesthetic and values beyond their context, ultimately putting the *real* back into comfortable, insulated modern lives.

The blues and the new American poetry of the 1950s and 1960s shared a sense of (sometimes jolting) authenticity that appealed to Dylan and other young songwriters.[12] The characteristics below can be found in particular songs and poems from different eras, but their widespread use—especially in conjunction with one another—in the blues and contemporary poetry helped make poetic song verse possible:

1. A conversational, accessible, style
2. An emphasis on the personal, or the "confessional"
3. An emphasis on the local
4. A use of the fantastic

These characteristics manifested themselves in different but complementary ways in the blues and poetry, a phenomenon that helped make poetic language available to many songwriters in the sixties. To understand how blues-based popular music and poetry came to share the first characteristic, a conversational style, we return to the early twentieth century and the sounds W. C. Handy first encountered in Tutwiler, Mississippi. Around 1900 blues and jazz emerged in the American South. New Orleans and the Mississippi Delta played particularly important roles. In New Orleans downtown Creoles were trained according to European traditions. For instance, training at the city's famed French Opera House began with a year or more of singing solfège, using "do, re, mi, fa, sol, la, ti" as a tool to distinguish steps on the European scale. This course of study provides students' hearing with valuable preparation for the intricate melodic and harmonic systems of European musical theory. But uptown Black musicians who migrated from the country seldom received any formal training.[13] In fact, they often made their own instruments, including diddley bows, washtub basses, fifes, other wind instruments, and various types of drums.

Like most ethnomusicologists, Gerhard Kubik, in *Africa and the Blues*, links timing and pitch in blues and jazz to African music, particularly sounds from Gambia, Senegal, Ghana, and Nigeria. Similarly, Robert Palmer traces the "deep blues" of the Mississippi Delta to various African traditions, particularly Senegambian "drumming, hand clapping, and group singing in call and response form" (1981, 27). As we've discussed, these characteristics became part of slave spirituals, field hollers, and work songs, all of which played a part in creating the blues. Perhaps even more importantly, early blues, ragtime, and jazz musicians picked up on speech patterns and other sounds they heard around them and incorporated them into their music. New Orleans horn players and Delta guitarists often played what they heard; they created music that emphasized spontaneity and audience participation, music that often had little to do with European scales and meters.

An analogous shift in poetry occurred after World War II when Creeley, the Beats, and others began to turn away from modernist and formalist verse practices.[14] A handful of poets—including Hughes, Brown, and Randall Jarrell—had moved in this direction earlier in the century, but from the late forties to the early sixties a new generation of poets—including Robert Lowell, Frank O'Hara, Anne Sexton, Sylvia Plath, Amiri Baraka, and James Wright—tempered modernism's emphasis on idiosyncratic metaphors and allusions, as well as formalism's stress on meter, and began to write poetry more closely aligned with speech patterns.[15] It's widely recognized among literary critics that in *Life Studies* (1959) Lowell moved away from the formally chiseled poetry of his first three books and toward more conversational, confessional poems. This shift is evident in "Memories of West Street and Lepke," a poem in which the narrator Lowell explains that in the "tranquillized fifties" he teaches on Tuesdays and lives in an affluent Boston neighborhood, but that in the forties he'd been a conscientious objector—a "fire breathing Catholic C.O."—who was tried and imprisoned for refusing to serve in the military:

> telling off the state and president, and then
> sat waiting in the bull pen
> beside a Negro boy with curlicues
> of marijuana in his hair

The blues' origins in the sound of the human voice and the turn of poets toward a conversational style are closely related to our second characteristic, an emphasis on the personal. A vital element of the blues can be identified by paraphrasing the great Irish poet William Butler Yeats. Yeats claimed that rhetoric results from conversations with others, but poetry springs from a conversation with oneself. Similarly, blues songs most often center on an internal dialogue concerning intimate thoughts and memories, a tendency that rock inherited and that left rock open to contemporary poetry's emphasis on the self. These qualities are what inform Eric Clapton's claim that "what really shook" him when he listened to Robert Johnson was that Johnson "didn't seem concerned with appeal at all. All the music I'd heard up until that time seemed to be structured in some way for recording ... he was just playing for himself. It was almost as if he felt things so acutely he found it almost unbearable."[16] We'll note that whether or not Clapton's impressions of Johnson's motivations are accurate is relatively unimportant for the development of poetic song verse—what matters is how Clapton and other young musicians experienced Johnson and other blues musician's music, and how it influenced their creative practices.

As the blues evolved in the twentieth century, the call-and-response format of work songs, field hollers, and spirituals was internalized into modes of self-questioning, interrogation, and confession. The dominant blues verse pattern of sets of identical or near-identical lines followed by a line that offers a comment or response often resulted in the types of reflective, private conversations that characterized much contemporary poetry. For instance, Furry Lewis unleashes his anger in "Furry's Blues" (1928):

> I believe I'll buy me a graveyard of my own
> I believe I'll buy me a graveyard of my own
> I'm gonna kill everybody that have done me wrong

In "Empty Bed Blues" (1928) Alberta Hunter sings of loneliness and sexual frustration:

> When my bed gets empty, makes me feel awful mean and blue
> When my bed gets empty, makes me feel awful mean and blue
> 'Cause my springs getting rusty, sleeping single the way I do

Allen Ginsberg's earliest poems are formal, full of allusions, and less than stellar, but the influence of William Carlos Williams, the blues, and jazz led Ginsberg to develop what he often called his own "natural prose poetry style." Like many blues songs, Ginsberg's poems blur the distinction between poet and the "I" figure who narrates the poem. "Kaddish" (1959) is dedicated to Ginsberg's mother, who had passed away.

> Strange now to think of you, gone without corsets & eyes, while I walk on
>   the sunny pavement of Greenwich Village.
> downtown Manhattan, clear winter noon, and I've been up all night, talking,
>   talking, reading the Kaddish aloud, listening to Ray Charles blues
>   shout blind on the phonograph
> the rhythm the rhythm—and your memory in my head three years after—

Anne Sexton's "The Double Image" (1959) provides another example of how, like most blues songs, much contemporary poetry diminishes the distance between poet and persona. The poem's dramatic situation involves a mother—very recognizably Sexton herself—contemplating her relationship with her daughter.

> I am thirty this November.
> You are still small, in your fourth year.
> We stand watching the yellow leaves go queer,
> flapping in the winter rain.

Again, we'd like to stress that the blues lyrics and the poetry we just examined are different. But both are written in conversational, accessible language; they give the impression that the poem's narrator is one and the same as the artist, and they emphasize the speakers' internal, private emotions.

Blues lyrics also tend to focus on the specific and the local—our third characteristic—rather than on the archetypal and the generic. Where in the nineteenth century field hollers, spirituals, and Black hillbilly songs often used archetypal settings and told tales of mythic engineers, animals, outlaws, heroes, demons, and saviors, blues songs often concerned particular locations, individuals, and events, reflecting Delta musicians' relatively small but fluid world.

During the first half of the twentieth century, Delta musicians tended to play venues scattered from New Orleans to Memphis. They performed for Black audiences on the streets of small towns, on plantations, in private homes, and occasionally for whites at parties and other social gatherings. Audiences enjoyed listening to songs that described places, events, and individuals with whom they were familiar. The names of the same small towns (Clarksburg, Greenville, Rosedale, Vicksburg, Yazoo, Natchez, Algiers), of specific plantations, streets, highways, trains, and personages, pop up in song after song. Like William Carlos Williams, who believed poetry should focus on "no ideas but in things," blues lyricists addressed the concrete and the particular.

Charley Patton, one of several musicians dubbed the "Father of the Delta Blues," lived and played on the Dockery Plantation. In "34 Blues" Patton laments what happened to him in 1934 and pleads for another bluesman's job: "They run me from Will Dockery's, Willie Brown, I want your job." In "Crossroads" (1936) Robert Johnson describes his attempts to "flag a ride" at an intersection. His lonely despair leads him to evoke the same Willie Brown, who often performed with Johnson and Patton.

> You can run, you can run, tell my friend Willie Brown
> You can run, you can run, tell my friend Willie Brown
> That I got the crossroad blues this morning,
> Lord, baby I'm sinking down

In 1900 Patton—who was born in Hinds County, Mississippi, and lived most of his life in Sunflower County, Mississippi—and his family moved to the Dockery Plantation, where his playing would influence Willie Brown, Tommy Johnson, Robert Johnson, Howlin' Wolf, John Lee Hooker, and other notable bluesmen. "High Water Everywhere" describes the Great Mississippi Flood of 1927. The flood was especially devastating for many African American sharecroppers, who were legally bound to landowners and prohibited from leaving (when consulting the full lyrics, note the phrase "I would go to the hilly country but they got me barred").

> Well, backwater done rose all around Sumner now, drove me down the line
> Backwater done rose at Sumner, drove poor Charley down the line
> Lord, I'll tell the world the water, done crept through this town

In subsequent verses Patton specifies Leland, Greenville, and Rosedale as places that are flooded and claims he's headed for Vicksburg and other "lands" where water "don't never flow."

Like Delta blues singers during the first half of the twentieth century, in the fifties and the sixties contemporary poets emphasized local settings and turned toward seemingly autobiographical poetry written in conversational language. In "Autumn Begins in Martins Ferry, Ohio" (1963), James Wright describes how sitting in his hometown high school football stadium leads him to consider the lives of people from nearby places whose sons play there.

> I think of Polacks nursing long beers in Tiltonsville,
> And gray faces of Negroes in the blast furnace at Benwood,
> And the ruptured night watchmen of Wheeling Steel,
> Dreaming of heroes.

Frank O'Hara, a poet associated with the New York School, lived and worked in Manhattan. His *Lunch Poems* (1964) often depict their narrator's day-to-day experiences. In "A Step Away from Them," the narrator O'Hara strolls on "to Times Square" and sees a man and a woman interacting:

> A blonde chorus girl clicks: he
> smiles and rubs his chin. Everything
> suddenly honks: it is 12:40 of
> a Thursday.

In addition to a stress on conversational language, the personal, and the local, blues music and the new American poetry often displayed an emphasis on the surreal or fantastic (our fourth characteristic and a topic we discuss in more detail in chapter 4). Where surrealism primarily entered mid-twentieth-century American poetry through the work of European artists, surrealistic imagery came to the blues via a mixture of African and Western religion and mysticism.[18] Blues lyrics often are surreal in terms of their nonlinear, associative, stream-of-consciousness character, much like the license so many twentieth century American poets take to jump around in a world as paradoxically death-haunted and jubilant, dark and hopeful, profound and terrifying, finished and nascent as the Old Testament. Blues lyrics often tend to address the actual world, but in language that is not of the real world, framing terrible or bizarre experiences in terms of fantastic events.

Like mid-century poets, blues lyricists used surreal imagery to describe individual's interior reality in terms of the fantastic. For example, Ma Rainey's "Black Dust Blues" (1928) describes romantic turmoil in terms of being cursed by a woman who claims the narrator "took her man." One morning she discovers black dust around her door and starts to "get thin" and experience trouble with her feet:

> Black dust in my window, black dust on my porch mat
> Black dust in my window, black dust on my porch mat
> Black dust's got me walking on all fours like a cat

In "Hellhound on My Trail" (1937) Robert Johnson likens evading emotional anguish to fending off a satanic beast with hoodoo:

> You sprinkled hot foot powder, mmm, around my door
> You sprinkled hot foot powder, all around your daddy's door
> It keeps me with rambling in mind rider
> Every old place I go, every old place I go

In American poetry the fantastic most often has been associated with surrealism's influence on Beat, New York, and Deep Image poetry, such as Robert Bly's "Waking from Sleep" (1962):

> Inside the veins there are navies setting forth,
> Tiny explosions at the water lines
> And seagulls weaving in the wind of the salty blood

And James Wright's "A Blessing" (1963):

> Suddenly I realize
> That if I stepped out of my body I would break
> Into blossom

However, as the sixties unfolded, many different poets also integrated the fantastic into their poems.[19] In "Lady Lazarus" (1965), Sylvia Plath, a poet usually identified with the Confessional school, claims,

Out of the ash
I rise with my red hair
And I eat men like air.

James Dickey, a southern narrative poet, created a form he called "country surrealism." Part of "The Sheep Child" (1965) is told from the point of view of a creature half-human and half-animal. For "a blazing moment" the sheep child sees the "great grassy world from both sides":

My hoof and my hand clasped each other,
I ate my one meal
Of milk, and died

The type of fantastical imagery associated with the blues and contemporary poetry influenced dozens of iconic rock songs, including the Rolling Stones' "Sympathy for the Devil," Santana's "Black Magic Woman," the Jimi Hendrix Experience's "Voodoo Chile (Slight Return)," and Led Zeppelin's "The Battle of Evermore." The emergence of psychedelic culture reinforced and altered this trend. The Beatles' "Lucy in the Sky with Diamonds" and "I Am the Walrus," the Jefferson Airplane's "White Rabbit," the Doors' "Break on Through (to the Other Side)" and "The End," and the Moody Blues' tribute to Timothy Leary, "Legend of a Mind," are among the many examples of blues-based psychedelic surrealism that drew on literary influences.

Poetry's turn toward more accessible language and the blues' origins in the sound of the human voice—as well as each genre's emphasis on the confessional, the local, and the fantastic—helped rock absorb poetic language and techniques and provided a catalyst for Dylan and others to change rock into a more lyrically and sonically sophisticated art form. Think about it this way: If you were a reasonably intellectual young musician who had been turned on to the blues, poems like John Crowe Ransom's picture-perfect metrical verse, or high modernist poetry such as T. S. Eliot's *The Waste Land*, might provide an idea of how to use allusions in a song, or provide strategies for intermingling certain types of imagery (as in some of Dylan's, Van Morrison's, and Joni Mitchell's verse). But the language in most modernist poems tends to be very different from the type of language that characterizes blues-based popular music. However, when that same blues-enthralled young musician heard Howlin' Wolf or Willie Dixon and read and heard Beat and other contemporary poets, he or she was exposed to rich, sophisticated language based on rhythms of speech (i.e., material that could serve as a powerful source for lyrics). As we'll discuss in chapters 2 and 3, with different twists and turns this essentially was the case for Dylan, Mick Jagger, John Lennon, Paul McCartney, Jim Morrison, and many others.

2

Bob Dylan, Chuck Berry, and the Evolution of Poetic Song Verse

Notoriously, and perhaps unsurprisingly, Bob Dylan dispatched Patti Smith to read his Nobel Prize acceptance speech and opted to release his own recording of another speech later.[1] Dylan's piano-accompanied talk is more than a lecture. Whereas Smith served as a buffer between Dylan and the public in the present, the recording allowed him to orchestrate what he leaves for posterity in a way that's unique among Nobel Prize winners in literature. In a performance reminiscent of Jack Kerouac and other Beat writers' recordings of the late fifties and early sixties, Dylan reflects on people and works that influenced him—Buddy Holly, Lead Belly, *Moby Dick*, *All Quiet on the Western Front*, and *The Odyssey*—and compares his professional practices to Shakespeare's. Essentially, Dylan invokes these artists and literary works to affirm the wider importance of rock 'n' roll, the rural blues, and literature to his creative practices. He asserts that he wanted his songs to "make it all connect and move with the current of the day."[2]

Dylan's emphasis on tying his songs to "the current of the day" played an essential role in poetic song verse's development. In chapter 1 we focused on the formal and aesthetic characteristics that helped make poetic song verse possible. In this chapter we'll discuss how the cultural landscape of the fifties set the stage for Dylan and other practitioners of poetic song verse in the sixties. It's well known that in the early sixties Dylan modeled himself on Woody Guthrie, and that in 1965 he reverted to his teenage passion for rock 'n' roll when he jettisoned his Guthrie-like folk style and opened *Bringing It All Back Home* with "Subterranean Homesick Blues," a song modeled on Chuck Berry's 1956 hit "Too Much Monkey Business." But the larger question of the blues' and rock 'n' roll's—and Berry's in particular—influence on Dylan only has been addressed tangentially. In 1955 the twenty-nine-year-old Berry—whom Dylan calls "the Shakespeare of rock 'n' roll"—embraced the persona of a rebellious teenager, an image that allowed him to sell records to adolescents and to cloak lyrics that defied mainstream values. Similarly, Dylan's return to rock 'n' roll propelled him to assume a new persona and to infuse his music with qualities that jolted his audience and the nation. We'll pay particular attention to how Berry's use of persona and his response to fifties culture influenced Dylan, and how the racially charged, politically transgressive dimensions of fifties rock 'n' roll helped spur Dylan and other songwriters' challenges to an array of social norms. Cultural shifts during the midsixties prompted Dylan to combine rock 'n' roll, the rural blues, and poetry, and to convey authenticity through an *aesthetic of disorientation*, changes that opened rock to new possibilities and ignited an explosion of poetic song verse.

Nick Tosches stresses that "rock 'n' roll was not created solely by whites or by blacks.... It evolved slowly." He also points out that by the "early thirties, rock 'n' roll was more than a fuck-phrase" (1999, 1, 6). But it wasn't until the fifties that rock 'n' roll became a phenomenon among white and Black teenagers, who embraced it as badge of independence against an older generation ossified by McCarthyism and terrified by challenges to racial segregation. Dylan, Joni Mitchell, John Lennon, Paul McCartney, Mick Jagger, Keith Richards, Stephen Stills, Van Morrison, and many others who were teenagers in the fifties have acknowledged their debts to rock 'n' roll; but during the fifties rock 'n' roll widely was considered a lesser musical form. Jazz—the sounds of Thelonious Monk, Dizzy Gillespie, Charlie Parker, Billie Holiday, Sara Vaughan, Sonny Rollins, Miles Davis, John Coltrane, Julian "Cannonball" Adderley, Abbey Lincoln, Dave Brubeck, Charles Mingus, and Ornette Coleman—was the sphere of virtuosos, the music that cool cats, hipsters, and sophisticated aficionados dug. The folk music and rural blues Dylan would embrace were the province of socially conscious purists, largely imbibed by a younger generation of middle-class, college-educated whites who mingled with the unwashed. Rock 'n' roll, on other the other hand, was regarded as adolescent kid stuff, music for rebellious, irresponsible, hormonal teenagers. In 1957 Frank Sinatra famously fumed that rock 'n' roll was "sung, played, and written for the most part by cretinous goons and by means of its almost imbecilic reiteration and sly, lewd, in plain fact, dirty lyrics it manages to be the martial music of every sideburned delinquent on the face of the earth."[3] Anglo-European and African American newspapers ran continuous features and editorials warning against its effects on adolescents. Shows were banned in cities all over the nation. Rock 'n' roll seemed so threatening that in 1958 the Mutual Broadcasting System dropped it from all network music programing.[4]

These sentiments were challenged as popular culture—in venues ranging from movies starring Elvis Presley to *American Bandstand*—sanitized, whitened, and profited from it. Grace Palladino points out that it was "one thing for teenagers to dance along to 'American Bandstand' while their mothers and kid sisters looked on. It was quite another when they danced on the seats at a live rock 'n' roll show in a mixed crowd of frantic teenagers" (1996, 155). In the public imagination, the decade remains characterized as a time of relative innocence and prosperity in dozens of constantly streaming bedroom comedies and other fifties films starring the likes of Doris Day, Cary Grant, Debbie Reynolds, and Rock Hudson, and in fifties TV sitcoms, including *The Honeymooners*, *The Adventures of Ozzie and Harriet*, *Father Knows Best*, and *Leave It to Beaver*. These shows, and many others, were founded on explicit and implicit assumptions of Anglo-European homogeneity. In a popular "mixed" fifties sitcom, *I Love Lucy*, the show's female star is married to a Cuban bandleader who resembles his white neighbors physically and shares their concerns and values.[5] Conversely, much fifties film noir and other ambitious movies, including *The Asphalt Jungle*, *In a Lonely Place*, *Sunset Boulevard*, *The Big Heat*, *Night and the City*, *A Touch of Evil*, *The Wild One*, *On the Waterfront*, *Rebel Without a Cause*, *East of Eden*, *Blackboard Jungle*, and *I Want to Live*, as well as many teen rock 'n' roll movies of the mid to late fifties—see (or don't) *Don't Knock the Rock*; *Shake, Rattle and Rock*; and *Dragstrip Riot*—offer portraits of a society filled with anxiety and corruption, and haunted by a plethora of paradoxical impulses.

The disparities between characterizations of the fifties as a nostalgic soundtrack for a bygone age of innocence or as the chords of social unrest are striking and increasingly have drawn critical attention. In *All Shook Up: How Rock 'n' Roll Changed America*, Glenn C. Altschuler details the pressures that led to differing images of that time: in the fifties there was a "pervasive, powerful, public ideology proclaiming the United States a harmonious, homogenous, and prosperous land," but "rock 'n' roll seemed to be everywhere during the decade, exhilarating, influential, and even pivotal to some, and an outrage to Americans intent on ignoring, wishing away, or suppressing dissent and conflict" (2003, 9). Reactions to rock 'n' roll were similar to those against hot jazz and bebop in previous decades, but intensified by mounting challenges to racial segregation.[6] Fear of Black and white youth fraternizing—and having sex—heightened, and music was deemed an accomplice. As Robert Walser asserts, "Racists attacked rock and roll because of the mingling of black and white people it implied and achieved, and because of what they saw as black music's power to corrupt through vulgar and animalistic rhythms" (1998, 358).

A seemingly endless roll call of people, incidents, and events reflects the tensions that underpin rock 'n' roll's well-documented legacy: Wynonie Harris's "Good Rockin' Tonight," Ike Turner's "Rocket 88," Jack Lait and Lee Mortimer's *USA Confidential, Brown v. Board of Education*, Beale Street, Sam Phillips, Arthur Crudup's "That's Alright," Elvis's "That's Alright," Big Mama Thornton's "Hound Dog," Elvis's "Hound Dog," WDIA, Rufus Thomas, WHBQ, Dewey Phillips, Specialty, Chess, Stax, Sun, Atlantic, the Fender Esquire Guitar, Asa Carter and "white citizens" groups' denunciations of white and Black teenagers dancing together, Alan Freed's Cleveland-based "The Moondog House" and his radio "Rock 'n' Roll Party," Norman Mailer's "The White Negro," Jack Kerouac's Sal Paradise wishing he were Black, Jerry Leiber and Michael Stoller wishing they were Black, New York congressman Emanuel Celler thinking that Leiber and Stoller were Black, Ginsberg's "negro streets at dawn," Fats Domino and other "crossover artists," Little Richard abandoning rock 'n' roll after recording eighteen hit singles in three years to enter the Oakwood Theological Seminary, and dozens of other people and phenomena fill chapters and footnotes.

Elvis was the most popular and controversial singer of the time, but nobody made a bigger impact on the development of rock 'n' roll lyrically than Chuck Berry. In interviews Berry often stressed that he played and wrote songs to make money, and his attempts to tap into larger markets in the fifties were part of a larger trend to expand rhythm and blues' appeal and grow the budding rock 'n' roll market. In the late forties Ahmet Ertegun and Herb Abramson had made efforts to open up the blues market to white audiences by signing African American musicians to their nascent Atlantic Records label. In 1949 Ertegun, Abramson, and Jesse Stone—"the first black person on the Atlantic payroll"—traveled to New Orleans, where Stone "put up a sign in the back of a black record shop saying that anyone who had a song should bring it to Cosimo Matassa's studio when the Atlantic Record Company would be there." Stone remembers that "songwriters lined up outside the door . . . like people going to a movie" (Greenfield 2011, 86). In Memphis, Rufus Thomas and other disc jockeys' success at WDIA airing blues by Howlin' Wolf, Muddy Waters, and others in the late forties inspired WHBQ to let the soon-to-be-infamous "Daddy-O" Dewey loose on *Red Hot and Blue*—by the midfifties roughly 100,000 listeners were turning in. At KOWH in Omaha, Nebraska, Bill Stewart and Todd Storz launched daily radio programming based on the jukebox and the popular weekly radio show *American Hit Parade*. Other radio stations across the country soon followed suit, playing the same songs several times a day. James Miller observes that the "Storz Top 40 format simply turned a radio station into *Your Hit Parade* writ large" (1999, 55). By 1953, 25 percent of the radio stations *Billboard* surveyed featured several hours of rhythm and blues programming weekly" (Jackson 1991, 58–59). In 1958 Sam Phillips reflected that in the early fifties, "you could sell a half-million copies of a rhythm and blues record. These records appealed to white youngsters" (Bertrand 2005, 65).

Critics and historians have documented how the appeal of beating drums and heightened emotions in rhythm and blues and rock 'n' roll sparked fears of miscegenation. Michael T. Bertrand notes that in the fifties Elvis's "merging of black music and culture with white symbolized similar trends occurring throughout the South," especially "volatile issues of class, race, and age" (2005, 23). Though Elvis didn't write songs, his recordings and performances incited fear and anger. As Eric Lott points out, "all the citizens' councils in the South called Elvis 'n----- music' and were terribly afraid that Elvis . . . was going to corrupt the youth of America" (MacLowry 2001). Racist paranoia spread all over the country. Shows were banned in Boston, New Haven, Jersey City, Minneapolis, Atlanta, and dozens of other cities. New York congressman Emanuel Celler, a Brooklyn Jew who usually possessed a liberal bent, blamed rock 'n' roll's popularity on payola[7]—which, in fact, was rampant—and insisted, "Rock 'n' roll has its place among the colored people. . . . The bad taste that is exemplified by the Elvis Presley 'Hound Dog' music, with his animal gyrations which are certainly most distasteful . . . are violative of all that I know to be in good taste" (Grualnick 1994, 384). In the mid to late fifties authorities in San Diego, several locales in Florida, and other places threatened that if Elvis moved at all during shows, he would be arrested for obscenity. In 1957 *The Ed Sullivan Show* famously filmed him from the waist up because executives feared his performance would be considered indecent.

But at least Elvis was white. Black artists who performed to mixed-race audiences were seen as manifestations of fears coming true, and reactions sometimes verged on hysteria. Responses to Little Richard's gender-bending sexuality—early in his career he had performed in drag in vaudeville shows—and his ecstatic, unpredictable, raucous performances were scorned by many whites and Blacks.[8] As Preston Lauterbach quips in *The Chitlin' Circuit and the Road to Rock 'n' Roll*, "funky and gay were definitely the wrong kind of black" (2011, 249). Little Richard claimed that his first hit song, the homoerotic "Tutti Frutti," was best suited to whites-only venues: "White people, it always cracked 'em up, but black people didn't like it that much." As a counterstrategy to potentially hostile Blacks and whites, he "decided that my image should be crazy and way out so that the adults would think I was harmless. I'd appear in one show dressed as the Queen of England and in the next as the pope" (Miller 1999, 111–12).

Chuck Berry and other rock 'n' rollers' response to mid-century American culture provided a rough template for Dylan and other sixties songwriters' lyric practices. Berry wanted to make and sell music that tapped into as many demographic markets as possible, but he soon recognized that rock 'n' roll was his ticket. Lauterbach notes that Berry's first hit, "Maybellene," "was destined to carry Berry over to a predominately white audience, making him the briefest tenured of the chitlin' circuit artists during rock 'n' roll's rise" (2011, 250). Berry recalled that the song "got me into the country market," but that when he showed up to play in Nashville, the promoters realized he was Black and "canceled the gig" (Flanagan 1987, 83). In "Johnny B. Goode" the phrase "little colored boy" was altered to "little country boy" in order to enhance sales, but the song didn't dent the country market; however, it was embraced by teenagers. Palladino observes that in the "days of swing" teenagers had been a "major part of the crowd, but adults participated, too." In contrast "rock 'n' roll stars, like Bo Diddley, Joe Turner, LaVern Baker, or Fats Domino played to racially mixed houses that would have surprised swing musicians" and had "only one audience to please . . . the thirteen- to nineteen-year-old crowd" (1996, 124).

Berry perceived that many teenagers' passion for rock 'n' roll was propelled by the racial, generational, and cultural tensions informing anxious parents and irate traditionalists' fear of it, a blueprint Dylan, Jagger, Jim Morrison, and many others employed in the sixties. Marlon Brando's riposte ("Whadda you got?") to the question "What are you rebelling against?" in *The Wild One* (1953) often is used to characterize a rebellious attitude among fifties youth, but Berry realized precisely what many teenagers were bucking against—their parents—and that rock 'n' roll served as a physical and emotional cynosure of their discontent. He observed, "Some of the white fathers didn't want my songs getting into the suburbs at all. A big hit would get right into the jukebox ... elite suburban parents didn't want kids to hear it. They'd call the radio stations and say, 'Don't play that record! We've got kids dancing to it'" (Flanagan 1987, 84).

Despite his insistence that songwriting primarily was a moneymaking venture, Berry—like Little Richard, Elvis, Bo Diddley, B. B. King, Jimmy Reed, and others—realized that his music was having a strong effect on race relations. In the PBS special *The History of Rock 'n' Roll: Rock 'n' Roll Explodes*, Carl Perkins expressed that at rock 'n' roll shows in the fifties kids of different races danced together and saw "no difference," and recalled that Berry told him, "We might be doing as much with our music as our leaders are in Washington to bring down the barriers." Changes in record sales over the course of the decade are telling. In 1954 Black artists represented 3 percent of the sales on the pop charts. By 1957 that number had increased to almost 30 percent (Bertrand 2005, 86). In his high school yearbook Dylan asserted his ambition "to join Little Richard" (Shelton 1997, 39). But whereas Little Richard's lyrics and persona often cloaked, blurred, and burlesqued issues of sexuality and gender, Berry's lyrics and image often masked racial and generational issues.

As we discuss later in this chapter, the stories Berry told in his verse provided Dylan and others with an example of how assuming a persona could serve as a catalyst for creating socially provocative popular music. In the midfifties Berry adopted the persona of a rebellious teenager, though he was thirty when "Roll Over Beethoven" hit the charts in 1956. His past had prepared him for the persona he adopted. He had grown up in a deeply religious middle-class family in a relatively prosperous African American neighborhood in St. Louis. Berry biographer Bruce Pegg describes the Ville as a "self-contained island of black enterprise and culture in a vast white, segregated ocean" (2002, 5). At a high school talent contest Berry sang "Confessin' the Blues" because, as Berry claimed, "everybody was playing it on the jukebox across the street and nobody was singing any blues in the show." During the performance his schoolmates' applause heartened the nervous fifteen-year-old, but he noticed that a look of "'How dare you?' showed on the faces of a couple of faculty members" (Berry 1987, 33–34). But by the time Berry wrote lyrics from the perspective of or about restless teenagers, his own life experiences had taken him well beyond his audience's ducktails and bobby socks. As a seventeen-year-old he was sentenced to ten years (he served three in a juvenile detention facility) for stealing a car and committing three armed robberies in less than a week. After several years of drifting from job to job, in the early fifties Berry, now married, joined a band and started playing regular gigs in East St. Louis, a rough-and-tumble city replete with musical talent, blues clubs, and violence.

After Muddy Waters introduced him to Leonard Chess in 1955, Berry signed with Chess records in Chicago, a city embroiled in a campaign against rock 'n' roll. Willie Dixon—whose blues songwriting prowess was of such stature that he credibly titled his autobiography *I Am the Blues*—was working at Chess. When he first heard Berry, Dixon "knew he was a very good poet" (Flanagan 1987, 73). Berry soon adopted a teenage persona, but he was well versed in a range of musical styles. He had studied and imitated Charlie Christian's and T-Bone Walker's guitar and performance styles. He had listened to blues, R&B, classical music, and white country musicians, especially Jimmie Rodgers and Bill Monroe. In 1953 he had joined pianist Johnnie Johnson's Sir John's Trio. Berry's first hit, "Maybellene" (1955), was a reworking of a traditional Appalachian fiddle tune that Bob Wills and His Texas Playboys had recorded as country swing song in 1938 and had recast as "Ida Red Likes the Boogie" in 1949. Berry's song shot to number one on the R&B chart and to number five on the pop chart.

"Maybellene" reflects Berry's penchant for misdirection, a technique he soon used to mask politically provocative lyrics and that influenced Dylan and other sixties songwriters. The song possesses one of rock 'n' roll's most recognizable refrains, "Maybellene, why can't you be true?" On the surface, "Maybellene" appears to be a typical "woman done me wrong" song; the type of song in country music wherein the narrator sings an inventory of grievances against his beloved and then describes how his heartbreak manifests itself over her misdeeds ("walking the floor," "cryin' over you," etc.). Musically, this is not a stretch: "Maybellene" is an exaggerated country two-step, simply faster and rawer (consider the rhythmic feel of Hank Williams's "Hey Good Lookin'" on steroids).

However, the country/blues trope of a woman-done-me-wrong song belies Berry's cunning use of framing and juxtaposition. Ironically, Berry's cool-under-pressure delivery of this breathless tale potentially veils the dynamic language and point-of-view strategies that edge "Maybellene" toward the poetic. Two elements distract the listener from the outset: First, the inauspicious introductory guitar lick (a "clam" in the vernacular: Berry and his studio team probably kept it because the ensuing take was so lively; there was no technology for overdubs in 1955), and second, the fact that the verses fly out of the gate at an impressive clip, generating a word tsunami that blurs comprehension. What can go unnoticed is that "Maybellene" actually is a detailed description of a car chase—or perhaps more accurately, a road race. The first verse opens in medias res with the narrator "motivatin' over the hill." He spots Maybellene in her Cadillac, determines nothing will beat his V-8 Ford, and pulls up next to her.

It soon becomes unclear if Maybellene is the driver or the passenger. If she's the passenger, who exactly is driving the car she is in? A rival racer? Or is Maybellene on the run with a lover? Berry frames the story with an almost throwaway couplet about a girl who is "untrue," only to push the listener into a heart-stopping action-film sequence. The subversion of expectations sets the song aloft. The language is that of a seasoned driver, active and in charge, matching Berry's measured delivery in the face of his many syllables: "motivatin'" instead of driving, binding machine and human intent together; chopping the make of the car in two in order to catch the rhyme and alliteration of the first couplet ("Coupe de Ville / Cadillac- . . ."), Ford vs. Caddy at 95 mph, "side by side." And who is the hero? Who is the villain? As the road and lyrics rush past, the pronouns begin to blur as well. "*She's* bumper to bumper" (emphasis ours) makes the listener wonder if the narrator is referring to "Maybellene" or the narrator's Ford ("she" in the parlance of vehicles and ships). The careful listener may wonder: What is *happening*? I thought I was going to hear you complain about your ex, and now I'm a spectator at a classic-car drag race?

Hence, the second chorus is draped in an entirely different context. "Maybellene why can't you be true?" now is the mantra of the concentrated madman behind the wheel, something he might be muttering to himself, or yelling at the car he's chasing, or at his own vehicle, urging it on—an apt metaphor for romance. The speed increases; the chase accelerates as the Cadillac speeds to a "hundred and four" and the Ford begins to overheat and can't go any faster. It looks like the narrator has fallen behind the Cadillac, which is now racing at an almost impossible speed. But in a melodramatic twist, the clouds open up and rain cascades down on the race/chase. It seems like it's curtains for our hero—but wait: he realizes rain is cooling his motor and that he *can* pass!

The story has a third act. The third verse returns to the terse, active language of the first. Once the engine cools the narrator finally hears "that highway sound," an unexpected but beautiful phrase that renders the driver's open-throttled confidence. As the listener ponders its sonic and pneumatic meanings, the narrator abruptly shifts to his behind-the-wheel perspective: "The Cadillac a-sittin' like a ton of lead / A hundred and ten half a mile ahead." You are there with the narrator, looking through the windshield; the Cadillac is no longer shrinking into the distance; its presence is maintained and presumably magnified by the narrator's own speed. He *catches* Maybellene "at the top of the hill"! The possible outcomes are manifold and unspoken.

Within months after the song's release, Berry turned toward politically charged topics and more poignant lyrics. Though there is little indication that literature influenced Berry's verse beyond the fact that he insisted that as a youngster he "wrote poems," not songs, he often stressed that a "song is written for the story" (Flanagan 1987, 80, 85). His ability to tell stories in verse by combining rhythm and blues with rockabilly led to a string of hits from 1956 to 1959 that shrouded controversial themes with playful rhymes and melodies, a tactic that Dylan, Jagger, Lennon, Mitchell, and others employed in manifold ways during the sixties. "Roll Over Beethoven," "School Days," "Rock and Roll Music," "Sweet Little Sixteen," and "Johnny B. Goode" all celebrated rock 'n' roll at a time when it was increasingly controversial. Berry's 1956 hit "Roll Over Beethoven" came on the heels of Elvis's first televised appearance and the release of the movie *Rock Around the Clock*, events that had been blamed for instigating riots and vandalism. Berry's prescription for the "rockin' pneumonia" dizzying American culture was a "shot of rhythm and blues" spiked with ingenious and provocative lyrics, a formula Dylan adopted and modified in the midsixties when he described Johnny "in the basement / mixing up the medicine" in "Subterranean Homesick Blues." Berry's 1957 single "School Days" hit the charts when many public and nearly all Catholic schools in Chicago—where Berry was recording—had banned it on school grounds and had cautioned parents to shield their children from it. Chicago radio stations were deluged with an estimated fifteen thousand letters protesting rock 'n' roll. Producer and guitarist T Bone Burnett calls "School Days" "a straight piece of journalism. He wasn't a kid—he was thirty years old when he wrote that. He was just writing about what he saw, the mood of the country, of the town" (Flanagan 1987, 53). The song cheers when "three o'clock rolls around" and students hurry "Right to the juke joint . . . / You gotta hear somethin' that's really hot." Berry's appeal that rock 'n' roll "deliver me from the days of old" and to the "beat of the drums, loud and bold" was a direct affront to critics like Jack Lait and Lee Mortimer, who in their bestseller, *USA Confidential* (1952), linked teenage degeneracy to "tom-toms and hot jive and ritualistic orgies of erotic dancing, weed-smoking and mass mania, with African jungle background"; they claimed "many music shops" that sold rhythm and blues and jazz were places where "white girls were recruited for colored lovers" (37).

Berry's most lyrically ambitious and provocative song of the fifties perhaps was "Brown Eyed Handsome Man" (1956), the B side of "Too Much Monkey Business." The song influenced Dylan and was covered by Buddy Holly, Johnny Rivers, Nina Simone, Waylon Jennings, and others. Like "Maybellene," "Brown Eyed Handsome Man" relies on misdirection. But whereas "Maybellene" manipulates point of view to divert and guide the listener, "Brown Eyed Handsome Man" cloaks its theme by adding an extra word, "eyed," each time the title is invoked, creating a phrase that wasn't specific enough to solicit charges of interracial sexual attraction, though the connotations are clear. The song depicts various instances of white women attracted to men of color, sometimes resulting in "a lot of trouble for a brown-eyed handsome man" and his female suitor: "Milo Venus," the Greek goddess of love and beauty, "lost both the arms in a wrestling match / To get a brown-eyed handsome man." It concludes with a brown-eyed handsome man belting a game-winning home run, a particularly compelling image in an era when Major League Baseball was being racially integrated. Like "School Days" and many of his songs of the mid to late fifties, the song also reflects Berry's response to his immediate environment, what we call the "local" in chapter 1. While frequenting a predominantly African American and Latino neighborhood in California, Berry had observed a Chicano man being threatened with arrest and a white woman demanding the police release him. Berry's own efforts at racial dissimulation—on his driver's license in the fifties he identified himself as "Indian," and his bandmate Johnnie Johnson claimed that Berry "wanted to be everything but a St. Louisian, but an Afro-American"—perhaps also are embedded in his cagey description of a "brown-eyed handsome man" (Pegg 2002, 47).

After the release of "Back in the U.S.A." in 1959, Berry had several minor hits in the early sixties, including "Promised Land" (1964), his first single after his release from prison for violating the Mann Act (he was accused of having sex with a minor and transporting her across state lines). In a brilliant analysis of the song, T. R. Hummer explains that the circuitous route the narrator takes—Norfolk, Virginia, to Los Angeles via several southern states—likely was inspired by the "tragic events in Birmingham" and in "the South generally." Hummer points out why the narrator "stopped in Charlotte and bypassed Rock Hill":

> It's no accident, then, that the Greyhound in "Promised Land" heads south (it could have traveled more directly west), and the reference to Rock Hill, S.C., where the bus does *not* go, is tellingly deliberate. Since 1955, Rock Hill had been a civil rights flashpoint. The desegregation of a Rock Hill Catholic school in that year had ignited racial friction that led to such an effective boycott of the Rock Hill bus company that it went out of business. Berry's "poor boy" could not have got there by bus. In 1960 a series of lunch counter sit-ins began, leading to the 1961 arrest and imprisonment of nine men, now known as the Friendship Nine. In that same year, John Lewis, then a young civil rights crusader and now a U.S. Representative, was badly beaten in Rock Hill by a Klansman when Lewis arrived there on a Freedom Rider bus. Rock Hill, then, has an undeniable place on the landscape, and in the history, of racial conflict in the U.S.—as well as a checkered relationship with buses. (Hummer 2019, 137)

Like Berry's protagonist in "Promised Land," many young songwriters went on the road in the sixties, heading for Los Angeles, San Francisco, New York, Boston, and others locales in search of a more tolerant social environment and a vibrant musical culture. The impetus behind Dylan's 1961 trek from Minnesota to New York City, where he honed his craft at Woody Guthrie's feet and adopted a persona that matched the new prototype of an "authentic" folk and rural bluesman, was part of a larger phenomenon that involved a shift away from rock 'n' roll. Suze Rotolo, Dylan's significant other in the early sixties, notes that "Rock and Roll was approaching adolescence and kids who had grown up with one foot in folk music and the other in rock were unsteady in their loyalties. Rock was tied to commercialism and selling out. Elvis was a flagrant example of that" (2008, 240). Dylan's sentiments in the liner notes to *Biograph* (1985) capture what many young folkies felt: he came to believe that rock 'n' roll "songs weren't serious or didn't reflect life in a realistic way. I knew that when I got into folk music, it was more of a serious type of thing. The songs are filled with more despair, more sadness, more triumph, more faith in the supernatural, much deeper feelings."[9]

Dylan returned to Berry and rock 'n' roll in the midsixties, but he was responding to the sanitized turn much rock 'n' roll took in the late fifties and early sixties, when Pat Boone, Frankie Avalon, Connie Francis, and Brenda Lee's singles flittered to the top of the pop charts. Like Dylan, many others—including Dave Van Ronk, Jack Elliott, Joan Baez, Peter Yarrow, Mary Travers, Phil Ochs, and Tom Paxton—also assumed the folk guise and embraced the authenticity they associated with it. The call of the rural blues was irresistible to the mostly young white musicians, intellectuals, and college students who were the engine behind the folk music revival. Aspirants sought to mimic the originators' sounds, endeavoring to sound archaic and idiosyncratic, note for note. For some, the blues became a university of otherness: poor, rural, and inflected with Black language, stories, and music; they reveled in immersing themselves in a culture foreign to them and feeling themselves honorary outsiders. Norman Mailer had grasped at this collusion of hipsterism, race, and transgressive behavior in his 1957 essay "The White Negro." Kevin Young observes that the "postwar fascination with the 'White Negro'" reflects a "dissatisfaction with America expressed through black culture" (2012, 255). And Keith Richards's assertion "We just wanted to be black motherfuckers" in his autobiography, *Life* (2010), suggests how this dissatisfaction transcended the United States' borders and why young European whites came to identify with the rural blues (Richards 2010, 104).

Guthrie's autobiography *Bound for Glory* (1943), Harry Smith's *Anthology of American Folk Music* (1952), Samuel Charters's *The Country Blues* (1959), and other media served as templates on how to become a folkie or bluesman. But it's important to note that Smith's anthology and Guthrie's autobiography essentially were works of the imagination (Smith cites his credentials as an experimental filmmaker and magician, suggesting his work was fanciful). Rather than a comprehensive musicological representation of rural American song, Smith's anthology reflects the favorite works of an eccentric music fan, Harry Smith, who organized the selections by genre, rather than by the artists' races, an unusual tactic at the time. Smith's liner notes became a Rosetta stone for deciphering the mysterious origins of music that, to young middle-class whites, must have appeared to transubstantiate from a sphere more like Mars than the USA, a place Greil Marcus in *Invisible Republic* described as "the old, weird America." Smith's notes are a whimsical collage, designed to resemble a perverse parlor music catalog: reproductions of sheet music, instructional diagrams for old-style banjos, Autoharps (some of which appear to be for sale), inky lithographs of artists such as Gus Cannon's Jug Stompers, and finally, a few choice quotes from the likes of controversial British occultist Aleister Crowley and theosophist Rudolf Steiner ("The in-breathing becomes thought, and the out-breathing becomes the will manifestation of thought"). Particularly amusing are Smith's capsule summaries of songs. Consider his description of the Carolina Tar Heels' 1932 rendition of "Got the Farmland Blues": "DISCOURAGING ACTS OF GOD AND MAN CONVINCE FARMER OF POSITIVE BENEFITS IN URBAN LIFE."

The idiosyncratic, imaginative quality of Smith's collection caught the attention of aspiring folkies seeking to reinvent themselves. Van Ronk observes that the collection became a touchstone for the young converts, who "all knew every word of every song on it, including the ones we hated" (2005, 47). Marcus stresses that "Smith's definition of 'American folk music' would have satisfied no one else. He ignored all field recordings, Library of Congress archives, anything validated only by scholarship or carrying the must of the museum. He wanted music to which people really had responded: records put on sale that at least somebody thought were worth paying for" (1998, 102). Marcus asserts that what the newly minted folkies found among the anthology's old-world folk songs, Appalachian ballads, Negro work songs, and country blues was "the call of another life" (101). By this we are meant to believe something much more mysterious, trenchant, and dangerous than the prescribed norms for American youth in the fifties and early sixties. John Cooke, a bluegrass guitarist and the son of journalist Alistair Cooke, remembers that "one of the things that made this music different and better than what everybody else was listening to was the fact that everybody *wasn't* listening to it. It was *anti*commercial music." But as David Hajdu points out, Cooke and other young folkies didn't realize that the "music they revered as noncommercial (or anticommercial), the sound of rural artists that struck them as exotic or obscure, was really nothing of the sort in its time and place. Every track that Harry Smith collected for his Smithsonian Folkways albums was originally a commercial record, produced and distributed for profit" (2001, 12).

Despite their blind spots, the folkies marched on, and they came to realize that this powerful music's progenitors still were alive, if often not well, and living among them as barely perceived apparitions. The race was on for fans, musicologists, and savvy promoters to seek out these living, breathing artifacts of another era in American music. Among the anthology's bluesmen soon to be rediscovered were Mississippi John Hurt, Sleepy John Estes, Furry Lewis, and Yank Rachell (who would later act as a musical companion and comedic foil to Howard Armstrong in Terry Zwigoff's film *Louie Bluie*), and many of them were more than willing to invent narratives and portray themselves in ways they thought would line their pockets.

Dylan had witnessed Berry's obvious adoption of a teenage persona in the 1950s—Berry was in his thirties, and like Little Richard, recognizably in costume—but when Dylan assumed the persona of a rural folk singer in the early 1960s, he was imitating Guthrie in ways he probably didn't imagine. Like many young folkies, Dylan was drawn to Guthrie's apparent authenticity. But authenticity is in the eyes of the beholder, and twenty years before the release of Smith's anthology, Guthrie's *Bound for Glory* had been embellished and fictionalized even by today's criteria for memoir. Hajdu notes that after reading the book during the fall of 1960, Dylan, then a freshman English major at the University of Minnesota, was "instantly and wholly consumed by idol worship.... Guthrie's music evidently never struck Bob as deeply as his picaresque tales of life on the road. In Guthrie Bob found more than a genre of music, a body of work, or a performance style: he found an image—the hard travelin' loner with a guitar and a way with words" (2001, 70).

Dylan's ability to create a seemingly authentic persona perhaps was unparalleled among the new generation of folkies. Folk singer Mark Spoelstra recalls that, when they met in the winter of 1961, Dylan possessed "a kind of theater about himself. Actually the very first time that I met him, he was really acting in a way, and that was good because you can go anywhere when you are somebody else" (Scorsese 2005). Suze Rotolo asserts that in the early sixties Dylan spent "much time... in front of the mirror trying on one wrinkled article of clothing after another, until it all came together to look as if Bob had just gotten up and thrown on something. Image meant everything. Folk music was taking hold of a generation and it was important to get it right—be authentic, be cool, have something to say" (2008, 9). Rotolo claims that

Dylan's obsession with creating an image was so strong that "trouble between us slowly grew out of his facility for not telling the truth." Dylan "didn't want people to just drop by" their apartment "unless he invited them himself.... He was on guard. His paranoia was palpable. It was as if he expected someone to show up and blow his cover and expose him" (95–96).

In Martin Scorsese's documentary *No Direction Home* (2005), Izzy Young, the proprietor of the Folklore Center who booked Dylan's first Greenwich Village shows, reads the young Dylan's resume aloud:

> I was born in Duluth, Minnesota, in 1941, moved to Gallup, New Mexico.... Lived in Iowa, South Dakota, Kansas, North Dakota for a little bit. Started playing in carnivals when I was fourteen. Arvella Gray taught me blues songs—a blind street singer from Chicago about four or five years ago. Used to know a guy named Mance Lipscomb from Navasota, Texas. Listened to him a lot.

As Young quickly points out, this is all "bullshit," but Dylan's statement suggests how early in his career he conflated his love of Guthrie's legend with his idea of a typical folk or bluesman's experiences. Mance Lipscomb was, indeed, a bluesman from Navasota, Texas, who had recently become one of the folk movement's rediscoveries. Like other bluesmen revived from Smith's *Anthology*—Hurt, Estes, Lewis, Rachell, et al.—Lipscomb was in his seventies and had left professional music behind. Wizened and knotted like old trees, they came to fifties and sixties folk audiences as celebrated curios: authentic, and to a certain degree fragile, if not harmless.

It's helpful to consider most bluesmen's reality in the "old, weird America" of the twenties and thirties, when as young men these artists recorded what became their famous musical sides. Elijah Wald points out that for whites "Mississippi has come to be singled out as" the blues' "unique heartland," but "if there is one place and time outside of slavery that black Americans have no romanticism or nostalgia about, it is Depression-era Mississippi" (2004, 82). Similarly, Benjamin Filene notes that Willie Dixon and Muddy Waters were "explicit about feeling that they no longer belonged in the southern culture of their youth. They treated their downhome past as a resource to be drawn on, a memory that they could share with their audiences. They saw no contradiction in reveling in these memories while having no desire to return to the culture of the past" (2000, 107).

In the twenties and thirties experienced bluesmen found it most lucrative to move from town to town to keep their audiences fresh (and any romantic and/or extralegal encounters well behind them). At a time when the average southern Black man was known about town, or "belonged" to a white man's plantation, bluesmen generally were men without a home, unattached to the land, and subject to much scrutiny and suspicion. As for transportation, an automobile—especially owning one—often was out of the question. Walking or hopping boxcars became the standard of travel. Howlin' Wolf claimed to be "the onliest one drove out of the South like a gentleman" (Segrest 2005, 102). Arrest for vagrancy or whatever crimes happened to be sitting unsolved on a precinct's register was a very real risk. It makes perfect sense that bluesmen usually chucked their given names to become "Muddy Waters," "Howlin' Wolf," or "Sleepy John." A still common backstage game among musicians is to create one's "blues name" by combining the name of your first pet with the name of the street on which you grew up.

Daytime often meant busking for change, with or without local law enforcement's permission. Nighttime could mean performing at a dance, or more likely, an illegal juke joint beyond the city limits and the law's jurisdiction. Alongside the good times, drunkenness, mayhem, and impromptu violence were the order of the evening. B. B. King's famous guitar, "Lucille," was named after a woman who inspired a brawl at an illegal juke joint where King happened to be playing. The fight knocked over a barrel of burning kerosene used to illuminate the place, and King and his guitar barely escaped the conflagration. Overall, the only upside to the blues life for a southern Black man or woman was a hard-won degree of social and artistic freedom. David "Honeyboy" Edwards, a contemporary and running mate of Robert Johnson and Charley Patton, wrote of his mentor Big Joe Williams: "[He] kept me out of the [cotton] field. He changed my life and I'm glad of it," adding that "running was the only way I could make that money. I didn't have a wife to work and take care of me; I didn't want that. I stayed on the road all the time and the only thing I carried with me was my guitar and harp and those dice in my pocket" (1997, 43, 87).

By the 1960s the musicians who survived the blues life of the Depression mostly had settled down in professions available to Black men of the era. Anecdotes concerning their rediscoveries are familiar to blues fans. The great Son House was living in Rochester, New York, and working as a Pullman porter. Mississippi John Hurt literally was found on a tractor after two twenty-something white blues fans, Dick Spottswood and Tom Hoskins, made an educated guess that Hurt's mention of "Avalon, my hometown" on his 1928 side "Avalon Blues" indeed was a reference to his hometown. They trekked to Avalon, Mississippi, and discovered him working as a farm laborer. As an undergraduate and fledging beat/folkie, Jim Dickinson read Samuel Charters's *The Country Blues* and returned to his hometown of Memphis, where he joined friends and looked up Gus Cannon, who was pumping gas at a filling station, and Furry Lewis, "who was living on Beale Street and working as a street sweeper for the city" (Dickinson 2017, 133). Dickinson went on to play with and produce Aretha Franklin, the Rolling Stones, Arlo Guthrie, Ry Cooder, and Albert King, and he cofounded the Memphis Country Blues Festival, where Cannon, Lewis, and many other older bluesmen performed.

The folkies idealized these legendary rediscoveries, so there were bound to be generational and cultural misunderstandings. Thus the mournful, almost hurt tone of Stephen Calt's *I'd Rather Be the Devil: Skip James and the Blues* (1994) and John Fahey's reminiscence of Skip James in his *How Bluegrass Music Destroyed My Life* (2000), both of which conveniently could be summarized as, "Hate to tell you folks, but Skip wasn't a very pleasant fellow." Another example of the tragicomedy of interracial blues errors is guitarist and Dylan sideman Mike Bloomfield's *Big Joe and Me* (1999), a now-classic description of a lost weekend trailing Big Joe Williams around Kansas City's murky streets, culminating in a slum apartment where the toilet facility is a hole in the floor that empties on the apartment below. Decades of grinding poverty and hand-to-mouth living on the edge of both white and Black society had molded these musicians, manifesting a psychological hurt not easily grasped by the young, white, and mostly college-educated folkies.

Treated as folk art, the blues can seem quaint, and as high art the music can be deemed unsophisticated, but treated as living art the blues open new vistas of creative energy and possibility. Like poetry, where one can, with hard work and discipline, master the technical aspects and cadences and yet remain a tourist in one's heart, the blues don't ask for utter compliance. The blues inhabit the willing and demand that one reveal the blues in oneself. The sense of authenticity that sixties songwriters associated with blues songs and legends was crucial to poetic song verse's creation. Authenticity was a marketing device, but at the same time Dylan, other musicians, and many listeners felt that the older performers they admired and their music were authentic—and many songwriters, including Dylan, crafted songs they hoped and felt were genuine artistic creations, even as they strove to sell themselves and their music.

The changes that Dylan's music and persona underwent from the early to the middle sixties became a template that others followed, much like older bluesmen's songs and images had guided him and other folkies. In the early sixties, Dylan and the folkies had closely imitated older musicians' dress and demeanor, and they composed songs that drew on the blues' emphasis on the conversational, the personal, the local, and the fantastic. As the decade progressed and conceptions of authenticity shifted in response to cultural pressures, Dylan and other sixties songwriters transformed their personae and songs by vigorously combining blues with poetry and rock (topics that we address more widely in chapters 3 and 4). Dylan's resume for Folk City was "bullshit," but John Hammond, the legendary talent scout, recognized something authentic and new in the young bard when he signed him to Columbia Records. Today Dylan is credited with bringing poetic seriousness to popular music. Volume upon volume is available to the student of Dylan's songs. What's missing, however, is a discussion of the distinctive blues presence in his early work, how it transformed into a poetics of disorientation when he returned to rock 'n' roll, and how these things contributed to the development of poetic song verse. One immediately recognizes the blues and poetic influences in Dylan's "late era" albums of the 1990s and 2000s: *Time Out of Mind* (1997), *Love and Theft* (2001), *Modern Times* (2006), *The Tempest* (2012), and *Rough and Rowdy Ways* (2020). But his first four albums—*Bob Dylan* (1962), *The Freewheelin' Bob Dylan* (1963), *The Times They Are a-Changin'* (1964), and *Another Side of Bob Dylan* (1965)—make evident, with the advantage of hindsight, that Dylan's whole career was a journey to and from blues-inflected verse.

Like many blues musicians, Dylan really is only interested in soul stories. On his first album, *Bob Dylan* (1962), Woody Guthrie's imprint is up-front on the talk/sung "Talkin' New York," on the folksy interludes in "Pretty Peggy-O," and on Dylan's glaringly direct homage "Song for Woody." Also apparent, however, is an unabashed blues presence. A glance at the credits reveals that Dylan interprets Bukka White's signature Delta blues "Fixin' to Die" and Blind Lemon Jefferson's "See that My Grave Is Kept Clean." But it is the hypnotic one-chord "In My Time of Dying" that clues us in to Dylan's immersion and understanding of the blues via the blue note–laden guitar picking, repetitive and driving, and Dylan's keening, high-lonesome singing. Although "Highway

51" and "Baby Let Me Follow You Down" may have found a more recognized place in the Dylan canon, "In My Time of Dying" might be the most moving performance on the album.

For his second record, *The Freewheelin' Bob Dylan* (1963), Dylan emerges as the singular songwriter who combined folk and blues with poetry to change music—and eventually literary—history. Allen Ginsberg remembers that the first time he heard Dylan's folk ballad "A Hard Rain's a-Gonna Fall," he wept because "it seemed like the torch had been passed to another generation from earlier bohemian or Beat illumination and self-knowledge" (Scorsese 2005). The song's accessible language, surreal imagery, and probing, personal, and exclamatory delivery dissolve the distance between the speaker and Dylan himself, qualities present in so much of his early work that he often was hailed as his generation's spokesperson. In "Hard Rain" Dylan draws on the traditional ballad "Lord Randal," but he uses the form to present a modern sensibility. Like "Lord Randal," Dylan's song begins with a question from a young man's parent and is followed by the son's answer. But each verse of "Lord Randal" is made up of four lines, while Dylan's verses offer a much more extended response. His decision to expand the traditional ballad's form reflects differences in the works' respective dramatic situations. Each ballad addresses a tragedy. In "Lord Randal" we discover that the young man has been poisoned. "A Hard Rain's a-Gonna Fall"—written in the wake of the Cuban Missile Crisis—concerns nuclear catastrophe. In other words, "Lord Randal" addresses the death of one person, while "Hard Rain" concerns a dilemma of much wider proportions. Christopher Ricks calls it "a vision of judgment, a scouring vision of hell. Hell on earth" (2004, 342). Both "Lord Randal" and "Hard Rain" maintain the question-response structure in subsequent verses, but Dylan's song presents a speaker's involvement with a larger landscape. He moves from "twelve misty mountains" to "six crooked highways" to "seven sad forests" to a "dozen dead oceans" to "ten thousand miles in the mouth of a graveyard." By specifying how many mountains, highways, and other entities will be affected, and moving toward an image of death devouring the narrator and the terrain, Dylan sets up the repetition of "it's a hard" and the awareness that calamity is imminent. Dylan repeats a similar pattern in the song's remaining verses. The shape of each verse, the repetition and variation of patterns within them, and the use of imagery, sonic effects, and other formal devices make the song powerful.

Similarly, "Blowin' in the Wind" combines folk music and poetic imagery, and may have done more than any other song of the time to bring poetic song verse to the popular audience. But Dylan's insistence on maintaining blues and blues-inspired material on his second album makes another type of impact: he is at once restating his commitment to the blues as an essential element of folk and unleashing the unedited blues idiom on an unsuspecting popular audience. In typical Dylan fashion, the songs on *Freewheelin'* with "blues" in their title—"Bob Dylan's Blues" and "Talking World War III Blues"—technically are not blues in form, tone, or inclination. However, "Down the Highway" is a pure country blues that would make Mance Lipscomb proud, and a version of Sleepy John Estes's "Corrina Corrina" has the insistent lope, blues form, and spare production that late-era Dylan gleaned from his heroes. A perceptive blues watcher would immediately be at home with Dylan's third-person self-referencing on "Bob Dylan's Dream."

The pattern continues on *The Times They Are a-Changin'* (1963). Having mastered folk's fundamentals, Dylan delivers his most austere collection to date. The previously slightly out-of-tune guitar is more in tune, and the snickering asides seem less like preemptive strikes at the Folk Police's accusations, more like simple fun. The guitar and the harmonica reign here as well, but fearlessly. "With God on Our Side" is a prime example. Dylan stretches the propriety of mechanical song length (around 3:30 for a vinyl single) to 7:04, as if to proclaim that the jukebox's dictates could not contain his verse, a conviction he pursued even more vigorously after returning to rock 'n' roll in 1965. Lyrically, the song lurches effortlessly from the universal to the local ("Oh, my name it ain't nothing / My age it means less / The country I come from / Is called the Midwest") as it also pitches in and out of traditional 3/4 ballad time into a quickstepping 4/4, sometimes to lengthen or strengthen a line, sometimes, seemingly, just because he can; the effect is disconcerting and powerful. The musician is in absolute control of his unwieldy message. This is music from a man who has little to prove and much to say. His recklessness is focused. The feeling in the singing and the singing *about* feeling are notable. The imprecation to a lover on "Boots of Spanish Leather" is delivered with a sensitivity and emotional depth that belie the words' simplicity:

How can, how can you ask me again?
It only brings me sorrow

The same thing I would want today
I will want again tomorrow.

Times is a political record with the lyrical and musical gravitas to back up its topics: the imminence of World War III, the murder of civil rights leaders, and the duplicity of American populism dividing class comrades with mythologies concerning race. Conceptually, musically, and in all other ways, the purest blues song on *Times* is the "Ballad of Hollis Brown," a one-chord vehicle that tells the story of a South Dakota farmer so eviscerated by poverty that he murders himself and his family. Dylan's description of Brown's pathetic circumstances tower over and above the murder's presumed denouement in classic AAB blues-verse form:

The rats have got your flour, bad blood it got your mare
The rats have got your flour, bad blood it got your mare
Is there anyone knows who knows? Is there anyone who cares?

In a deft move that amplifies the song's context, Dylan sings of a destitute farmer from South Dakota in a style usually reserved for poor Blacks of the American South. Similarly, "North Country Blues" is not strictly a blues, but more of a ballad in the Appalachian strain, relating the tale of a young mother-turned-beggar, and yet Dylan likely is referencing the open-pit iron ore mining of the Mesabi Range in his native northern Minnesota.

By late 1963, Dylan's posturing as a folkie had begun to backfire. He had been stung when the activist and entertainer Dick Gregory covered his ears during Dylan's performance at a massive civil rights rally at the Lincoln Memorial in Washington, DC, on August 28, 1963. Gregory publically chided him, asking "What was a white boy like Bob Dylan there for?" and declared, "If Bob Dylan and Joan Baez and whoever the hell stood out there with the crowd and cheered for Odetta and Josh White, that would be a greater statement than arriving in their limousines and taking bows" (Marqusee 2005, 13). Two months later, an article in *Newsweek* revealed that Dylan was not an orphaned hobo, but a well-to-do suburban Jewish boy whose parents were alive and well.[10] Dylan's friend and biographer Robert Shelton recounts that the article "threw Dylan into a depression" and prompted him to go "underground" (1997, 193, 195).

These events and others contributed to his discomfort with the folk movement and compelled him to turn from writing songs to working "all day for weeks... on writing poetry and prose-poems" (Hajdu 2001, 183–84). The change was predictable in many ways and would have a dramatic impact on poetic song verse's development. Besides searching for Woody Guthrie when he came to New York City in January of 1961, Dylan asserts that he was "looking for what" he had "read about in *On the Road* (1956)... looking for what Allen Ginsberg had called the 'hydrogen jukebox world'" (Dylan 2004, 235). However, Dylan didn't meet Ginsberg until late in 1963, when he attended a "welcome home" party for the poet. Dylan had recently been honored by the Emergency Civil Liberties Committee, but as Ginsberg's longtime friend and biographer Bill Morgan points out, in his award acceptance speech Dylan asserted his "independence from all political allegiances, which upset many on the committee, but the statement intrigued Allen. The two talked about poetry and politics, and about how poetry should be a reflection of the mind, independent of politics" (2006, 383).

Like many folkies who had embraced rock 'n' roll as teenagers in the mid to late fifties, Dylan was a devotee of Ginsberg's poems and of Beat poetry in general.[11] The Beats' use of free verse dazzled him, and he began to draw on it more vigorously after retreating from the folk scene. His statement in the liner notes to *Biograph* that in New York he "fell in with the Beat scene, the Bohemian, the Bebop crowd, it was all pretty much connected... it had just as big of an impact on me as Elvis Presley, Pound, Camus, T. S. Eliot, e. e. cummings" suggests his desire to combine Beat and other forms of literature with and rock 'n' roll.[12] Rotolo recalls that at the time she was "reading Rimbaud and it piqued" Dylan's "interest... when Bob searched for more, Allen Ginsberg took him further with his great spontaneous knowledge of all the poets" (2008, 199). Dylan also "loved the breathless, dynamic bop phrases that flowed from" Jack Kerouac's "pen," and had witnessed him and other writers read poetry and prose infused with the syncopated sounds of Parker, Gillespie, and other bebop artists (Dylan 2004, 57). Ginsberg, who would appear in the video of "Subterranean Homesick Blues" a few months after meeting Dylan, also was a fan of rock 'n' roll. In 1957 he had watched Little Richard and Fats Domino play to a capacity crowd of more than 15,000 in New York City. Ginsberg biographer Morgan notes that the "power of music to reach a whole generation of listeners was not lost on Allen" (2006, 233). It wasn't lost on Dylan, either. Hajdu observes that "when he started writing songs in earnest again, he picked up where his work for the page had taken him, eschewing topical and political themes to write songs in a new style—introspective, ruminative work about his own life, with dense symbolic lyrics, and music drawing equally upon folk, blues, rhythm, and pop influences" (2001, 202).

On his fourth album, *Another Side of Bob Dylan* (1964), his new practices informed two deliberate blues numbers. "Black Crow Blues" stands out as the first song on which Dylan accompanies himself on piano in a kind of inexpert barrelhouse style, his foot stomps audible on the open harmonica microphone. This is a straight-up blues stylistically, except for the manner in which Dylan hangs up the AAB form, holding out on the "five" (B) for one, and sometimes two, measures longer than necessary, or even returning to the "five" and lingering there as a sort of prelude to the proper form, much like Jerry Lee Lewis pedals the five before he returns to the verse on "Great Balls of Fire."

The other blues number, "Motorpsycho Nitemare," is a straight-ahead twelve-bar blues strummed up-tempo on an acoustic guitar. Lyrically, it's Dylan's first full venture into the aesthetic of disorientation that would characterize his next three albums and that would revolutionize poetic song verse. On its surface the song is a retelling of the old "farmer's daughter" tale: On a rainy night a traveling salesman breaks down on the road; he finds a farmhouse; the farmer allows the stranger to stay but warns against disporting with his unusually attractive daughter. Mayhem ensues. Sometimes the salesman gets away. Sometimes he is an unwilling participant in a shotgun wedding. However, in Dylan's telling the rhythm of the story immediately is amiss, recalling Berry's use of misdirection in "Maybellene," "Brown Eyed Handsome Man," and other songs, but filtered through a playful, hyperbolic, Beat-like narrative.

> I pounded on a farmhouse
> Lookin' for a place to stay
> I was mighty, mighty tired
> I had come a long, long way
> I said, "Hey, hey, in there
> Is there anybody home?"
> I was standing on the steps
> Feeling most alone
> Well, out comes a farmer
> He must have thought that I was nuts

He immediately looked at me
And stuck a gun into my guts

I fell down
To my bended knees
Saying, "I dig farmers
Don't shoot me, please!"
He cocked his rifle
And began to shout
"Are you that travelin' salesman
That I have heard about?"
I said, "No! No! No!
I'm a doctor and it's true
I'm a clean-cut kid
And I been to college, too"

The narrator claims he is a new type of traveler. He's not a salesman; he's a purported "doctor" who roams the back roads on a motorcycle and "digs farmers." Employing cinematic allusions, Dylan amplifies and distorts the traditional tale. He describes the narrator's inevitable run-in with the farmer's comely daughter by referencing Anita Ekberg in Federico Fellini's 1960 masterpiece, *La dolce vita*, an experimental dramatic comedy that challenges conventional presentations of plot and character. In the next verse Dylan signals a change by altering the clichéd phrase "sleeping like a baby" to "sleepin' like a rat" as Rita makes her scripted pass at the dormant traveler. Then the narrative abruptly cuts to another film, Alfred Hitchcock's *Psycho* (1960), and the farmer's strikingly attractive daughter appears as a cross-dressing homicidal maniac:

Then in comes his daughter
Whose name was Rita
She looked like she stepped out of
La dolce vita
I was sleepin' like a rat
When I heard something jerkin'
There stood Rita
Lookin' just like Tony Perkins

By this point, listeners begin to realize they are accomplices to the narrator's nightmare: a litany of god-awful, timeworn clichés like the "farmer's daughter." The narrator, now partnered with an audience who presumably understands his cutting-edge film references, obviously considers himself too erudite to become a character in such a corny story and realizes that the only escape is to create another narrative.

> I said, "Oh, no! no!
> I've been through this movie before"
> I knew I had to split
> But I didn't know how
>
> I had to say something
> To strike him very weird
> So I yelled
> "I like Fidel Castro and his beard"

He announces to the farmer that he's such a fanatical communist that he has pledged his allegiance to "Fidel Castro *and his beard*" (emphasis ours). Listeners come to realize that the premise of this particular joke—or nightmare—doesn't primarily rest on the traditional Town vs. Country dichotomy that typically informs farmer's daughter jokes, but on Cold War sociopolitical antagonisms of Young vs. Old—or perhaps more accurately, Hip vs. Square.

"Motorpsycho Nitemare" is a postmodern blues that upends conventional narratives, and it represents arguably the first time poetic song verse transformed the authenticity associated with the blues into an aesthetic of disorientation. It uses the bedrock of American musical forms, the blues, to narrate an escape from popular tropes, popular themes, and popular song itself. Hung among such obvious genre classics as "All I Really Want to Do," "Chimes of Freedom," and "It Ain't Me Babe," "Motorpsycho Nitemare" would become the touchstone for the amped-up blues and hallucinatory poetic wordplay of Dylan's upcoming watershed albums.

Called on the carpet by a press that exposed him, admonished by Dick Gregory and others who questioned his motives, chastised by folkies for breaking the rules, and buoyed by his friendship with Ginsberg and other Beat writers, Dylan threw a fit on his next album, *Bringing It All Back Home* (1965), by returning to rock 'n' roll and adopting the persona of a rebellious youngster, à la Chuck Berry. Like Berry's songs vaunting teenage rebellion and the Beats' poetry—which was more popular than ever in the midsixties—Dylan's albums appealed to a generation chafing against conformity and middle-class values. Kenneth Rexroth, who helped start the San Francisco Renaissance and inspired the Beats, could have been talking about Dylan's transition from folk to rock when he claimed it was "very important to get poetry . . . out of the hands of the squares" (Charters 1992, 229).

Other songwriters—including Mick Jagger, John Lennon, Paul McCartney, Jimi Hendrix, Van Morrison, Jim Morrison, Joni Mitchell, David Crosby, Neil Young, and Stephen Stills—who also had embraced the blues and Beat coffeehouse culture, quickly followed Dylan's lead. The magnitude of Dylan's influence is reflected in Jagger's observation that in the midsixties, "Everyone looked up to" Dylan "as being a kind of guru of lyrics. It's hard to think of the absolute garbage that pop music really was at the time."[13] As discussed in chapter 1, rock 'n' roll's roots in the blues and contemporary poetry's turn toward accessible language had made the two forms more compatible. Laurence Coupe correctly asserts that the "Beat vision" of Ginsberg, Kerouac, Corso, and others "of the 50s lies behind the Beat sound of the next decade," including the songs of Dylan, the Beatles, Jim Morrison, Mitchell, Cohen, and others (2007, 1). (The similarities between Ginsberg reciting/singing his poetry and Dylan singing/reciting his lyrics in Martin Scorsese's fanciful 2019 film *Rolling Thunder Revue: A Bob Dylan Story* are striking.) To repeat: if a relatively well-educated young songwriter enthralled with the blues or rock 'n' roll looked to modernist or older poetry for lyric inspiration, he or she might be rewarded with an image or an allusion, or occasionally might strike gold, as with Dylan and "Lord Randal." But if that person looked to Beat and other forms of contemporary poetry, he or she could discover a wide range of vivid language based on contemporary speech rhythms that could be sculpted for blues-based sonics.

As Simon Warner amply details in *Text and Drugs and Rock 'n' Roll: The Beat and Rock Culture* (2013), as teenagers Dylan and others had consciously and subconsciously absorbed these lessons on the jukebox and in Beat coffeehouses and cafes. After putting rock 'n' roll aside for folk music for a handful of years, many sixties songwriters returned to the rebellious rhythms of fifties rock 'n' roll and associated them with contemporary poetry. In the midsixties Dylan's rock 'n' roll–Beat poet persona strengthened his already active sense of the possibilities between poetry and music and led to *Bringing It All Back Home* (1965), *Highway 61 Revisited* (1965), and *Blonde on Blonde* (1966).

When Dylan went electric at the Newport Folk Festival in July of 1965 the issue wasn't, as is often alleged, that he played electrically amplified music—Muddy Waters had played electric guitar there since 1960, and Howlin' Wolf had played electric guitar the day before Dylan plugged in his Stratocaster—but that he played rock 'n' roll. Dylan's infamous set—during which the audience booed and Alan Lomax and Pete Seeger tried to disconnect his amplifier—can be likened to the often-cited moment in which Robert Lowell showed his friend and mentor Allen Tate the manuscript of *Life Studies* (1959) and Tate declared, "But Cal, it isn't poetry!" In both instances traditionalists were telling younger artists that they had adulterated a revered form. Like *Life Studies*—which mixes free verse, metered verse, and prose poems—Dylan's albums of the midsixties aggressively blend a variety of forms. On *Bringing It All Back Home*, "Mr. Tambourine Man," with its "magic swirling ships," evokes Rimbaud. "Bob Dylan's 115th Dream" begins as an acoustic ballad but stops. Then laughter ensues before the tune recommences as an electric blues that describes the European discovery of America through an emphasis on the fantastic, commingling fact, fiction, locations, and chronological time. The playful, freely associative lyrics of "Subterranean Homesick Blues," "Maggie's Farm," and others songs clearly are indebted to the Beats. "On the Road Again" alludes to Kerouac's novel and is chock-full of the types of fantastical imagery and double entendre found in blues songs:

> Well, I go to pet your monkey
> I get a face full of claws
> I ask who's in the fireplace
> And you tell me Santa Claus

The album's first song, "Subterranean Homesick Blues," sets the direction and tone. Like Berry's "Too Much Monkey Business" and Bo Diddley's "Who Do You Love?"—both released in 1956—Dylan's tune is a rock 'n' roll number born from the blues; the songs share a compositional and performance strategy that only can be described as rapid-fire talk-singing. Comparing the three songs suggests how Dylan combined the blues, rock 'n' roll, and Beat poetry to create poetic song verse informed by an aesthetic of disorientation. In each song the lyrics are delivered in swift staccato bursts that are half-sung, half-spoken. The words' speed and volume diminish melodic possibilities, resulting in one-note patterns with slight modulations. In passing, one occasionally catches a word or a phrase, but interestingly, the effect isn't off-putting. Rather it draws the listener closer: "Excuse me: Say *what*?"

All three songs are entertaining and Machiavellian. The musical strategy at once is self-conscious and self-serving. Since there almost is no conceivable way—on first listen—to comprehend individual lines, much less a coherent narrative, the breakneck delivery compels the listener to the performance and commands repeated listening. In effect, misapprehension impels collusion—a clever trick, if vaguely manipulative, and on the outer edge, unkind, but one that works. To what ends are these means justified?

"Too Much Monkey Business" is a seven-verse complaint with shifting points of view, scaled to varying degrees. The brisk delivery complements effervescent internal rhymes and jarring shifts in perspective, setting, and tone. Here are snapshots from American life that cumulatively say: Whatever you do, whatever someone says, no matter the situation, the other shoe always will drop. It's rock 'n' roll Murphy's Law: anything that can go wrong, will.

The song's form approximates the harmonic intervals of a traditional blues—the fourth and fifth steps—but only on the chorus. In the first two verses the narrator rejects working-class life and bourgeois home life: a good-looking blonde wants him to marry her, buy a home, "settle down, write a book." And here, after each two-line scenario, Berry adds a disgusted "Ahh!" (or is it "nahhh"?) before he sings the refrain "Too much monkey business . . ." The message is that he's above all this quotidian nonsense. Beyond urgency, the song's speed gives the listener an overriding sense that something is being said that only the informed or initiated understand. (This from the guy who has "no kick against modern jazz / Unless they try to play it too darn fast.") It's akin to being with two native speakers who know you are marginally competent in their language and suddenly fog the conversation with patois in order to speak beyond or around you. A word is caught here or there, but your feeble grasp of the language doesn't help. Maybe you should have studied harder before you left home? Nahhh!: "Same thing every day, gettin' up, goin' to school." Even the phone company is against you: "Ought to sue the operator for telling me a tale, ahh." Perhaps I'll join the army? Done that: "Army bunk, army chow, army clothes, army car, aah."

The narrator is *hip to how the world works*; and now the attentive listener is, too. Perhaps we finally understand why he feels the need to encode his story via speed. He has made a leap from being irritated with daily life's small indignities to slighting some of the United States' most cherished institutions: our army and the wars we fight, our puritanical work ethic, and the dream of middle-class stability. It's one thing to complain about bills, unscrupulous salesmen, tradition-bound spouses, and broken pay phones. It's quite another to throw your hands up and say, "It's *all* bullshit! Wars. Work itself. Monkey business is our general condition. Who would deign to participate in this nonsense?" A radical idea, especially in 1956—but one also expressed in Ginsberg's *Howl and Other Poems* in that same year and in Kerouac's *On the Road* a year later.

Bo Diddley, Berry's labelmate at Chess Records, released his similarly verbose hit "Who Do You Love?" within a month of "Too Much Monkey Business." There's some confusion if Ellas McDaniel named himself Bo Diddley or was bestowed the nickname. Regardless, McDaniel owned the moniker, using it to bolster his reputation as the ur-self-mythologizer of rock, or rather, as the first "crossover" rock 'n' roller to effectively employ the blues' grand tradition of self-mythologizing. Note how many of his hits include singing about himself in the third person: "Bo Diddley," "Diddley Daddy," "Hey! Bo Diddley."

One senses a direct link between nickname and style: The diddley bow is a precursor to the guitar, a "primitive" instrument strung by slaves, often consisting of a wire and a broom handle or a cigar box. The main feature of Bo Diddley's style, which he didn't invent but certainly popularized, is the African clave beat: "Duh. Duh. Duh. Duh-DUH!" If McDaniel's nickname was meant as an insult—denoting "simplistic"—he was able flip the script and inhabit the name, proclaiming himself more blues than the blues itself, rudimentary in his power like the diddley bow; his signature clave rhythm, Africa unfiltered.

As a bluesman Bo Diddley's use of sonic effects was unique; the tremolo on his guitar is so overdriven it often hangs beyond the strummed chord, subtly interfering with the song's rhythm (not unlike the tremolo baritone guitar on much of Johnny Cash's early Sun Records work). He also toyed with electric blues bands' traditional instrumentation: There is no bass on much of his early work; percussion and an unlikely yet omnipresent maraca player occupy the space left in the lower register. This configuration results in an atmospheric, hollow sound; ghostly and ominous, shamanistic.

We should note that Bo Diddley's custom signature square electric guitar did not attempt to replicate a classic guitar figure. (Perhaps a nod to early twentieth-century rural bluesmen's homemade cigar-box guitars.) His sound and presentation are freakier than that of Berry, the ambassador of teen rebellion and disparager of the quotidian. In "Who Do You Love?" the fantastic is in full force. The narrator tells Arlene, the object of his passion, that he uses a "cobra snake for a necktie" and possesses a home built from "rattlesnake hide," with a chimney culled from a "human skull." He declares that he's young but doesn't "mind dying," that he rides a lion into town, and uses a rattlesnake for a whip.

What kind of come-on is this? Cobras, rattlesnakes, lions, and skulls aren't exactly romantic selling points. It seems the narrator wants to frighten Arlene into loving him. Yet one always must be on the lookout for misdirection, especially in blues recorded for a mass—meaning mostly white—market. Cobbling together images that tear by, we recognize a supernatural theme, a world not quite our own, one that contains a "tombstone hand" and a "graveyard mind," strikingly effective images that evoke a common subject in the blues: the power of folk magic, or hoodoo.

From here, it isn't much of a stretch to recognize the songwriter's play on words: It's not "Who do you love?" It's "*Hoodoo* your love." We've moved from a question to a statement. The narrator is *working* his black magic on Arlene. Once the listener makes the leap, the preceding verses make perfect sense: We are seeing the world as Arlene sees it; as one under a spell, afflicted by hoodoo. With Arlene we tour another realm, a surreal cityscape of horrors and curiosities, a guided hallucination. The night is "dark," but the heavens remain "blue." An "ice-wagon" hits a bump, someone screams, and the verse ends with "You should have heard just what I've seen / *Hoodoo* your love."

We are arm in arm with Arlene in the shadow world, where our senses fail us; where our knowledge and experiences no longer serve to guide us. Night is day. What's *heard* is *seen*? But the kicker comes when Arlene takes the narrator by the hand and exclaims " . . . Ooowee boy / You know I understand." Arlene *likes* it. She *gets* it and, by extension, so do we. If this is what getting *hoodooed* is all about, Bo Diddley's young white audience certainly caught the bug. And he might be forgiven for disguising his intentions from their parents with his incantatory, race-for-the-prize delivery and sly wordplay—an inscrutable poetry intelligible only to its intended audience.

Released eight years later, "Subterranean Homesick Blues" shares the galloping patter of "Too Much Monkey Business" and "Who Do You Love?" Structurally, "Subterranean Homesick Blues" is more of a traditional blues than either of its predecessors; a sort of padded or extended blues form that slouches around the tonic, moves to the fourth and back, and finally descends from the fifth to the fourth for that familiar blues resolution. However, unlike the other two songs, in Dylan's tune the ear never rests on a familiar refrain. The chorus is foresworn. The jazzy wordplay of Beat-like poetry propels the narrative, doesn't look back, and refuses to repeat itself. If you miss something, sorry; the train has left the station. The listener's experience mirrors the narrator's sense of disorientation.

The tale spun in "Subterranean Homesick Blues" manages to fall somewhere between the frustrated hipster complaint of "Too Much Monkey Business" and the hoodoo phantasmagoria of "Who Do You Love?" It is a contemporary urban story, involving drugs and the counterculture, or in keeping with the title, "underground" culture: Johnny is in the "basement" preparing the "medicine," while the narrator is up on the "pavement" considering the "government." He's paranoid, and rightfully so. He wants to avoid trouble but must deal with a corrupt undercover cop in a "trench coat" and a drug dealer in a "coonskin cap" attempting to put the squeeze on him. The counterculture supposedly brings freedom, but not here. Our man is on the run: Maggie tells him the cops have tapped their phone and planted drugs, and of rumors concerning DA arrest quotas. Whether or not one participates in illegal activities—"don't matter what you did"—mere association with this scene indicts one in the authorities' eyes.

The language is brisk and convoluted, not elevated for heightened discourse like traditional poetic diction; rather it is *enervated*, shot through with tension; a wise, wayward chatter, like a speed freak reciting Beat poetry. Where Berry's narrator rejects the corrupt and deadening dimensions of middle-class existence, Dylan's narrator yanks back the curtain on hipsters' alternative lifestyles. And unlike the alluring portrait of occult romance in "Who Do You Love?," the fantasy presented in "Subterranean Homesick Blues" is utterly unappealing and terribly real. The song addresses the treadmill of Grub Street, where everyone is an aspiring poet and a potential criminal ("Hang around an inkwell / Hang bail . . ."). Its soundtrack is one long woozy, bluesy, drug-fueled romp. If you can't hack it, there's always the army. But even if counterculture manages to stay afloat and out of the slammer, they will get "hit" by street hustlers, "losers, cheaters," and "six-time users." One imagines the girl near the "whirlpool" looking for a new mark, muttering her junked-out wisdom about not following "leaders" and watching the "parking meters." It's enough to make the narrator homesick for his youthful innocence—when one learned to "dance," "dress," and become a "success"—before he encountered the big city and the cutting edge. Yet he realizes that a traditional existence entails two decades of schooling before confinement to the "day shift."

Man, Chuck Berry could have told you that years ago! What is one to do? Where is one to go? Maybe leap into a "manhole" and light a "candle." Ralph Ellison and Fyodor Dostoevsky mapped this terrain long ago: Become *invisible*, go *underground* (Dylan wants to go underground even from the *underground*). Into the sewer it is, with the voice of the mad junkie girl filtering from the above manhole, complaining that the "pump" doesn't work because "vandals" filched the "handles." On "Subterranean Homesick Blues" Dylan brought it all back home by returning to the rock 'n' roll he relished in high school and the verse he'd encountered in Beat coffeehouses around the University of Minnesota and in Greenwich Village.

The title of Dylan's next album, *Highway 61 Revisited*, reflected his determination to keep pushing blues-based rock's poetic boundaries. US Highway 61, the "blues highway," which runs from New Orleans to Memphis, frequently was cited in blues songs and legends. On the recording Dylan revisits the Delta blues and injects it with a range of poetic influences. For instance, in "Desolation Row," the eleven-minute song that closes the album, Dylan takes the blues' and the Beat's focus on the local and combines it with a modernist emphasis on allusion. Al Kooper, who played on the album, points out that Desolation Row was 8th Avenue in New York City (Cott 2006, 61). Essentially, Dylan takes people who lived in and frequented the area and transforms their identities, a technique that allows the song to remain tied to the local while evoking larger cultural contexts. Dylan describes his method in the song's final verse: "I had to rearrange their faces / And give them all another name." Hence the narrator's female companion becomes "Cinderella"; as night descends "Cain and Abel" and the "hunchback of Notre Dame" wander the street; a twenty-two-year-old street preacher who speaks of the hereafter is "Ophelia"; people presumably championing art become "Ezra Pound and T. S. Eliot / Fighting in the captain's tower." In "Ballad of a Thin Man" Dylan directly addresses the aesthetic of disorientation that characterizes much of his work of this period. The song is an edgy, surrealistic, and mocking indictment of a conventional individual baffled by the cultural changes occurring around him. Mr. Jones—a traditional, well-educated man—encounters the developing counterculture. Dylan coveys Mr. Jones's incomprehension by describing him in the midst of a bewildering circus scene.

Less than a year after *Highway 61 Revisited*, Dylan released *Blonde on Blonde* (1966), rock's first double LP. The record featured the influence of Beat, Confessional, and Continental poetry filtered through raw-edged electric blues. The album opens with the boozy sound effects of "Rainy Day Women #12 & 35." Its chorus, "Everybody must get stoned," recalls the blues trope of "having the blues" and the Beat trope of "feeling beat." In "Stuck Inside of Mobile with the Memphis Blues Again," allusions and surrealistic imagery abound: "Shakespeare is in the alley." Railroad men "drink up your blood like wine," smoke the narrators' "eyelids," and "punch" his "cigarette." "Sad Eyed Lady of the Lowlands," a love song that never mentions the word *love*, consists of five highly alliterative verses. It closes the album and is the first rock song to span an entire album side.

Dylan's experiments established him as rock's premier lyricist and ignited an explosion of poetic song verse. His influence became, and remains, immense. Robbie Robertson claimed that Dylan "showed" other songwriters "that anything goes," and Paul Simon noted that without Dylan's influence he "can't imagine" how he would have made the transition from his early pop songs to lyrically sophisticated verse in works like "Sound of Silence."[14] In 1987 Warren Zevon remarked that he'd "always felt" that Dylan "invented my job."[15] As songwriter Lucinda Williams—poet Miller Williams's daughter—observes, "After those Dylan albums everybody wanted to be an artist instead of an entertainer."[16] In essence, rock became a genre that drew on sundry art forms and valued sophisticated innovations. Like Dylan, many lyricists approached their craft with the diligence of a skilled poet.[17]

Stephen Stills and Joni Mitchell are two of many songwriters who moved from performing covers to composing carefully patterned verse after encountering the Greenwich Village folk and Beat scene and witnessing Dylan's evolution. In "Helplessly Hoping" (1969) Stills uses variations of phrases and syntactical patterns, rather than conventional meters or blues structures, to supply his lyrics' rhythms. The song's dominant sonic pattern involves front-loaded, alliterative words. The recorded performance possesses an idiosyncratic formality: the tight-knit harmonies and spare acoustic accompaniment evoke a gently controlled environment—made more so by deliberately odd vocal filigrees ("fly-y," "goodby-y-y-y-y-y-ye," and "hello-o-o-o"). These effects—and a meager running time of 2:37—call attention to the song itself as delicate, made thing:

> Helplessly hoping
> Her harlequin hovers nearby
> Awaiting a word
> Gasping at glimpses
> Of gentle true spirit
> He runs
> Wishing he could fly
> Only to trip at the sound of goodbye

Stills arranges consonant and vowel sounds, and uses internal and end rhymes, to give the verse a distinctive cadence. In the first two lines, "h" sounds are foregrounded. In line three the long "a" that begins "Awaiting" is repeated within the word and in the word ("a") that follows, creating a slight, lingering pause when the trio sings it. Line four stresses "g" sounds and shadows the previous line. "Gasping" rhymes with the first word ("Awaiting") of the previous line, and the short "a"s in "Gasping at" echo and modify the long "a"s ("Awaiting a") that begin line three. The couplet that closes the first verse creates an end rhyme with line one and is highlighted by lifting and repeating the long "y" in "fly" and "goodbye."

The second verse opens by emphasizing "w" sounds and proceeds to echo the "h" sounds that open the song. Again, the vocals lift and repeat the long "y" in "goodbye," and the verse ends by accenting and extending the "o" in "hello":

> Wordlessly watching
> He waits by the window
> And wonders
> At the empty place inside
> Heartlessly helping himself to her bad dreams
> He worries
> Did hear a goodbye?
> Or even hello?

A similar—but not identical—pattern marks the third verse:

> Stand by the stairway
> You'll see something
> Certain to tell you confusion has its cost
> Love isn't lying
> It's loose in a lady
> Who lingers
> Saying she is lost
> And choking on hello

As in the first and second verses, Stills doesn't stick to a strictly regimented pattern, but the "s," "c," "t," and "l" sounds that fill the verse raise the lyrics' resonance. The strong rhyme that concludes the first verse and that's used to emphasize "goodbye" is not repeated. However, the "hello" that ends the third verse plays off the heavy use of "o" sounds in the verse and provides an ironic, "choking" counter to "goodbye."

Stills alternates the verses above with the chorus, which employs wordplay to express the unity and dissatisfaction felt by people involved in a triangular love affair:

> They are one person
> They are two alone
> They are three together
> They are for each other

The song's movement between two distinct patterns varies its rhythm and adds to its emotional texture. The highly alliterative verses are detailed, concrete, and evocative, while the chorus consists of four relatively terse declarative sentences that summarize the situation. Whereas Stills, Crosby, and Nash sing the verses in harmony, the vocals in the chorus are staggered to emphasize the song's subject. "One person"—Stills—sings the first line; Nash joins him on the second line; and they all sing the third and fourth lines. It's not unlike the reality-unreality of a dramatic performance: a construct that feels organic and is reminiscent of medieval troubadours' stories of harlequins and their ladies.

In Mitchell's "Both Sides Now" (1969) the heavens serve as a Rorschach for the narrator's shifting state of mind.[18] Mitchell, who went on to publish poetry in the *New Yorker* and other prominent venues, opens every other verse with sonically resonant imagistic patterns. Verses one, three, and five begin with strong rhymes: "Bows and flows," "Moons and Junes," "Tears and fears." Each of the first lines forms a grammatical unit with the second line, which is punctuated with a caesura. The caesura is followed with a similarly phrased comment—"I've looked at clouds that way," "I've looked at love that way," "I've looked at life that way"—and each third line begins with "But" and continues with an observation about life's uncertainties for the rest of the quatrain. The verses that form the chorus also are cast in quatrains, but the lines are shorter, consisting of eight syllables in a rough iambic pattern. Unlike the irregular rhyme scheme of the other verses, the refrains use an A/A B/B pattern and feature shifts in phrasing that echo the preceding verse's movement from "clouds" to "love" to "life."

Many other musicians also took note of Dylan's ability to inflect rock with a seemingly endless amount of influences, and they were inspired to expand the range of their source materials and engage in more ambitious lyric and sonic practices. The Beatles, who met Dylan in August of 1964, moved from pop toward greater complexity on *Revolver* (1966) and *Sgt. Pepper's Lonely Heart's Club Band* (1967). The Doors (1967)— a name inspired by Aldous Huxley's *The Doors of Perception* (1954) and William Blake's line "If the Doors of perception were cleansed everything would appear to man as it is, infinite"—featured lyrics inspired by Beat, Romantic, and Symbolist poets and often used the organ as a lead instrument. Albert King's electric blues, African and Western mysticism, Beat poetry, and surrealism influenced Jimi Hendrix's *Are You Experienced?* (1967). *Songs of Leonard Cohen* (1967) drew on a wide range of poetry, mythology, surrealism, and religion. On *Days of Future Passed* (1967) the Moody Blues, influenced by James Joyce's *Ulysses*, created a song cycle based on the events of a single day and employed a classical orchestra. Lou Reed, John Cale, Sterling Morrison, and Maureen Tucker's *The Velvet Underground and Nico* (1967) meshed blunt street poetry with sonic distortion. Van Morrison's *Astral Weeks* (1968) fused impressionistic Beat-inflected lyrics with blues, jazz, folk, and classical music to create a song cycle. Florida-bred Gram Parsons joined the Byrds and helped record the first country rock album, *Sweetheart of the Rodeo* (1968). The Who created the first rock opera, *Tommy* (1969). Langston Hughes and poets associated with the Black Arts Movement influenced Gil Scott-Heron's lyrics on *Small Talk at 125th and Lenox* (1970).

In 1971 David Bowie's "Song for Bob Dylan" appeared on *Hunky Dory*. It's an homage from a younger, enigmatic rock shape-shifter to the original "superbrain" whose "words had truthful vengeance / That could pin us to the floor." In 2016 Bowie, ill with cancer, knew *Blackstar* would be his last album. The final track, "I Can't Give Everything Away," is a confession and an apology to fans—as if to say, "My tricks, knowledge, secrets, artistry. I must keep something for myself and for my legacy." In June of 2020, at the age of seventy-nine, Dylan released *Rough and Rowdy Ways*, his first album of original material in eight years. We hope it's not his swan song, but like Bowie's *Blackstar* or Zevon's *The Wind* (2003), the album possesses a clear motif of an aging narrator looking back, reminiscing, and taking stock. Throughout the ten tracks, Dylan employs a dense network of allusions, a technique he's used since the midsixties and has expanded on his late-career albums. His success with the approach is a timely rebuke to contemporary songwriters—spanning genres from "bro country" to pop to R&B and rap—who sing lists of merchandise and brand names and compare themselves to cultural figures and events far more significant than themselves. In Dylan's repertoire, the breadth of cultural knowledge, of matters both "high" and "low," renders much more complex and intriguing landscapes. His references, allusions, winks, and asides turn the songs on *Rough and Rowdy Ways* into collages that toy with memory and context, begetting further scrutiny. On title track, "I Contain Multitudes"—appropriately and straightforwardly lifted from Walt Whitman's *Song of Myself*—the allusions parade. But whereas Whitman's narrator encompasses people, places, and events in his present, the United States of 1855, in a spirit of soaring optimism, Dylan's absorbs "Today and Tomorrow and Yesterday, too," in a melancholy pseudo–love song in which artistic allusions are threaded to personal ruminations. Edgar Allen Poe, Mott the Hoople, Anne Frank, Indiana Jones, the Rolling Stones, William Blake, Beethoven's sonatas, and Chopin's preludes become part of the narrator's unsettled self. Dylan's untamed vision and ability to synthesize disparate and improbable elements of our culture into poetic song verse still feels potent, if not new. The dilemma of Dylan's potential final or near-final career chapter reflects his disciple Bowie's, yet remains unique unto himself: He can't give everything away; there's simply too much left to say. He contains multitudes.

Bowie and the other songwriters of the mid to late sixties and seventies that we noted are indebted to the blues, rock 'n' roll, and especially Dylan's albums of the midsixties. At the dawn of the sixties, if we had the gift of foresight—not forecasting or guesswork but the ability to peel back the world's opaque skin and glimpse the future—we may have peered at Dylan in his "late era": *Time Out of Mind* (1997), *Love and Theft* (2001), the inscrutable film *Masked and Anonymous* (2003), *Modern Times* (2006), *Together Through Life* (2009), *The Tempest* (2012), and *Rough and Rowdy Ways* (2020). The upstart folk singer of the early sixties, hailed as the bellwether of the young generation now was this: the mustachioed drifter draped in a silver nudie suit, in what we guess might be called a "video" for *Love and Theft*, throwing cards and smoking cigars with grifters. We might reach into the future to spin 1997's *Time Out of Mind* on a compact disc (!) and hear the distinct echo of Screaming Jay Hawkins on "Love Sick," or on "Dirt Road Blues," a pretty damn near pitch-perfect amalgamation of Muddy Waters, Howlin' Wolf, and Little Walter on their finer Chess sides, and witness a musician and persona spun through with reverb, cobwebs, mystery, and menace. What other surviving artist of Dylan's era could be picked up by the police in 2009 while on tour in Long Branch, New Jersey, for "walking around looking at houses"—a shabby sixty-eight-year-old, carrying no identification, absorbing a turn-of-the-century neighborhood that had long since transitioned to a Latino community in the 1970s? In a twenty-first-century version of perceived vagrancy, he persuaded the officers to accompany him to the concert site so that they could verify his story, and then asked that if his story turned out to be true, would they be kind enough drive him *back* to that Long Branch neighborhood so he could continue looking at houses?

Knowing this in the sixties, we would have said to ourselves, "Of course!" This grizzled, uncompromising, vagabond-like bluesman and bard, could he have emerged as anyone else? Had he ever been anyone else? The list of Dylan's personae is long: the Woody Guthrie protégé, the voice of a generation, the Beat poet rocker and counterculture martyr, born-again Jesus freak, the hippie King Lear foundering in the digital wilderness. Dylan may have been all of these things and none. But his forging of a persona as a vehicle for yoking together the blues, rock 'n' roll, and poetry in the sixties changed the relationship between music and poetry, and as we'll discuss in the next chapter, took on new dimensions in his and other artists' work.

3

Myth-Making, Personae, and Poetic Song Verse

The Beatles, the Rolling Stones, and the Doors

Reflecting on the changes in rock during the sixties, Mick Jagger observed that when the Rolling Stones formed in 1962, "popular music wasn't talked about on any kind of intellectual level. . . . But suddenly popular music became bigger than it had ever been before. It became an important, perhaps the most important, art form of the period, after not at all being regarded as an art form before."[1] The transformation Jagger mentions largely was due to many songwriters' shift from reverential devotion to folk music as a marker of authenticity to emphasizing sensational, often shocking aspects of their public images and creative practices. Instead of portraying themselves as the descendants of Woody Guthrie, Bukka White, and Pete Seeger, artists returned to the theatrics of Chuck Berry, Little Richard, and Jerry Lee Lewis but retained the cerebral, self-consciously artistic emphasis that characterized songs and poetry in folk and Beat coffeehouses. This combination released Bob Dylan and others from songwriting conventions that ranged from the length of individual songs to how albums were conceptualized, recorded, and produced. In essence, the Rolling Stones, the Beatles, the Doors, the Who, Jimi Hendrix, the Kinks, and others followed Dylan's lead and expanded fifties rock 'n' rollers' sounds and emphasis on performance, assuming often extravagant yet artistically resonant personae that resulted in songs and albums replete with ambitious wordplay and sonic arrangements.[2]

The poet James Dickey's observation in "The Self as Agent" (1965) concerning the "creative possibility of the lie" readily applies to many sixties songwriters:

> The I-figure's actions and meaning, and indeed his very being, are determined by the poet's rational or instinctive grasp of the dramatic possibilities in the scene or situation into which he has placed himself as one of the elements. To put it another way, he sees the creative possibilities of the lie. He comes to understand that he is not after the "truth" at all but something that he considers better. He understands that he is not trying to tell the truth but to *make* it, so that the vision of the poem will impose itself on the reader as more memorable and value-laden than the actuality it is taken from. In the work of many a poet, therefore, the most significant creation of the poet is his fictional self. (Dickey 1971, 156)

Dickey suggests how artists' invention of "fictional" selves, or personae, interacts with their creative practices and their desires to perform on and off the page. The "I-figure" becomes part of the process of creating a "truth" that's "more memorable" and "value-laden" than literal truth. Artists—from Lord Byron to Walt Whitman to Lead Belly—had promoted images that complemented their works' themes, but in the mid to late 1960s many artists proved particularly adept at exploiting this phenomenon in an era often characterized by Marshall McLuhan's assertion the "medium is the message." In this chapter we'll discuss how the "creative lies" the Beatles, the Rolling Stones, the Doors, and others cultivated helped turn them into larger—often more notorious—celebrities and had a profound influence on the form and substance of their art.

Two classic works of literary criticism—T. S. Eliot's "Tradition and the Individual Talent" (1921) and Harold Bloom's *The Anxiety of Influence* (1973)—provide a further context. In his essay, Eliot considers how writers draw on traditions and are subject to the pressures of their time. He discusses how exceptional artists are able to use and extend previous creative practices, altering existing forms and creating new modes that give expression to their age. Bloom's book posits a Freudian model, coupling Eliot's insights into the relationship between formal developments and the cultural landscape with an emphasis on how particular writers enter into psychological and creative struggles with other writers. Great artists must appropriate and distance themselves from previous and competing figures who serve as inspiration and menace; through readings and misreadings of powerful figures, they strive to slay their creative progenitors in order to assert their own identities.

In the sixties the "anxieties" between artists took on an increasingly public dimension, largely due to the media boom. Songwriters' turn toward ambitious, often surreal verse frequently was accompanied with an emphasis on personae—and the proliferation of musical and promotional technologies heightened the possibilities of and need for novel expression and exploitation. Simply put, the development of more sophisticated production techniques, and the expansion of television, radio, print media, and photography, made it increasingly compelling to appear different from others.[3]

The Beats and the artists they identified as their creative predecessors—especially Walt Whitman, William Blake, Arthur Rimbaud, and other Romantic or Symbolist poets—played a vital role shaping this dynamic, which often balanced theatricality and authenticity. In the fifties and early sixties Ginsberg and his fellow Beats had taken American poetry to new levels of showmanship, but the folkies and many fledging rock musicians found them authentic and appealing. When Little Richard had dressed as the pope or the queen of England, it was considered burlesque, but the Beats' eccentricities, like the folkies' embrace of rural music and dress, were perceived as genuine, though there was a calculated dimension of salesmanship to it.

Ginsberg—the most visible of the Beats—crafted and revised his life story in his poetry and in the press throughout his career. In the fifties he invented his own *Künstlerroman* and cast himself as the central character. Similar to Dylan's mimicry of Woody Guthrie several years later, Ginsberg latched on to Walt Whitman in 1955. That fall he studied Whitman's poetry at the University of California, Berkeley, and began composing what would become *Howl and Other Poems* (1956).[4] In these poems he cultivated a prophetic, Whitman-like style, beginning lines with the same words and similar syntax, and creating catalogs that he recited like incantations (see "Howl," "Footnote to Howl," "America," "Tears," "In the Baggage Room at Greyhound," and "Psalm III"). His first public reading was at an arts festival in San Francisco in late September of 1955. The audience's positive reaction to "A Supermarket in California"—in which he dubs Whitman his "dear father, graybeard, lonely old courage-teacher"—emboldened his new poetic identity. The arts festival appearance was followed by a reading at Six Gallery on October 7 (an evening that's famous in Beat lore) and other events, during which he became increasingly animated.[5] At Six Gallery Ginsberg read from the unfinished manuscript of *Howl*, and Jack Kerouac cheered him on—a moment Kerouac enshrined in *The Dharma Bums* (1958) when his fictional alter ago, Ray Smith, "followed the whole gang of howling poets to the reading at Gallery Six that night ... the night of the birth of the San Francisco Poetry Renaissance ... Alvah Goldbrook was reading his wailing poem 'Wail' ... everybody was yelling 'Go! Go! Go!' (like a jam session)."

Like Whitman, Ginsberg created a transformation myth about his change into a prophetic bard. In section 5 of *Song of Myself* Whitman describes his body and soul making love to each other on a "transparent summer morning," an experience that changes him into a visionary seer who recognizes the unity of all things. In "Howl," "Sunflower Sutra," and other poems, Ginsberg attributes his transformation to hearing the eighteenth-century poet William Blake recite his poetry. In "Howl" Ginsberg passes "through universities with radiant cool eyes hallucinating Arkansas and Blake-light tragedy among the scholars of war" (a phrase that links the civil rights movement and anti-war sentiments to his poetic transformation), and in "Sunflower Sutra" he recalls his "memories of Blake—my visions—Harlem / and Hells of the Eastern rivers." In interviews and essays he comments on these lines and asserts that the mystical moment allowed him to recognize the interrelatedness of all things.[6]

After the publication of *Howl and Other Poems*, and a widely publicized trial on charges of pornography, Ginsberg was heralded as the quintessential Beat poet.[7] His emphasis on performance was in sharp contrast to Robert Frost, T. S. Eliot, Wallace Stevens, Marianne Moore, John Crowe Ransom, and other established poets who projected aloof, decorous demeanors, but it appealed to many young musicians and their fans.[8] Like Robert Lowell, Anne Sexton, Sylvia Plath, and other Confessional poets of the period, Ginsberg wrote poems that presented private experiences in an often shocking manner, but in the sixties he also began embedding his poetry in a tapestry of popular culture, a tactic that helped him communicate material—allusions to classical myth, canonical literature, and Romantic philosophy—usually intended for a high-art crowd to a wider audience that included Dylan, John Lennon, Paul McCartney, Jim Morrison, and other songwriters.

In June of 1965 the BBC interviewed Lennon about the publication of his second novel, *A Spaniard in the Works* (his first was *In His Own Write*). During the interview Lennon claimed, "If I hadn't been a Beatle ... I might have been a Beat poet!" (Coupe 2007, 131). Within months Ginsberg added the Beatles to the list of rock musicians with whom he'd cultivated a friendship, a development that enhanced Ginsberg and the Beats' visibility and put them at the center of popular culture. Simon Warner points out that "rock's endorsement of Ginsberg, Burroughs, Kerouac and others encouraged fans of the great singers and groups of the day to familiarize themselves with Beat literature. If you were listening to *Blonde on Blonde* or *Revolver*, you were most likely also intrigued to know what 'Howl,' *Naked Lunch* and *On the Road* may offer by way of background" (2013, 15). In early 1964 Ginsberg attended Dylan's concert in Princeton, New Jersey, and was photographed wearing a top hat. The picture ended up on *Bringing It All Back Home*, and he appeared in *Don't Look Back*, the documentary film of Dylan's 1965 UK tour. Ginsberg visited the Beatles' home turf of Liverpool in 1965 and in the press claimed that it was "at the present moment the centre of the consciousness of the human universe." Soon after, he was filmed dancing around a hotel room and falling into people's laps at a party with the Beatles. Later that year Ginsberg and his lover, Peter Orlovsky, posed hugging each other in the nude for widely circulated media photos, and he joined Ken Kesey and the Merry Pranksters on their infamous trip to Timothy Leary's commune for psychedelic experiments. He met John Cale and other members of the Velvet Underground, and he befriended Andy Warhol, the Byrds, Robbie Robertson, and Phil Spector. He performed with the Fugs—a group of poets turned musicians—and became a fixture at the Dom, the Electric Circus, the Balloon Farm, and other East Village poetry and rock clubs (see Ginsberg's poem "Consulting I Ching Smoking Pot Listening to the Fugs Sing Blake"). His notebooks show that he was becoming more and more infatuated with the Beatles' mass appeal, and rock stars began showing up in his poems. In "Portland Coliseum" (1965) he pictures "Goofed Ringo," "Silent George," "Short black-skulled Paul," and "Lennon the Captain" transforming the "million children / the thousand worlds" into "one Animal / in the New World Auditorium." "Beginning of a Poem of These States" (1965) describes a journey up the West Coast. The narrator Ginsberg listens to the "Beatles crying / Help! Their voices woodling for tenderness," and to "Dylan" end "his song 'You'd see what a drag you are'" as he passes by "Pacific Gas high voltage antennae" and "over last hump to giant orange Bay." Similarly, "First Party at Ken Kesey's with Hell's Angels" (1965) describes "at 3 a.m. the blast of loudspeakers / hi-fi Rolling Stones Ray Charles Beatles." He became close friends with Paul

McCartney, and in 1968 they created an experimental spoken word label called Zapple—a play on the Beatles' new label, Apple.⁹

Rock music helped transform Ginsberg from a Beat who romantically celebrated his marginalization from society into a celebrity, counterculture mystic. At the same time, Ginsberg and his fellow Beats helped promote and influence rock music. He professed that together rock and poetry would change the United States' social structure and often paraphrased Plato's claim that "when the mode of music changes, the walls of the city shake." He gained notoriety as a prototype counterculture radical, venturing into South and Central America, dabbling in politics, and taking well-publicized trips to India, the Middle East, Africa, Cuba, Eastern Europe, and the Soviet Union (to his dismay and surprise, he was deported from Cuba and Czechoslovakia). After participating in experiments with Timothy Leary at Harvard University, they hatched a not-so-secret "plot to get everyone in power in America high" (Morgan 2006, 321). He testified before Congress, advocating the legalization of drugs, and when speaking at the Arlington Street Church in Boston, he urged the clergy and teachers to tell "everyone in sound health over the age of 14" to use LSD "at least once" and advised community leaders to host orgies on the Boston Common (431). He opened shows for rock musicians and contoured his poems as prophetic statements. "Bayonne Turnpike to Tuscarora," written in 1967 during the Summer of Love, ends by combining Ginsberg's love life and rock music with images of the American landscape and war. While driving, the narrator declares that he could "split Peter's skull" with an "ax" and describes motel's signs as "Satanic Selfs covering nature." The song "'Devil in the Blue Dress' exudes over the radio" and intermingles with the "crash of machineguns, ring of locusts, airplane roar."

Like Ginsberg, in the mid to late sixties Dylan, the Beatles, and other rock musicians adopted personae that influenced the form and substance of their art. The authenticity that had been founded on premises of unadorned simplicity in early sixties rock 'n' roll (including the Beatles' early recordings), or on sincerity in traditional folk and blues, became infused with elements that suggested an inability to comprehend existence in terms of cause and effect. Society, culture, media, and government became symbolic constructs to be deciphered, and conveying a sense of disorientation became a sign of authenticity. Disorientation reflected a world that no longer was comprehensible—nuclear bombs hovered, spies were in the midst, fluoride in the water was a chemical agent designed to manipulate minds, TV commercials and print ads contained subliminal clues that determined behavior—and psychotropic substances were needed to break down barriers of consciousness.

As often was the case, Dylan helped rearrange the musical landscape, despite the fact that, as Joni Mitchell has asserted (and as discussed in chapter 2), Dylan "is not authentic at all: He's a plagiarist, and his name and voice are fake. Everything about Bob is a deception. We are like night and day, he and I."[10] Mitchell's point is well taken in the sense that Dylan has drawn from sundry sources to transform himself and his music—a process that has continued throughout his career—but so had Mitchell and every other rock musician influenced by the blues or rural folk music. In Martin Scorsese's faux documentary of Dylan's midseventies performance tour, *Rolling Thunder Revue: A Bob Dylan Story* (2019), Dylan claims that when a person is "wearing a mask, he's going to tell you the truth," but if he's not, "it's highly unlikely" (we should note that Dylan isn't wearing a mask when he made the remark). As Scorsese's film suggests, authenticity largely is a function of performance, perception, and point of view. The metamorphosis of Dylan's early-to-mid-sixties personae reflects shifts in *conceptions of authenticity* implied by changes in his album covers. On *Bob Dylan* (1962) he's pictured in a dark corduroy cap and tan coat holding up his guitar by the frets, a shot that suggests unadorned simplicity. *The Freewheelin' Bob Dylan* (1963) displays him dressed casually, strolling arm in arm with his girlfriend Suze Rotolo down the middle of a street in New York City on a blustery day, an image that accents his ties to the Greenwich Village folk scene. Similarly, the black-and-white cover of *The Times They Are a-Changin'* (1964) features his folk roots with a shot of him from the shoulders up, hair mussed, dressed in an open collar workingman's shirt, and looking down thoughtfully. On the transitional album *Another Side of Bob Dylan* (1964), a dark overcoat replaces the workingman's garb. The picture of Dylan against a cityscape, posed with one knee up, one arm balanced upon his thigh and his other arm reaching back with his hand set on his hip, looks more self-consciously staged than his previous covers and gives the air of an artiste. The differences between the cover of his next album—the first in which he goes electric—and those of his first three albums are more striking. The cover of *Bringing It All Back Home* (1965) imposes a circular iris that at once distorts and focuses a square color photograph. The scene is decidedly tongue-in-cheek bohemian upscale, with a decadent air. Dylan is seated in the foreground wearing a dinner jacket over a striped shirt with cuffs; his legs are crossed, and he's hugging a kitten perched on an entertainment magazine. Reclined on the far end of a long divan, a young black-haired woman dressed in red holds a cigarette in her hand and, like Dylan, stares toward the camera. Behind her is a copy of *Another Side of Bob Dylan* and an ornate fireplace. Various magazines, albums, and pictures are scattered around the room, but one element is decidedly out of place: in the foreground, bottom left, traversing the iris, is an askew yellow and black sign that warns, "FALLOUT SHELTER."

Dylan's midsixties personae helped change the ways in which musicians thought about themselves and conceptualized their public images in relation to their art. The Beatles, the Rolling Stones, the Doors, and other bands followed Dylan's lead, using the perspective of a psychedelic bluesman and loading it with ambitious poetic song verse that challenged social values and rock music's status as strictly entertainment. After encountering Dylan, the Beatles gradually moved away from simple, melodic love songs and began a transformation that eventually resulted in becoming a "fake band" for *Sgt. Pepper's Lonely Hearts Club Band* (1967). Like Dylan, the Beatles and other musicians coupled previous notions of authenticity with sensationalistic enhancements that effected and created a more distinct synergy between their music, public images, and performances. John Lennon recalled that Paul McCartney purchased *The Freewheelin' Bob Dylan* in early 1964, and for "three weeks in Paris we didn't stop listening to it" (Sptiz 2005, 533). But Al Aronowitz, the music critic and promoter who introduced the musicians in New York City later that year, remembers that at the time Dylan had "no interest in the Beatles ... it was almost as if I had to drag him kicking and screaming." Dylan thought the Beatles' music was "Bubblegum" (Aronowitz 1995).

Lennon was equally reluctant to meet Dylan, but for a different reason: he wanted to wait until he was Dylan's "ego-equal." Aronowitz observes that "Dylan's magic had stopped an entire Counterculture dead in its tracks, and John, too. In effect, Dylan had tapped John on the shoulder and made him turn around to look. John recognized that he had been outdistanced by Bob in plumbing his own depths" (1995). The counterculture to which Aronowitz refers had already flowered in poetry but barely had begun to bud in music. Dylan had separated himself from the folk scene, and he increasingly brought Beat and other poetic techniques into his work. In contrast, the Beatles still were packaged as smiling clean-cut kids with pleasing harmonies, and Andrew Oldham—the Stones' then-current and the Beatles' former manager—had begun to market the Stones as their rough-and-tumble opposites, hooligans with the street cred to play the down-and dirty-electric blues of Mississippi, Memphis, and Chicago.[11]

Soon after meeting Dylan, Lennon wrote and recorded "I'm a Loser," a folk rock tune that he later claimed was indebted to Dylan.[12] Similarly, McCartney observed that "You've Got to Hide Your Love Away," from *Help!* (released in August 1965), reveals "John doing a Dylan . . . heavily influenced by Bob. If you listen, he's singing it like Bob."[13] "Nowhere Man," from the band's next LP, *Rubber Soul* (released in December 1965), signals a further attempt to shift away from a vocal style the Everly Brothers and Buddy Holly had inspired, and from love songs that had sent millions of teenage girls into hysterics. The song was written and recorded in the months after the release of Dylan's *Bringing It All Back Home* in March of 1965, his controversial performance at the Newport Folk Festival on July 25, and the release of *Highway 61 Revisited* in August of 1965. Like Dylan's "Ballad of a Thin Man," "Nowhere Man" concerns an individual disconnected from his environment. However, where Dylan's song is an edgy, surrealistic, and mocking indictment of a conventional individual baffled by the cultural changes occurring around him, Lennon's song is a melodious, sympathetic lament loaded with angst.

> Doesn't have a point of view,
> Knows not where he's going to,
> Isn't he a bit like you and me?

The Beatles' next album, *Revolver* (August 1966), followed Dylan's *Blonde on Blonde* (May 1966). Like Dylan's album, *Revolver* signaled a shift to a more vigorous psychedelic sound. *Revolver* also reflects the Beatles' movement toward more sophisticated wordplay and poetic, allusive lyrics. On "Tomorrow Never Knows"—a song inspired by *The Tibetan Book of the Dead*—suggestive lyrics and Indian music guide and instruct the listener toward transcendence. The first line of each verse ends with a noun—in verse three "within" is ingeniously used as a place and a concept—and the second line ends with a gerund that links the verses sonically and functions as the line's subject, suggesting an evolving process (e.g., "dying" instead of die or dead).

> Turn off your mind, relax and float down stream,
> It is not dying, it is not dying

Lay down all thought, surrender to the void,
Is it shining? Is it shining?

McCartney's "Eleanor Rigby" recalls E. A. Robinson's poems—then standards in most high school and college anthologies—in its formal regularity and description of ordinary individuals' isolation and despair. McCartney moves from speculating about "all the lonely people" to describing two specific cases, Eleanor Rigby and Father McKenzie. In the verses devoted to the two characters, McCartney begins with a long line that details the empty tedium of their lives and follows it with a short line that provides a pithy reflection on their emotional state. In the penultimate verse he juxtaposes Rigby and McKenzie:

Eleanor Rigby died in the church and was buried along with her name
Nobody came
Father McKenzie wiping the dirt from his hands as he walks from the grave
No one was saved

The band's most powerful breakthrough occurred with *Sgt. Pepper's Lonely Heart Club Band*, which is widely regarded as rock's first concept album. McCartney recalls, "It was an idea I had, I think, when I was flying from L.A. to somewhere. I thought it would be nice to lose our identities, to submerge ourselves in the persona of a fake group."[14] The Beatles' reasons for creating personae were different from most artists, who used personae to enhance their fame; the Beatles were world-famous by the time of *Sgt. Pepper*. McCartney wanted to use the "fake" band to "put some distance between The Beatles and the public" (Spitz 2005, 643). His hopes to escape the pressures of Beatlemania were naïve to the point of fantasy, but the Beatles' use of this persona transformed their art. Before *Sgt. Pepper*, the band's label, EMI, had insisted the Beatles release four singles and two LPs a year. But for *Sgt. Pepper* the band decided to seclude itself in the studio at Abbey Road and take its time, playing no concerts and scheduling no other commitments.

The album was groundbreaking, melding blues, folk, Indian, jazz, British dance hall, and classical music into psychedelic rock. The band members' desire to create alter egos freed them to submerge in a sea of experimentation that changed popular music. The use of orchestras and the inclusion of non-Western musical traditions spread. Bands on both sides of the Atlantic began making concept albums. Elaborate and painstakingly engineered, including the first use of automatic double tracking, *Sgt. Pepper* revolutionized the way records were produced. The cover art drew an enormous amount of attention and changed how albums were designed and marketed. But McCartney's idea of making an entire album from the perspective of a "fake band" drifted away after the creation of the first two songs—"Sgt. Pepper's Lonely Hearts Club Band" and "With a Little Help from My Friends"—and the penultimate tune, a harder-edged version of the title track. However, the theme of a culture in flux unifies the album. The surrealistic "Lucy in the Sky with Diamonds," "Fixing a Hole," and "A Day in the Life" make reference to consciousness-altering drugs. "Getting Better," "She's Leaving Home," and "Good Morning Good Morning" chafe against bourgeois conformity. And "Being for the Benefit of Mr. Kite," "When I'm Sixty-Four," and "Lovely Rita" provide humorous digs at traditional conceptions of courting.

The album's capstone, "A Day in the Life"—which *Newsweek* dubbed rock's equivalent of T. S. Eliot's *The Waste Land*—involved over two hundred instruments. It's been widely noted that a newspaper account of the death of Tara Browne, a rich socialite with whom Lennon was friendly, inspired the song, but the decision to keep the person's identity anonymous is telling. Instead of focusing on Browne, the song presents the narrator's descriptions of everyday life and suggests that alternatives are available.

> I read the news today, oh boy
> About a lucky man who made a grade
> And though the news was rather sad
> Well, I just had to laugh
> I saw the photograph
>
> He blew his mind out in a car
> He didn't notice that the lights had changed
> A crowd of people stood and stared
> They'd seen his face before
> Nobody was really sure if he was from the House of Lords
>
> I saw a film today, oh boy
> The English army had just won the war
> A crowd of people turned away
> But I just had to look

> Having read the book
> I'd love to turn you on . . .

The song's first three verses are similar in form and content, beginning with three unrhymed lines before closing with a couplet. The unrhymed lines describe a situation in a casual, conversational tone. In contrast, the rhymed couplets call additional attention to themselves, emphasizing the narrator's tone and perspective. In the first verse the expression "oh boy" and the use of "rather" to modify "sad" signal that the narrator is perusing the news, not mourning an individual. As he sings, Lennon halts and extends the "a" sounds (his voice is heavily reverbed) in "photograph" and "laugh," reinforcing the rhyme in a manner that causes a sense of irony and disorientation. In the second verse the longish line "Nobody was really sure if he was from the House of Lords" is strung out and accompanied by psychedelic sounds that reinforce the ironic laughter that closes the first verse. The movement from a person's death to describing a film—note the similarities between the first line of the first and third verses—reflects the narrator's attitude that he's discussing everyday things, rather than, say, mourning an individual. "I'd love to turn you on," a phrase that suggests drug use but also indicates initiation into a new way of viewing the world, signals a shift in pace and tone. The song wends from piano, guitar, bass, and drums to a swirling orchestral arrangement that mounts before giving away to a persistent, monotonous thumping E chord on piano and the sound of an alarm clock ringing, signaling the inception of another day of drudgery.

> Woke up, fell out of bed
> dragged a comb across my head
> found my way downstairs and drank a cup
> and looking up I noticed I was late
>
> Found my coat and grabbed my hat
> made the bus in seconds flat
> found my way upstairs and had a smoke
> and somebody spoke and I went into a dream

The verses above end with contrasting sound effects. "Late" is followed by panting sounds and "dream" is followed with Lennon singing "Ahhhh, ahhhha

..." mixed in a fade that suggests soaring into an alternate state. A classical horn section intercedes and returns the song to a verse that resembles the opening three verses. In this instance, the daily news concerns the many potholes in a road, which the newspaper article presumably alleges would be enough to fill Albert Hall. The sardonic reflection on the triviality of counting potholes stresses the monotonous and dissatisfying quality of conventional life and contrasts it with the possibility of being "turned on" to an enlightened perspective, the theme that underpins and unifies *Sgt. Pepper*:

> I read the news today, oh boy
> 4,000 holes in Blackburn Lancashire
> And though the holes were rather small
> They had to count them all
> Now they know how many holes it takes to fill the Albert Hall
>
> I'd love to turn you on . . .

The Beatles' use of personae transformed their art, but their image still oscillated between that of serious artists and insightful social commentators and that of playful lads from Liverpool. The BBC special *Magical Mystery Tour* (1967) and the animated film *Yellow Submarine* (1968)—in which the music-loathing Blue Meanies besiege the underwater paradise Pepperland and the Fab Four come to the rescue—reinforced the latter. Tom Wolfe, practitioner of the New Journalism and chronicler of Ken Kesey and the Merry Pranksters in the *Electric Kool-Aid Acid Test* (1968), succinctly, and famously, summarized the continuing differences between the Beatles' and the Rolling Stones' images: "The Beatles want to hold your hand, but the Stones want to burn your town."

★ ★ ★

The differences between the Beatles and the Stones were more than just marketing ploys—they reflected actualities that were exaggerated and used for publicity purposes which in turn affected the artists' work. When the Beatles witnessed the Stones play the Crawdaddy Club in Richmond, England, in 1962, Lennon observed that the Stones' charging electric blues were "a bit more radical" than the Beatles' pop sounds (Spitz 2005, 408).

Jack Hamilton points out that the Stones "presented a vision of the music obsessively rooted in tradition, and a black musical tradition specifically" (2016, 251). He notes that in the midsixties the African American press and Black bluesmen, including Muddy Waters, praised the band for its authenticity (254).

In 1963 the Stones' manager, Andrew Oldham, a former publicist for the Beatles, encouraged the band to start writing original songs and began selling the Stones as the Beatles' opposites with the widely publicized question, "Would you let your daughter marry a Rolling Stone?" Five years later, on "Monkey Man" (1968), the Stones provided a wry comment on the band's image as seedy, scruffy Londoners with a bent for Mississippi mysticism, à la Robert Johnson:

> Well, I hope we're not too messianic
> Or a trifle too satanic
> We love to play the blues

Like the Beatles, in the midsixties the Stones felt Dylan's influence and began creating more ambitious songs. When Beatlemania arrived in New York City on August 13, 1965, Mick Jagger was on a yacht on the Hudson River dancing to an advanced copy of "Like a Rolling Stone" (Spitz 2005, 574). The Stones were several years away from approximating Dylan's lyrical sophistication, but Jagger and Keith Richards had begun writing songs that focused on cultural trends in ways that pointedly promoted their image as bluesmen. After watching television commercials in a Florida motel room while on tour in May of 1965, the band went to Chess studio in Chicago to cut "Satisfaction," which was immediately released as a single in the United States and vaulted to number one on the charts. Oldham remembers that for the Stones going to Chess was like "telling the Pope you can go to the Vatican" (Appleford 1997, 29). The Doors' Ray Manzarek observed that when the Stones "assimilated the blues aspect *into* the band," rather than doing covers, was "when it really happened for me.... The first time I heard 'Satisfaction' on the radio I couldn't believe it. The lyrics were so terrific, they were talking to all young American males" (Jackson 2015, 86). Like Dylan, the Stones were writing updated, original blues whose authenticity was affirmed by the way listeners related to it. The song's narrator is watching television,

> And that man comes on to tell me
> How white my shirts can be
> But he can't be a man 'cause he doesn't smoke
> The same cigarettes as me

In 1966 the Stones followed with the single "19th Nervous Breakdown," a song that, like Dylan's 1965 hit "Like a Rolling Stone," lambasts a self-absorbed, privileged young woman. That same year another single, "Mother's Little Helper," addressed a contemporary woman's addiction to barbiturates. But unlike the first-person confessional narrative of, say, Anne Sexton's poem "The Addict," Jagger and Richards challenge a hypocritical older generation's claim that youths had changed for the worse, accusing mothers of abnegating familial duties. Later released on *Aftermath* (1967), "Mother's Little Helper" reflects Jagger's and Richards's developing sense of lyrical arrangements. The song opens with the pronouncement "What a drag it is getting old," which is followed by an instrumental sequence that initially separates it from the rest of tune. However, the line keeps resurfacing in increasingly loaded refrains. Except for the refrains, each verse begins with the narrator quoting a contemporary housewife. After the opening couplet, the narrator engages in ironic accounts of housewives' behavior. These verses also contain various internal rhymes, including the repeated combination of "shelter" and "helper," two words usually associated with protection and nurturing that take on a caustic twist.

> "Life's just much too hard today"
> I hear every mother say
> The pursuit of happiness just seems a bore
> And if you take more of those, you will get an overdose

The Stones, Dylan, and the Beatles all stopped touring for several years during the late sixties, but for different reasons. Dylan's hiatus resulted from his discomfort with continued scrutiny of his biography in the press, a motorcycle accident, and his unease at being cast as the "voice of his generation." The Beatles had grown weary of Beatlemania and had begun fighting with one another over revenues. The Stones were beset with legal issues and drug problems. But in each case the lull created space for spectacular innovations that audiences rapidly absorbed and other bands copied.

Jagger remembers the period as a time when he was "just writing a lot, reading a lot. I was educating myself. I was reading a lot of poetry. I was reading a lot of philosophy."[15] After ventures into pop with *Between the Buttons* (1967) and psychedelia in the disastrous *Their Satanic Majesties Request* (1967), the Stones returned to the band's blues roots on *Beggar's Banquet* (1968), but with an expanded sense of composition that resulted in a remarkable string of albums recorded in quick succession: *Beggar's Banquet* (1968), *Let It Bleed* (1969), *Sticky Fingers* (1971), *Exile on Main St.* (1972), *Goat's Head Soup* (1973), and *It's Only Rock 'n' Roll* (1974). *Beggar's Banquet* also marked the band's venture into country music—largely due to Gram Parsons's influence—but the country-inflected songs often took a comic, satiric tone. In contrast, their return to blues-based rock was emotionally charged, elaborately conceived, and an affirmation of their persona as outsiders who flirted with danger, death, and the devil.

The album's first track, "Sympathy for the Devil," is a brilliant extension of a longtime blues theme. Blues artists—including Charley Patton, Robert Johnson, Brownie McGhee, Skip James, and Peetie Wheatstraw—had used Satan as a metaphor for an enemy, an oppressor, a faithless woman, or evil, but in "Sympathy for the Devil" Jagger writes a dramatic monologue from Lucifer's perspective. (One of Jagger's sources of inspiration was Russian writer Mikhail Bulgakov's mid-century novel *The Master and Margarita*, a tale of a devil-like gentleman and his minions descending on Moscow to wreak gleeful mayhem.) The song's title drips with irony, as the devil introduces himself as a sophisticated, cosmopolitan individual—"a man of wealth and taste"—who opportunistically infiltrates human history. He "was *around* when Jesus Christ" experienced "doubt and pain," and "*Made damn sure* that Pilate / Washed his hands and sealed his fate" (our emphasis). Similarly, he "*stuck around* St. Petersburg" when he noticed "it was time for a change," and he proceeds to murder the "Czar and his ministers" during the Russian Revolution. Satan recounts his role in other historical atrocities—the Hundred Years' War, World War II—and challenges listeners to puzzle over the "nature" of his "game." His "game" becomes clear when he cites a contemporary instance, the Kennedy assassinations, and points out humans' complicity in evil ("it was you and me").

The need for "restraint" Satan cites later in the song involves people's tendency to view evil as separate from themselves, but the phrase "heads is tails" and the question ("who? who?") that ends several verses suggest that Satan has infiltrated history with humanity's help. The "courtesy," "sympathy," and "taste" he invokes are the smoke screens humans use to deny their own complicity, a charge emphasized by the play of "politesse"—derived from the Latin (via French), "to cleanse or polish"—and "waste." In essence, decorum helps shield humanity from its own corruption, a pointed observation at a moment when heads of state were ordering the bombing of civilians in Southeast Asia.

In November of 1969 the Stones embarked on the band's first tour in three years. Bassist Bill Wyman recalled, "In '69, they listened. It was the first time audiences actually listened to us." Likewise, Keith Richards observed, "The audience used to be composed of ninety percent chicks twelve and thirteen. My first thought on this tour was, 'Where are they now?' The audiences are much more intimate now. They listen more. We can play much better" (Russell 2009, 59).

The tour in support of *Let It Bleed* (1969) provided the opportunity to play blues-based rock laced with poetic song verse in front of more sophisticated listeners. The albums' first track, "Gimme Shelter," picks up where "Sympathy for the Devil" left off, commenting on the ominous danger encircling a world besieged by wars, assassinations, and mayhem. Like "Sympathy for the Devil," the song consists of short, declarative lines interspersed with resonant imagery. The "fire" in the third verse is strewn with surreal images that simultaneously capture clashes with authorities during riots in the United States and Europe, of napalm searing Vietnam, and of Satan's inferno:

> Oh, see the fire is sweeping
> Our very streets today
> Burns like a red coal carpet
> Mad bull, lost its way

Like "Sympathy for the Devil," "Midnight Rambler" draws on a well-known blues theme, in this case the midnight man, a mysterious, libidinous creature with a dangerous air. Jagger and Richards take the theme to an extreme, drawing on the account of the Boston Strangler, Albert DeSalvo, whom a prison psychiatrist had diagnosed as possessing a split personality. During DeSalvo's highly publicized 1967 trial, the psychiatrist testified that the defendant lusted for fame and "badly wanted to be the Boston Strangler." Jagger and Richards portray DeSalvo's psychology by creating a semi-covert dramatic monologue that Richards calls a "blues opera in four parts."[16] The song opens as a straight Chicago blues, with Jagger moving between harp and vocals. During the first movement the narrator speaks of himself in the third person ("Did you hear about the midnight rambler?"), sounding a warning that implicitly suggests his desire for fame and notoriety. The narrator calls the strangler the "one you've never seen before" but is able to describe his actions in detail:

The one that shut the kitchen door?
He don't give a hoot about warning
Wrapped up in a black cat cloak
He don't go in the light of the morning
He split the time the cock crows

In the second movement the song slows before speeding up again, with the vocals taking on an urgent but hushed tone. "Don't you do that . . . Oh don't do that . . ." is repeated with increased fervor until the music diminishes and the vocals become louder. The song comes to a near standstill, and the third movement commences with the tune cast as a slow blues that signals the narrator's groaning acknowledgement of his identity. He shifts back and forth between describing himself in first and third person, reflecting his fractured desire to deny and affirm his identity:

We're talking about the midnight . . .
The one who closed the bedroom door
I'm called the hit-and-run, rape-her-in-anger
The knife sharpened tippy-toe . . .
Or just the shoot them, brain-bell jangler

The final movement surges, with the harp increasing in intensity, and bursts into an emphatic, almost celebratory swing, as the strangler menacingly announces his attack ("Well he's pouncing like a proud black panther") and passionately outs himself ("I'm gonna smash all your plate glass windows"). The narrative heaves to an abrupt conclusion as the last line of the final verse breaks the series of hard end rhymes leading up to it, altering the flow and calling attention to the rambler's addiction to sexual violence with a disturbing double entendre: "I'll stick my knife right down your throat baby, and it hurts."

Jagger's and Richards's bluesman personae empowered them to broach almost any topic, a quality reflected in "Brown Sugar," a song that addresses taboo subjects and creates disturbing ties between the past and the present.

To record the song, the Stones ventured to an apt location, as was often the band's practice. Soon after fleeing the tragic scene at the Altamont Speedway in Livermore, California—a post-Woodstock festival during which the audience rioted and a man was murdered during the Stones' performance—the band flew to Muscle Shoals, Alabama, to record at FAME, the studio that had been home to Joe Tex, Aretha Franklin, Wilson Pickett, and Otis Redding. Jagger describes "Brown Sugar," the opening track on *Sticky Fingers* (1971), as a song that combines "all the nasty subjects in one go."[17] "Brown Sugar"— a metaphor for Black women, oral and anal sex, and heroin—moves from slave traders' masochistic lust ("Scarred old slaver know he's doing all right / Hear him whip the women just around midnight") to an upper-class white woman's craving for a Black servant ("Drums beating, cold English blood runs hot / Lady of the house wondering where it's going to stop") to the contemporary narrator's liaison with a "Black girl."

As noted in chapter 2, almost any topic is allowed on the sacred patch of the blues as long as it possesses an authentic ring. The bad boy Stones had transformed themselves into actual rock 'n' roll outlaws by early 1967, when Jagger and Richards were imprisoned and Brian Jones was placed on probation for drugs.[18] But the personae Jagger—the band's primary lyricist—and Richards assumed upon their return to recording also had been primed with poetic influences that enriched their understanding of verse. After the Stones' contract with Decca expired in 1970, the record company insisted that the band owed it one more song. The band sent "Cocksucker Blues," which Decca declined to release (Hepworth 2016, 110). Besieged by tax and drug problems, as well as by paternity suits, after recording *Sticky Fingers* the Stones fled Great Britain for France, where Richards rented a large villa, Nellcôte, in Villefranche-sur-Mer, and the band worked in the basement through a drug-induced haze to extend its string of masterfully composed albums, with the fittingly titled *Exile on Main St.*

★ ★ ★

Ray Manzarek claimed that—like Dylan, Joni Mitchell, Stephen Stills, and others—the Doors "had a beatnik foundation" (Doors and Fong-Torres 2006, 96). Perhaps no one embraced the myth-making outlaw rock poet aesthetic more than Jim Morrison. Morrison was the son of a career US naval officer who had participated in the Gulf of Tonkin incident off Vietnam's coast in

1964 and within the year had been promoted to admiral and commander-in-chief of US Naval Forces, Europe. Jim disapproved of his father's profession, and after spending Christmas with his family in 1964, never saw his parents again. On the biographical profile Elektra Records used to promote the Doors' first album, he claimed his entire family was "dead," though they were all alive and healthy.

From the midsixties to the early seventies Morrison played the part of bard and shaman, fronting a quartet that fed—and sometimes choked—on his lyrical intensity and theatrics. In 1965 Morrison graduated with a major in theater arts and a concentration in film from UCLA, where he had developed his own version of the "creative lie." Morrison's friend Phil O'Leno recalls that as undergraduates they "had a theory of the True Rumor, that life wasn't as romantic and exciting as it should be, so you tell things that are false because it is better that images be created. It doesn't matter if they are true, so long as they are believed." Another friend and classmate, John DeBella, remembers they also were "into the shaman: the poet inspired" (Hopkins and Sugerman 1980, 45, 46). Manzarek, then an MFA student in film at UCLA and a classically trained musician with whom Morrison founded the Doors, wanted to combine poetry and rock.

Morrison had little musical training but had read and written poetry with enthusiasm since high school. His sister, Anne, recalls that as a teenager Jim "loved Bob Dylan," but throughout high school and college Morrison didn't think a career in music was possible. He later observed that the "birth of rock 'n' roll coincided with my adolescence, my coming into awareness. It was a real turn-on, although I could never allow myself to rationally fantasize about ever doing it." His younger brother, Andy, notes that as a youngster Jim was "more than anything into reading, writing, and drawing" (Doors and Fong-Torres 2006, 10). Morrison's high school English teacher observed, "Jim read as much and probably more than any other student in the class. His work was excellent. But everything he read was so completely off-beat" that he had to confirm Morrison's sources on research papers at the Library of Congress (Hopkins 1992, 40). When he graduated, Morrison asked his parents for Friedrich Nietzsche's complete works; the aphoristic quality of Nietzsche's writing and his embrace of Dionysian creative forces would influence Morrison's verse, performances, and outlook (at one point, the Doors' drummer, John Densmore, claimed that Nietzsche's influence killed Morrison).

Morrison lived in six different cities before his family settled in Alexandria, Virginia, during his high school years. He kept his bedroom stuffed with "hundreds and hundreds" of books. His friends recalled that he'd close his eyes, tell them to pick any book and start reading at the beginning of any chapter, and he would identify the book and its author (Hopkins and Sugerman 1980, 29). Manzarek remembers that Morrison played the same game at UCLA, but was betting on beer and telling people to "open the book" to "any page"; he wowed them, winning "95 percent of the time" (Manzarek 1998, 79). Morrison and Manzarek "read everything we could get our hands on," including Donald Allen's *The New American Poetry, 1945–1960* (1962), a then-controversial anthology that highlighted experimental poetry and had been published as a counterattack on Donald Hall, Robert Pack, and Louis Simpson's *New Poets of England and America* (1957), which included an introduction by Robert Frost and stressed more traditional, formal poetry (Manzarek 1998, 68). In contrast, Allen's volume emphasized the imagistic, "open field" poetics developed by Ezra Pound and William Carlos Williams and practiced by the Beat, San Francisco Renaissance, and Black Mountain poets.

Morrison's interest in Allen's anthology is telling. Although he'd filled notebooks with poetry since his mid-teens, he was much more interested in imagery than meter, a proclivity suggested by his enthusiasm for the visual arts. In high school he painted copies of de Kooning nudes, self-portraits, and impressionistic representations of friends (Hopkins 1992, 40). While at UCLA, inspired by Sergei Eisenstein's films, he covered the walls of his student apartment with collages of photos that formed surrealistic rather than linear narratives (81). He loved Tennessee Williams's symbolic stage sets and immersed himself in experimental film, particularly the works of Ingmar Bergman. Morrison and Manzarek studied directing with Josef von Sternberg, the auteur of *The Blue Angel*, *Shanghai Express*, and *The Devil Is a Woman*. Morrison's capstone student film was an erotic, imagistic homage to Sternberg's leading lady, Marlene Dietrich, sans a traditional plot.

The vast majority of Morrison's poetry is undistinguished, but his dedication to poetry helped him become one of rock's most poetic and original lyricists. When composing songs, the other band members would "listen to Jim chant-sing the words over and over and the sound that should go with them would slowly emerge" (Densmore 1990, 37). In his memoir *Light My Fire: My Life with The Doors* (1998), Manzarek writes that months after graduation,

> Jim was coming up with more variations and permutations on his lyrics that required more and more invention on the keys from me. I loved it. He was exploding with ideas, and I was constantly pushing myself to try different and more imaginative chord changes, harmonic patterns, solos, rhythms, funk grooves, blues riffs and jazz and classical modes of playing to support and embellish his poetry. (Manzarek 1998, 113)

Even at the height of his fame as a rock star, Morrison never lost his desire to be an esteemed poet. In the spring of 1969, Morrison told *Rolling Stone* that to be a published, recognized poet had "always been" his "dream" and remained his "greatest hope" (Hopkins 1992, 228). Beat poet Michael McClure read Morrison's poems and liked them "very much, particularly the ones that are pure image."[19] At McClure's urging, in 1969 Morrison privately printed a book of poems, *The New Creatures*, and a beautifully designed chapbook, *The Lords*. To Morrison's delight, his full name, James Douglas Morrison, graced both covers, but to his dismay "Jim Morrison" was used on the commercial Simon & Schuster edition that combined both works. McClure noted that "Morrison wanted to be known as a poet. . . . Jim was very serious about being a poet, and he didn't want to come in on top of being Jim-Morrison-the-big-rock-singer." In the fall of 1970, roughly a year before he died, Morrison speculated about financing and publishing a "little magazine . . . like the ones the Surrealists and Dadaists used to put out" (Hopkins 1992, 234). Danny Sugerman, the Doors' manager, observed that "Jim's dying wish was to be taken seriously as a poet" (Doors 1978, 14).

After graduation from UCLA, Morrison and Manzarek met on Venice Beach, where Morrison had spent two months living on a rooftop. Morrison had dropped thirty pounds and sculpted his physique. Like centuries of young romantics before him, he was preoccupied with sex, death, and transformation. He recited the verses of "Moonlight Drive," a love song filled with sensuous, visionary imagery that takes on connotations beyond a nighttime car ride. Volition and control vanish as the lovers step into a "river" at the end of the first verse and the narrator claims he can't be his partner's "guide" at the end of the second verse. Throughout the song a series of reversals results in the type of otherworldly imagery characteristic of Romantic poetry. In the second verse the verb "swim," which typically would be used in conjunction with "tide," and "climb," which usually would be used with "moon," are reversed. By switching them Morrison creates a dreamlike quality that continues with the behest to "surrender to waiting worlds that lap / Against our sides," a phrase that suggests change through sexual ecstasy and death. The couplet "Easy to love you as I watch you glide / Falling through wet forests on our moonlight drive" extends the Romantic trope of surrender, transformation, and dying as sexual climax.

The lyric's imagistic, dreamlike qualities reflect Morrison's career-long interest in Romantic transcendence. He drew on Aldous Huxley's *The Doors of Perception* (1954) for the band's name and often quoted William Blake's *The Marriage of Heaven and Hell* (1793): "There are things known & there are things unknown & in between are the Doors." He embraced Blake's first "Proverb of Hell," "The road of excess leads to the palace of wisdom," and viewed his songs and performances as portals that brought the audience face-to-face with him into a transformative ritual. "See, there's this theory about the nature of tragedy," Morrison claimed, "that Aristotle didn't mean catharsis for the audience, but a purgation of emotions for the actors themselves. The audience is just a witness to the events taking place on stage" (Hopkins 1992, 86).

Morrison's Romantic ethos permeated the band's live act, resulting in new forms of song, but during early appearances at fraternity parties and other small gigs he was so shy he wouldn't face the crowd, opting to turn his back to the dance floor. When he did turn around, he closed his eyes and clutched the microphone tightly. He soon started to overcome his fear through substance abuse. Buttressed by drugs and drink, he focused on visual performance, telling others he witnessed a car accident when he was five years old and the spirit of a dying American Indian entered him. This "creative lie" led to what his bandmates call his "shaman's dance." Morrison believed the "shaman" was an "unusual individual" who would "put himself into a trance by dancing, whirling around, drinking, taking drugs—however. Then he would go on a mental travel" and "describe the journey to the rest of the tribe" (Hopkins 1992, 86–87).

Morrison's description of Aristotelian theory and the shaman's trance turns the performer into the conduit for what he perceived as authentic experience. Tapping into sixties culture's emphasis on psychological and spiritual transformation, he used live concerts to catapult the audience into romantic ecstasy. He punctuated songs with poetic monologues, frenzied dances, and long dramatic pauses, during which he likened watching the crowd to "watching a mural. There's movement and then it's frozen. I like to see how long they can stand it, and just when they're about to crack, I let them go" (Hopkins 1992, 134). He drew on Norman O. Brown's theories concerning the sexual neuroses of crowds and French Surrealist Antonin Artaud's *The Theatre and Its Double* (1938), in which Artaud insisted that dramatic action should be cathartic, likening it to the plague, creating a context in which the audience "will be terrified and awaken." Similarly, Morrison claimed that his audiences' sometimes turbulent reactions demonstrated how "people like to get scared. It's exactly like the moment before you have an orgasm. Everybody wants that. It's a peaking experience" (134).

All four band members—and many in the audience—believed LSD and other psychotropic substances were catalysts for divining new states of consciousness. While their desire may seem naïve today—a conclusion Morrison expressed in 1971—in the sixties such ideas had an air of legitimacy in many, though certainly not all, sectors of society. Beat and Deep Image poets wrote prizewinning books that detailed substance-induced journeys into states of spiritual awareness. Psychiatrists and other physicians used LSD to treat patients, and laws against recreational use of the drug weren't in effect until California banned it in October of 1966 and other states followed suit. Timothy Leary and Richard Alpert conducted experiments at Harvard University in the early sixties and toured college campuses throughout the decade and beyond, advocating the spiritual benefits of psilocybin. Carlos Castaneda's accounts of peyote use and shamanism earned him a PhD at UCLA and were applauded by a host of respected academics. *Time* and *Life* magazines' cofounder Henry Luce and his wife, Clare, were LSD enthusiasts. In the midsixties both publications featured articles and editorials discussing the drug's psychological and spiritual benefits. The September 1966 cover of *Life* featured "LSD ART" (Siff 2008).

Early in 1966 the Doors became the house band at the London Fog, a small club on Los Angeles's Sunset Strip. Jac Holzman, the talent scout who signed the Doors to Elektra Records, recalls seeing the band during the "summer of 1966, and the place was the Sunset Strip, which had suddenly morphed before everyone's astonished eyes into the hippie navel of the universe." At the London Fog, the quartet honed its repertoire and quarreled with the club's management over pay and other issues, including Morrison's stage antics. The band played before sparse crowds, but Densmore notes that "at the London Fog" Morrison "literally turned it around, you know, got the nerve to develop the audience and developed his own thing" (Doors and Fong-Torres 2006, 53).

The band soon was hired at the top club on the Strip, the infamous Whisky a Go Go, and surged into prominence after the single "Light My Fire" catapulted to the top of the charts. *The Doors* (1967), the group's superb first album, begins with an injunction to "break on through to the other side" and concludes with "The End," a piece that exemplifies the band's goal, in their manager Danny Sugerman's words, of achieving "musical alchemy—they intended to unite rock music unlike any ever heard before with poetry and that hybrid with theater and drama" (Doors 1978, 4).

"The End"—a twelve-minute opus that moves from summoning the nation's youth westward to Oedipal drama—exemplifies how disorientation became a trope for authenticity. The song combines the erotic, the mythic, the psychedelic, and the fantastic with allusions to depth psychology and Greek drama in an effort to usher the performers and the audience into a new, more authentic reality. It alludes to Cold War–era conflicts but wraps them in myths and archetypes that Morrison-the-visionary-shaman believed were embedded in Western consciousness. Like many psychedelic songs, it captured psychotropic drugs' disorienting effects. The Doors' guitarist Robby Krieger observes that the piece was Morrison's "favorite song on acid" (Doors and Fong-Torres 2006, 58). Producer Paul Rothchild—whose credits include Paul Butterfield, Neil Young, Joni Mitchell, Janis Joplin, and Bonnie Raitt—explains that "The End" was a "very complex piece to record . . . it was the most awe inspiring thing I'd ever witnessed in the studio" (71).

In "The End" Morrison balances singing and poetic recitation. The song begins with a sinewy fifty-five-second instrumental in which cymbals, guitar, and keyboards float off and around one another before he announces, in a carefully modulated tone,

This is the end, beautiful friend
This is the end, my only friend
The end of our elaborate plans
The end of everything that stands
The end
No safety or surprise
The end
I'll never look into your eyes again

Though the lyrics begin by seemingly addressing an individual, the line "The end of everything that stands" provides a key to its broader focus. "The End" concerns endings that manifest in new beginnings. Morrison's concept of "revolution" suggests his intent. When he mentioned the word in the media, he almost always referred to existential acts instead of political action. He claimed, "It just seems that you have to be in a constant state of revolution, or you're dead. There always has to be a revolution, it has to be a constant thing, not something that's going to change things, and that's it. . . . It has to be everyday" (Doors and Fong-Torres 2006, 233). In the Elektra Record biography used to promote the album, he drew on the ideas of Rimbaud and the French Symbolists and claimed, "I like ideas about the breaking away or overthrowing of established order—I am interested in anything about revolt, disorder, chaos, especially activity that seems to have no meaning. It seems to me to be the road to freedom."

"The End" draws on myths and archetypes to explore how culminations result in freedoms. Surrounded by a burgeoning counterculture, Morrison regarded California—"the west"—as the edge and limit of Western civilization. His voice and Manzarek's organ soar as the song presents the possibility of hope and renewal in a "desperate land," a country in the midst of social unrest and the war in Vietnam, one that needs a "stranger's hand"—presumably Morrison-as-shaman—to guide it toward renewal.

> Can you picture what will be
> So limitless and free
> Desperately in need of some stranger's hand
> In a desperate land

A drumroll and a quickening instrumental bridge follow before the pace slows, and rather than, say, making an explicit political comment à la Pete Seeger, the vocal resumes with surreal lyrics that liken the country's social turmoil and young people's actions to a barbarian uprising.

> Lost in a Roman wilderness of pain
> And all the children are insane
> And all the children are insane
> Waiting for the summer rain, Yeah!

In consecutive lines Morrison announces that people are "Lost in a Roman wilderness of pain," that the youth are all "insane," and that they await renewal, "the summer rain." He sings the first line in a manner that slightly extends and accents the words *lost*, *Roman*, *Wilderness*, and *pain*, and continues even more pronouncedly in next line, in which every syllable except "the" is drawn out to create an unnerving, uncanny tone by the time he reaches the word *insane*. Then the line concerning the "summer rain" is delivered in a heightened, quickened manner and followed with the affirmation "Yeaaaaaah!"

A brief but intense instrumental interlude follows before Morrison issues an eerie decree for people to take the nation's highways west in a contemporary version of the California Gold Rush.

> There's danger on the edge of town
> Ride the King's highway, baby
> Weird scenes inside the gold mine
> Ride the highway west, baby
> Ride the snake
> Ride the snake
> To the lake
> The ancient lake, baby
> The snake he's long, seven miles
> Ride the snake
> He's old and his skin is cold
> The west is the best
> The west is the best
> Get here and we'll do the rest

Again, the vocal is carefully pitched between poetic declamation and song, with a particular note of abandon given to the line "Weird scenes inside the gold mine," a phrase that a half century later is still used in popular culture to suggest strangeness (the BBC used the phrase for the title of a 2012 radio program that looks at the "antidote to the peace and love generation of mid-60's America" by exploring "the darker side of the underground music scene"). The line's placement between calls to take to the "highway" and the directive to "ride the snake" stresses the journey's fantastic qualities. Snakes—long associated with evil, sexuality, wisdom, fertility, and the underworld—fascinated

Morrison-the-shaman, who provocatively told the press that people "evolved from snakes ... I used to see the universe as a mammoth peristaltic snake ... I think the peristaltic motion is the basic life movement and even your basic unicellular structures have this same motion. It's swallowing, digestion, the rhythms of sexual intercourse" (Hopkins 1992, 242). When Morrison issues the mandate "Get here, and we'll do the rest," it becomes clear that "The End" entails departure from the known, a process that takes on the connotations of a mythic journey replete with all the qualities Morrison associated with serpents and that wends toward the "ancient lake," the Pacific Ocean, at whose rim Western civilization expires and the sun sets.

His summons segues into a voyage into the subconscious with the invocation of the "blue bus" and a "driver" who is "taking us" into an unknown realm. At this point Morrison stops singing and enters into a dramatic speech about a killer who wakes before "dawn" and takes a "face" from the "ancient gallery." The killer proceeds to visit his sister and brother before encountering his parents in a room further down the hall, where he asserts that he wants to kill his father and have sex with his mother.

> The killer awoke before dawn
> He put his boots on
> He took a face from the ancient gallery
> And he walked on down the hall
>
> He went into the room where his sister lived
> And then he paid a visit to his brother
> And then he walked on down the hall
> And he came to a door
> And he looked inside
> Father?
> Yes, son?
> I want to kill you
> Mother, I want to ... !

This Oedipal drama addresses another "end," an excursion into the subconscious where the killer confronts and destroys his past. The line "He took a face from the ancient gallery" suggests the scene is a reenactment of a symbolic purgation that has occurred many times. The motion down the hall and the opening of doors draw on images widely associated with Freudian psychology. The scream that marks his interaction with his mother replaces the expletive sometimes used during live performances and expresses the pain of confronting and attempting to eradicate the past, particularly parental ties. The band explodes as Morrison shrieks, reinforcing the moment's cathartic intensity. It's worth noting that Morrison had one brother and one sister, reflecting the family structure in the song, and that the line asserting that the narrator wants to "kill you" echoes the "creative lie" expressed in Morrison's Elektra Records biography, in which he falsely claimed his family was dead.

The pace slows and the vocal resumes in a different tone. In contrast to the dreamlike crooning that dominates the song's first part and the spoken drama that marks the Oedipal section, the vocal becomes ever more aggressive as he compels his presumed lover and the listener to "take a chance with us" three times and insists on being met at the "back of the blue bus." The instrumental pace surges forward, with "fuck, fuck .. come on, alright" persistently repeated in a hushed and quickened tone beneath increasingly cacophonous music, before returning to lyrics and a pace that echo the song's beginning by invoking his "beautiful" and "only friend."

> This is the end
> Beautiful friend
> This is the end
> My only friend, the end
>
> It hurts to set you free
> But you'll never follow me
> The end of laughter and soft lies
> The end of nights we tried to die
> This is the end

The couplet expressing that it's painful to "set you free," but that the narrator's friend and lover, as well as the listener, can "never follow me," suggests the necessity of change, with the "end" resulting in new freedoms and possibilities. The possibilities include taking a "chance with us" and presumably experiencing a new reality by entering Morrison's world of mythic, fantastic transformations.

"The End" was one of many dramatic pieces the Doors staged during live performances. The band would pause at junctures within songs, and

Morrison would interject additional lines of poetry and philosophy and engage the audience in dialogue. In a 1969 interview for public television, Densmore told the *Village Voice*'s Richard Goldstein, "We'll play the structure of the song and then we'll get into a free part and we'll improvise musically and he'll improvise lyrically and that will probably be just straight poetry" (Hopkins 1992, 214).

In his effort to create dramatic intensity, Morrison cultivated an image that was erotic, intellectual, and outrageous. He wore tight leather pants, rested the microphone against his crotch, assumed the fetal position, entered into frenzied dances, fell into the crowd, recited Rimbaud, quoted philosophers, chided the police, challenged audiences' motivations for attending concerts, and paced the stage speaking of art and altered consciousness. He claimed, "The only time I really open up is on stage. The mask of performing gives it to me, a place after I hide myself when I can reveal myself" (Hopkins 1992, 132).

Morrison also became expert at manipulating the press. The band's promoter, Danny Fields, observes, "He was so smart. He gave such great interviews and such fabulous quotes. . . . [The press] took him perfectly seriously" (Hopkins 1992, 142). In one of his final interviews, at a time when he was attempting to transition away from rock and into poetry and film, Morrison admitted, "I was very good at manipulating publicity with a few little phrases like 'erotic politics' . . . I knew instinctively what people would catch on to. So I dropped those little jewels here and there—seemingly very innocently" (255). He cultivated a Steve McQueen smile, a Marlon Brando brood, a James Dean saunter, and a Paul Newman swagger; he posed in fur coats, bare-chested, and in snakeskin suits. His hair and gaze were drawn from Plutarch's description of Alexander the Great. He sometimes aimed a camera at photographers, playfully accenting the self-consciousness involved in creating an image. He encouraged rumors of his own death, leading people to believe his death in Paris in 1971 was a hoax, and that like his hero Rimbaud, he had disappeared from the public eye after creating a body of visionary verse. On September 17, 1967, he sang, "Girl you couldn't get much *higher*," on *The Ed Sullivan Show*, after agreeing to alter the line, a breach that infuriated Sullivan but resulted in tremendous publicity. On December 9, 1967, he was arrested onstage after inciting a crowd by announcing that a police officer had sprayed him with mace backstage. *Life* ran a feature and included a picture of the singer offering a stone-faced officer the microphone.

Blessed with movie-star good looks, Morrison exploited sexuality more successfully than any singer or poet of the era. With Mick Jagger on the sidelines due to the Stones' legal issues, Morrison became rock's hottest sex symbol in the late sixties. When the Doors ventured to New York City—where Morrison spurned Andy Warhol's advances and had a widely noted affair with Nico—Howard Smith vaunted his sex appeal in the *Village Voice*:

> There really hasn't been a major sex symbol since James Dean died and Marlon Brando got a paunch. Dylan is more of a cerebral heartthrob and the Beatles have always been too cute to be deeply sexy. Now along comes Jim Morrison of the Doors. If my antennae are right, he could be the biggest thing to grab the mass libido in a very long time. I've never seen such an animalistic response from so many different kinds of women.[20]

In the last verse of "The Crystal Ship" Morrison wrote, "The Crystal ship is being filled / A thousand girls, a thousand thrills / A million ways to spend your time." The band's press ranged from teenage girls who melted over photographs of Morrison in *16* to intellectuals who pored over his quotes in the *New York Times* and features on him by Joan Didion and other notable writers. In their biography of Morrison, *No One Here Gets Out Alive*, Jerry Hopkins and Danny Sugerman point out, "At all times Jim was aware of image and press. Before each concert he asked one of Elektra's publicists which writers were in the audience and who read the publications they wrote for" (Hopkins and Sugerman 1980, 143).

Manzarek claimed that the band's second album, *Strange Days* (1967), was "not so much" a comment on the "hippie era" but a "commentary on post–World War II America. . . . We had a beatnik foundation, a literary foundation, a film foundation" (Doors and Fong-Torres 2006, 96). That album, and the two that followed, *Waiting for the Sun* (1968) and *The Soft Parade* (1969), became gold records, and as the band's audience grew its live act increasingly became performance-oriented, leading Harvey Perr to claim in the *Los Angeles Free Press* that the "art of the Doors is more and more removed from those standards of art by which rock music is measured" (Doors 1978, 103). "When the Music's Over," "Not to Touch the Earth," "Shaman's Blues," "The Unknown Soldier," "The Soft Parade," and other songs often were presented as extended performance pieces, sometimes to audiences' dismay. Morrison became increasingly impatient with his rock star status, and his longtime girlfriend and common-law wife, Pamela Coursan, reputedly urged him to give up singing and devote himself to writing poetry. Rothchild recalled difficulties in the recording studio during the late sixties: "Jim was really not interested. He wanted to do other things like write. Being lead singer of the Doors was really not his idea of a good time now" (Doors and Fong-Torres 2006, 129). In 1968, Morrison, whose drinking was increasingly out of control, announced that he wanted to quit, only to be talked out of it by the other band members. At the Hollywood Bowl on July 5—with Jagger in the audience, hoping to learn about handling a large crowd and stage space in preparation for the *Let It Bleed* tour—Morrison stood still at the microphone, singing and reciting poetry but refusing to engage in his usual theatrics. During many performances he recited "Celebration of the Lizard," a 133-line poem that the other band members and Rothchild had jettisoned in the recording studio during the *Waiting for the Sun* sessions (Morrison had also wanted to record short poems between songs for the album but had to settle for "Celebration" being printed on the record sleeve). During a European tour that fall he disappeared for four days and entered into a heated dispute with his bandmates over their desire to sell Buick the rights to use "Light My Fire" in a television commercial (Morrison prevailed and the commercial was canceled). Frustrated with his image as a sex symbol—he had assiduously helped create it—and increasingly alcoholic, he gained weight, grew a bushy beard, and taunted audiences, whom he felt overlooked his lyrics. On December 13 at the LA Forum, he jeered the audience and performed a forty-minute version of "Celebration of the Lizard" to a frustrated and angry crowd.

Morrison's desires to move in a new direction were reflected in a conversation with classical composer Fred Myrow, whom he told, "If I don't find a new way to develop creatively within a year, I'll be good for nothing but nostalgia" (Hopkins 1992, 220). In February of 1969, Morrison attended the entire five-night run for the Living Theatre's performances at the University of Southern California. The troupe's act involved directly confronting the audience with a series of statements—"I am not allowed to travel without a passport," "I don't know how to stop the wars," "I'm not allowed to take my clothes off"—and a finale in which the actors disrobed. On March 1 at the Dinner Key Auditorium in Miami, an inebriated Morrison refused to sing, talked over the band's attempts to play songs, and pointed at his crotch, asking, "What do you want from me?" He pulled off his shirt and attempted to take down his pants, but Vince Treanor, the band's equipment manager, "got behind Jim and put my fingers into his belt loop and twisted them so he couldn't unbuckle them" (Doors and Fong-Torres 2006, 165–66). Morrison summoned the crowd onstage, and Densmore and Krieger jumped offstage as a "security guard flipped Jim like a black-belt karate expert, head over heels into the audience, thinking he was a fan." His bandmates "looked down from a balcony" and watched "Jim . . . now in the middle of the auditorium, leading a snake dance with ten thousand people following him" (Densmore 1990, 217).

On March 5 the Florida State Attorney's Office issued a warrant for Morrison's arrest, charging him with

1. LEWD AND LASCIVIOUS BEHAVIOR (FEL)
2. INDECENT EXPOSURE (MISD)
3. OPEN PROFANITY (MISD)
4. DRUNKENNESS (MISD)

Tour dates were canceled, and in an interview with *Rolling Stone* a few weeks later Morrison refused to discuss the incident, declared that rock had run its course, discussed literature and film, and finished by reciting his poem "An American Prayer." Morrison's legal defense would center on the claim that the event was a theatrical performance and covered by laws of free speech. He was found guilty of profanity and public exposure, innocent of lewd behavior, and acquitted on public drunkenness. In October of 1970 Morrison was sentenced to sixty days for profanity, six months for exposure, and fined $500.

While awaiting trial the Doors recorded *Morrison Hotel* (a titled inspired by the name of a skid row hotel in Los Angeles), a strong blues-based album that resulted in the band's fifth consecutive gold record, but the supporting tour was disappointing. On December 12, 1970, in New Orleans Morrison gave his last concert, a show in which he pounded the microphone into the stage, flung it into the audience, and sat down. Before leaving for Paris in March of 1971—he would die there on July 3—Morrison wrote and recorded "L.A. Woman," his love/hate tribute to the city where he'd found fame. Based on a poem he'd written for Diane Gardiner, a journalist and sometime lover, the song assumes the perspective of a man on the prowl, venturing into Los Angeles, the "City of Night," and considering its dualities.

As he drives through the suburbs, his view of the city's surroundings conjures a surrealistic red-haired lover—"I see your hair is burning / Hills are filled with fire"—with whom he's had a stormy relationship. In the next verse, the view reveals Los Angeles's seedy underside before expressing the desire to "change the mood from glad to sadness" and the invocation of "Mr. Mojo risin,'" an anagram for "Jim Morrison" that Wallace Fowlie called a "deliberate secret code, an unknown character except for the initiated," and that suggests Morrison's persona as a brooding, sexually provocative bluesman (Fowlie 1994, 104–5). Mojo—a hoodoo bag of magical charms—is alluded to in many blues songs, including Muddy Waters's famous "Got My Mojo Working," and is associated with confidence and sex appeal, qualities reinforced by the double entendre "Risin' risin', goin' right in, right in." Like Dylan, Lennon, McCartney, Jagger, Richards, and other rock singers and performers of the sixties, Morrison had wedded the blues and poetry to discover inspiration and license to transform his art.

In July of 1981, ten years after Morrison's mysterious and controversial death, *Rolling Stone* featured him on the cover with the subtitle "He's Hot, He's Sexy, He's Dead." In the cover story, Bryn Bridenthal, vice president of public relations for Elektra/Asylum Records, claimed, "The group is bigger now than when Morrison was alive. We've sold more Doors records this year than in any year since they were first released." *Rolling Stone* credited the publication of Hopkins's and Sugerman's best-selling biography of Morrison, *No One Here Gets Out Alive (1980)*, which concludes by speculating that Morrison had staged his death and might return, with helping spur the phenomenon.

The Morrison persona and the poetic song verse it engendered had triumphed beyond the grave.

The Fantastic
Beyond Surrealism and Psychedelia

At the end of a recent tour, one of this book's authors, Mike Mattison, found himself on a plane bound for Los Angeles seated next to a chatty navy ensign who was on the first leg of a long journey back to duty on an atoll in the Indian Ocean. As Mattison's band put its instruments into the overhead compartments, the ensign, recognizing that he was surrounded by musicians, asked him about their style of music. He worked back from contemporary R&B and Mattison worked up from the blues until they finally met at Ray Charles. The ensign said music meant a lot to him and that he listened to it constantly on the atoll. He paused a moment, and added: "In fact, without music, none of this"—he gestured at the passengers, the stewards, the airplane, and California spread below them—"means shit."

Much has been made of the ecstatic and reinvigorating powers of music and poetry, modes of expression that are, at their most elemental, transformative. Ancient poets tell us that Orpheus, the father of poetry and song, could make trees and stones dance, alter the very course of rivers, and literally go to hell and return to tell the tale. In this chapter we'll examine the ways in which the fantastic was used—with varying degrees of success—to invigorate language and sound in poetic song verse. Properly plied, poetic song verse can bring the listener to the outer limits of familiar reality, to the fantastic.

The fantastic has been realized in the particular, potent mixture of blues, rock, and poetry that developed in the mid to late 1960s. As discussed in previous chapters the blues, contemporary poetry, and sixties poetic song verse often emphasized the surreal. But we should stress that the fantastic and surrealism are not one and the same. Surrealism is a tactic, an artistic approach that employs the juxtaposition of unlikely elements to stress the primacy of the subconscious mind. According to André Breton's 1924 surrealist manifesto, surrealism seeks creation "in the absence of any control exercised by reason, exempt from any aesthetic or moral concern."[1] The fantastic encompasses surrealism and other approaches that result in the iteration of multiple stimuli that coalesce in an altered, even elevated sense of reality. Surrealism primarily entered American poetry through the work of French- and Spanish-language artists, and surrealistic imagery came to the blues through African and Western mysticism. Both manifestations of the fantastic melded in rock during the mid to late sixties and played a vital role in the development of poetic song verse.

Tzvetan Todorov's distinction between the fantastic and fantasy highlights a crucial difference between works that alter an audience's preconceptions concerning reality and those that use the preternatural to entertain. In his seminal study, *The Fantastic: A Structural Approach to a Literary Genre* (1973), Todorov cautions against confusing the fantastic in literature and art with what is merely marvelous, uncanny, or tinged with the supernatural. The fantastic is not fantasy. In its most exalted form, the fantastic is an aesthetic device that conjures and maintains reality and unreality simultaneously. It is ephemeral, and therefore difficult to employ successfully, its effect difficult to describe:

> The fantastic . . . lasts only as long as a certain hesitation: a hesitation common to reader and character, who must decide whether or not what they perceive derives from "reality" as it exists in the common opinion. . . . The fantastic therefore leads a life full of dangers, and may evaporate at any time. (Todorov 1973, 41)

This type of creative collision underpinned much poetic song verse during the latter half of the sixties. It's an apt description of the genius Bob Dylan brought to the fledgling—and floundering—genre of rock 'n' roll in the early sixties. As we've noted, after World War II rock 'n' roll sprang from a convergence of American song forms, most notably electric blues, country, folk, and jazz. By the time Dylan arrived on the scene in the early sixties, the genre—which in the latter fifties had coalesced as a cultural force of dynamism and change—largely had been reabsorbed into the pop milieu. The shock and energy of Elvis Presley, Chuck Berry, and Little Richard had lost ground to the pabulum of Pat Boone and Connie Francis. Even the injection of the British Invasion groups in the early 1960s was a matter of recycling and reselling American rock 'n' roll back to the next generation of white teenagers. In its early days, the British Invasion brought very little to songwriting beyond hand-holding and girl-longing. Indeed, the overarching themes of early sixties rock 'n' roll were the mercurial quality of adolescent love, how much fun it is to surf, and odes to specific models of American-made cars. But, to push the digression further, these "Little GTOs" and "Daddy's T-Birds" inverted the blues conception and Beat philosophy of travel-as-revelation, turning them into vehicles for achieving the sanitized, quotidian, suburban teenage dream of prom dates, letter sweaters, and chaste kisses. (In the seventies Bruce Springsteen would restore American hot rods to their rightful place as existential getaway cars.) To repeat Mick Jagger's observation, "It's hard to think of the absolute garbage that pop music really was" before Dylan reinvigorated the genre.

Dylan's coupling of poetry and rock in the midsixties suggests how the fantastic extends and alters people's conceptions of reality. D. A. Pennebaker's documentary *Don't Look Back* (1967) captures the intense rage, shock, and sense of abandonment Dylan's audience expressed at his return to rock 'n' roll by "going electric." The film documents Dylan's 1965 European tour to promote *Bringing It All Back Home*. The most notorious moment occurs when an audience member apparently shouts an accusatory "Judas!" at Dylan. Like this accuser, many believed his "going electric" meant he'd abandoned folk traditions and poetic lyricism for straight rock, for teenaged kid stuff.

Sonically, Dylan's "going electric" only was a modest innovation in the context of folk, unlike what the Beatles or Jimi Hendrix would do with rock in the studio, deeply changing production techniques and values. But Dylan was bringing poetry to *rock*, a change that many people had difficulty perceiving or understanding. The film's most revealing confrontation occurs between Dylan and a condescending and genuinely puzzled press corps that can't comprehend where Dylan fits.

During the interview Dylan's carefully cultivated persona becomes a vehicle for what Roger Caillois, in *Au coeur du fantastique* (1965), identifies as "a break in the acknowledged order, an irruption of the inadmissible within the changeless everyday legality" (Todorov 1973, 41). His interaction with *Time* magazine's London correspondent results in a disquisition on the concept of media itself, riddled with Dylan's Zen-like koans: "I'm not questioning you, because I don't expect any answer from you." Or, "Who wants to go get whipped? And if you do want to go get whipped, are you really being entertained?" Beside the caustic comic value, the real revelation is Dylan's frustration with and acknowledgement of the fact that the media and the general public had less interest in his work than in the persona he projected, a persona that, as we've discussed, Dylan had energetically, connivingly, and mischievously conceived of and promoted. Dylan addresses *Time*'s man with growing confidence: "[Opera singer Enrico] Caruso is a pop singer. And I'm just as good a singer as Caruso. Have you ever heard me sing?" The interviewee has turned the tables on the journalist, who becomes the unwitting subject of the interview. It is a virtuoso performance, and Dylan isn't even playing guitar or singing.

The moment encourages one to wonder, Who is this man? Is he an artist, pure and true? Or is he a charlatan, a snake oil salesman, the worst sort of politician, a poseur, a crank? What type of pop singer—especially in 1965—wonders aloud to his backstage entourage, "Are there any poets around here like Allen Ginsberg?" as if asking, "Is there any good Chinese takeout in the area?"

Perhaps it's most helpful to identify Dylan's behavior as that of a trickster. In *Trickster Makes This World* (1998), Lewis Hyde writes of the Greek god Hermes:

> [What] tricksters quite regularly do is create lively talk where there has been silence, or where speech has been prohibited. Trickster speaks freshly where language has been blocked, gone dead, or lost its charm. Here again Plato's intuition—that deceit and inventive speech are linked—holds, for usually language goes dead because cultural practice has hedged it in, and some shameless double-dealer is needed to get outside the rules and set tongues wagging again. (Hyde 1998, 76)

Like the trickster, Dylan cunningly reanimates our cultural narrative. His provocative persona and his use of language and sonics manifest new modes of asserting individuality and communicating in popular culture. The documentary's introductory music video suggests his intentions. He flips cue cards in synch with the lyrics of "Subterranean Homesick Blues"—that confounding, alluring story, "Johnny's in the basement mixing up the medicine / I'm on the pavement thinking 'bout the government"—while Ginsberg, looking like a rabbi, gesticulates in the background, dressed in a tallit or prayer shawl, while having a back-alley deliberation with musician and painter Bob Neuwirth. Perhaps it's an inside joke, or a bit of impish nonsense. Or perhaps we are meant to construe that Dylan embodies a new way of approaching song.

The scene is a postmodern Chautauqua on how high art and popular culture are joined in the counterculture. Dylan's playful, enigmatic, imagistic song mirrors the tone and imagery of Beat poetry. Behind Dylan, Ginsberg enacts the ancient Jewish tradition of Talmudic debate: open-ended and indefinite, much more like poetry itself than the mainstream press's predictable, pandering proclamations. The lyrics dash by as Dylan nonchalantly tosses each card aside. The surreal gush of words becomes even more perplexing as the cards only can accommodate every third or fourth rhyme, all of this precariously riding on what the loquacious and shamanistic Ginsberg cannot utilize: a backbeat commensurate with anything Elvis or the Beatles put down. The cumulative effect is baffling, intriguing, off-putting, charming, menacing, and humorous. Unreality becomes a new reality; the fantastic emerges from the nexus of Dylan's persona, poetic language, and sonic palette.

Martin Scorsese's *No Direction Home* (2005), which appeared thirty-eight years after Pennebaker's film, covers much of the same European tour with mountains of additional footage and contextual interviews. In the grand finale, on May 17, 1966, at London's Royal Albert Hall, Dylan prepares to lead his electric band in his new hit "Like a Rolling Stone," a song that compels a formerly well-to-do young woman, who once "dressed so fine" and "threw the bums a dime," to consider a bewildering new existence:

> Ahh you've gone to the finest schools, alright Miss Lonely
> But you know you only used to get juiced in it
> Nobody's ever taught you how to live out on the street
> And now you're gonna have to get used to it
> You say you never compromise
> With the mystery tramp, but now you realize
> He's not selling any alibis
> As you stare into the vacuum of his eyes
> And say, do you want to make a deal?

Three months earlier Dylan had told an interviewer that "'Like a Rolling Stone' changed it all; I didn't care anymore after that about writing books or poems or whatever. I mean that it was something that I myself could dig."[2] But before the band plays a note, the infamous shout "Judas!" resounds, and Dylan responds to his critic, "I don't believe you! You're a liar!" But the real trump he holds is the musician's indulgence: he looks over his shoulder and yells to his band, "Play it fucking *loud*!" The audience—under the spell of the performer's confounding persona and the synergy between poetic language and amplified sounds—finds its perceptions altered and is beckoned to confront a fantastic, newly ordered world, one in which the music has changed and the high and mighty have been exposed and displaced.

> Ahh princess on a steeple and all the pretty people
> They're all drinking, thinking that they've got it made
> Exchanging all precious gifts
> But you better take your diamond ring, you better pawn it babe
> You used to be so amused
> At Napoleon in rags and the language that he used
> Go to him now, he calls you, you can't refuse
> When you got nothing, you got nothing to lose
> You're invisible now, you've got no secrets to conceal

Whether one is for or against it, it's a new reality, a "language" not previously envisioned, a revelation and a revolution. The words dance, balancing alliteration, rhyme, and allusion with blunt, declarative statements, followed by the chorus's confrontational call for self-awareness and re-evaluation, a rhetorical question that famously binds the whole song together: "*How does it feel?*" Poetic street talk has exploded and imaginatively not only unmasked Miss Lonely—a character of privilege who was certain she had a firm grasp on the workings of the world—but the protocols of popular songwriting itself.

As the decade unfolded, psychedelia abetted the confluence of high and popular culture that Dylan, the Beats, and others advanced, a phenomenon that further unsettled people's assumptions and helped energize language and sonics in rock and poetry. The aesthetic of disorientation we discussed in chapters 2 and 3 was coupled with an aesthetic of transformation in the Doors' and others' psychedelic art. What we now call "psychedelic" music was a byproduct of the introduction of psychotropic drugs—mainly lysergic acid diethylamide, known as LSD, and marijuana (a Beat generation staple)—into midsixties counterculture, and from that entry point, into youth culture and rock. Chemist Albert Hofmann, working with the drug company Sandoz to create a respiratory stimulant, had originally synthesized LSD in Switzerland in 1938. Its psychotropic effect caught the attention of the psychiatric community for possible clinical applications. Eventually the CIA tried to develop it as a mind-control agent.

While rock musicians championed LSD, the rise of its popularity originally was a literary phenomenon. Novelist Ken Kesey and his Merry Pranksters— an unlikely assortment of writers, academics, and Beat-era hipsters—began hosting "acid tests," events promoting the communal ingestion of LSD and celebrating its consciousness-altering effects. In 1964, in honor of the publication of Kesey's novel *Sometimes a Great Notion*, the author and his Pranksters took their mind-bending experiments on the road in an elaborately colored "Magic Bus," whose destination marquee read, aptly, "FURTHUR." Their exploits were notoriously documented and popularized in Hunter S. Thompson's *Hell's Angels: The Strange and Terrible Saga of the Outlaw Motorcycle Gangs* (1966) and Tom Wolfe's *The Electric Kool-Aid Acid Test* (1968), both exemplars of the New Journalism. However, in his relatively recent memoir, *Prime Green: Remembering the Sixties* (2007), novelist and acid test participant Robert Stone suggests that Wolfe "did not *see* the bus back then at all but is extremely accurate with the facts" (emphasis ours). To Stone, the Magic Bus trip was something approaching what we might deem the core aspect of the fantastic, something akin to revelation:

> Like everything that was essential to the sixties, the Kesey cross-country trip has been mythologized. If you can remember it, the old saw goes, you weren't there. But the ride in Ken's multicolored International Harvester school bus was a journey of such holiness that being there—mere vulgar location—was instantly beside the point. From the moment the first demented teenager waved a naked farewell as Neal Cassady threw the clutch, everything entered the numinous. (Stone 2007, 119)

Inspired by Kesey's tests, or at least their legend, Pete Townshend of the Who wrote "The Magic Bus" in 1966 (although it was not officially released until 1968).

Utilizing the clave beat that long had been germinating in American blues, and that Bo Diddley pushed to prominence in rock 'n' roll during the late fifties, the Who's "Magic Bus" gently turns the rock trope of teenage romance on its ear. It begins as an innocuous, danceable song about getting in the "queue" to take affordable public transportation to visit one's girlfriend, but we soon realize that the group-sung response "Too much!" probably is more akin to "Far out!" than a complaint about the actual price of the fare. As the verse ends, however, there's an unexpected twist when the teenage narrator, beyond cheeky, thanks the driver for the ride and promises him an inspectorship if he can "buy" his "magic bus."

The rest of the song conflates driving-as-sex and haggling over the obviously impossible purchase ("Give me a hundred / I won't take under"), but the recurring theme is "I want it, I want it, I want it / You can't have it!" The depiction of teenage sexual frustration is real, but played out under the rubric of Kesey's Magic Bus, the major theme that develops is a yearning for one's own journey above and beyond the quotidian and familiar lives reserved and planned for young people in 1960s England, and into the mysteries of counterculture, the destination proclaimed on the Pranksters' original Magic Bus: Furthur. Soon after, other rock acts also began to pick up on the metaphor, and "magical" album-length journeys appeared from the Beatles in *Sgt. Pepper's Lonely Hearts Club Band* and *Magical Mystery Tour*; the Rolling Stones in *Their Satanic Majesties Request* and their unaired television special *The Rolling Stones Rock and Roll Circus*; the Moody Blues in *In Search of the Lost Chord* (1968); and the Who's *Tommy* (1969).

Kesey's influence was particularly visible on the United States' West Coast. Kesey had graduated from the University of Oregon and gone on to study creative writing at Stanford University with editor and essayist Malcolm Cowley, who helped him develop his first novel, *One Flew Over the Cuckoo's Nest* (1962), and novelist Wallace Stegner, who thought Kesey a reprobate and denied him a fellowship. Cowley's support was justified by the novel's success, and Stegner's misgivings deepened as the San Francisco Bay Area became the epicenter of Kesey's acid tests and their cultural emanations.

Chief among the participants were Jerry Garcia and the Grateful Dead, whose images, performances, and music courted and marketed the fantastic via the psychedelic. The group first formed as the Warlocks, a blues-tinged jug band. As the band's horizons shifted so did its moniker, and the Grateful Dead became ensconced at the vanguard of San Francisco's psychedelic scene, largely due to the notoriety of Kesey's acid tests, at which the Warlocks had performed regularly. Garcia's childhood friend Robert Hunter became the main lyricist for the band, penning most of the lyrics for the Dead's early seminal albums, including *Workingman's Dead* (1970) and *American Beauty* (1970). One lyric in particular, from the song "Truckin," came to define the Dead's ethos/mythos: "What a long, strange trip it's been," invoking—much like travelers in blues and their modern Prankster counterparts—the marvels of travel unavailable to those who fail to tread beyond their native geography or psychological terra. (Hunter would go on to publish poetry in his own right, as well as translations of Rilke's *Duino Elegies: The Sonnets to Orpheus*.)

To this day, the Grateful Dead inspires fanatical loyalty on one hand, and heated derision on the other. To their fans, the Dead have unlocked music from its moors and brought them closer to infinity. To their detractors, the Dead are a serviceable electrified bluegrass band who never properly mastered their instruments. At play in this argument is the Dead's use of improvisation. The Grateful Dead arguably are the first and most dedicated purveyors of long-form improvisation in rock. By improvisation, we mean a conversation traded among musicians who individually leave the proscribed melody to solo above and around the stated chord progression. However, as in jazz, at times even more than one player—or even all—of the Dead tend to improvise over the chord progression at once, creating a polytonal effect. Taken even further, there might not even *be* a chord progression that the group improvises over, or even a set rhythm. This effect, quite distant from the norms of American popular music, has led to characterizations of the Dead as pointless noodlers. To the jazz or classical ear, perhaps it is not the Dead's improvisatory ambition, but the harmonic confines of the basic pentatonic scales the band employs and the general lack of rhythmic ingenuity and/or agility—their music certainly does not swing—that can be a turn-off. For our purposes, regarding the fantastic and the Dead's ongoing popularity, perhaps we can venture to say that their improvisatory, polyphonic "conversation" is easier to understand, or perhaps most intriguing to, those who have experienced psychotropic substances.

While the Dead did not perform at the 1967 Monterey Pop Festival, the event is widely considered the coming-out party for the psychedelic scene, or what a slightly misplaced Otis Redding termed from the stage, "the love crowd." D. A. Pennebaker, again, captured this seminal rock event on film in *Monterey Pop* (1968). While wild and intriguing performances by Jimi Hendrix, the Who, Big Brother and the Holding Company featuring Janis Joplin, and Ravi Shankar are musical highlights, the real stars of the documentary are the attendees, whose flamboyant dress and carefree antics epitomize the psychedelic San Francisco counterculture: face paint, fur hats in June, and Edwardian cravats. (And who's that older man in the white tunic clapping along to the Jefferson Airplane's "Somebody To Love"? Why, Allen Ginsberg, of course!) Rock royalty—including George Harrison and Brian Jones—stroll through the grounds as if giving their benediction to the scene, which seems to be straining as a community toward, as Robert Stone put it, "the numinous." Pennebaker's film documents the psychedelic era's high point, when drug use became a core part of the musical experience and music took on an aesthetic of transformation toward other worlds and realms. The psychedelic equation for attaining this experience, then, presents itself as "the right music plus the right drugs equals the fantastic." This equation produced innovative sounds and affected how they were experienced, but it soon became predictable and often destructive.

The eponymous track of Jimi Hendrix's first album, *Are You Experienced?* (1967), encompasses how psychedelic music and verse successfully broached the fantastic. Starting with a rhythmic guitar scratch that's recorded backwards—using a technique called "backmasking" that the Beatles pioneered on *Revolver* (1966)—the effect creates a disorienting yet persistent "sucking" sound. Next, a military tattoo–style drum pattern underlies a one-chord drone, topped off with a plinking piano on the high octave. While the song eventually reveals itself to contain multiple chord changes, the initial impression is modal—a nod to saxophonist John Coltrane's melding of jazz with Indian classical technique, in which the performer plays set scales or "modes" over a single anchor tone—quite a departure from Western conceptions of scales, melody, and harmony. Shankar, through his association with George Harrison, would become an ambassador to rock for Indian classical music, making spellbinding appearances at Monterey Pop and at Harrison's 1971 *Concert for Bangladesh*. The use of Indian modes and instruments such as the sitar first appeared on the Beatles' *Rubber Soul* (1965) and would become *de rigueur* in psychedelic music, sometimes integrated seamlessly and to great effect, at other times used as a naïve attempt at exoticism, and, occasionally, employed to the point of self-parody.

However, on "Are You Experienced?" Hendrix employs imagistic poetic song verse to ask listeners if they are "experienced," and asserts that he is. As if to assure the listener that the performer and his music are a spirit guide to worlds less "measly," he says, "Uh, let me prove it to you" and slides into a solo that's surprising in its combination of fluidity and abrupt starts and stops, a product of backmasking. He ends the song by proclaiming that he hears "trumpets" and "violins" in the "distance," and by telling listeners that if they don't already hear the instruments, he can escort them into a world of new sounds and perceptions. The song ends as he again asks, "Have you ever been experienced?" and clarifies what he means: "Not necessarily stoned, but beautiful."

The last line is perhaps necessary to distinguish the *type* of experience the pursuit of the fantastic in rock music required. The "experienced" are "tuned in," "with it," and know "where it's at." As we've mentioned, Jim Morrison named his band the Doors after British poet and writer Aldous Huxley's *The Doors of Perception* (1954), a treatise on the writer's first mescaline trip and a title that Huxley himself lifted from suspected drug-user William Blake's long poem and illustrated book, *The Marriage of Heaven and Hell* (1793). Thus, truly experiencing psychedelic music seemed to require an initiation, the sacraments of which often were psychotropic drugs. The idea is that drugs combined with psychedelic rock open a doorway to a new reality, other realities, or the *real* reality. Initiates, the "experienced," turned up their noses at drugs that did not widen an individual's spiritual or artistic horizons. The Rolling Stones' "Mother's Little Helper" is a derisive put-down, stereotyping the housewife who "goes running for the shelter of her mother's little helper" (i.e., tranquilizers) "to get her through her busy day." Or as the Jefferson Airplane's Grace Slick sings in "White Rabbit," casting a psychedelic trip against Lewis Carroll's *Alice in Wonderland*:

> One pill makes you larger
> And one pill makes you small
> And the ones that mother gives you
> Don't do anything at all

To reiterate, for many artists and folks associated with the counterculture, the fantastic was not fantasy; it wasn't escapism or make-believe. It embodied the cumulative effects of a journey toward—or an attempt to breach—the limits of reality, a distinction that sometimes mystified people who were, at least partially, sympathetic to the counterculture's social agenda.

Differences between poets and writers of the post-WWII generation, who generally leaned toward the political spectrum's liberal end, and artists associated with the counterculture, or the New Left, suggest the extent to which openness to the fantastic typified the new generation. Norman Mailer addresses this intergenerational dance in his lengthy reportage, *Armies of the Night: History as a Novel, the Novel as History* (1968). It is the story—through Mailer's highly subjective lens—of the hundred thousand–strong October 21, 1967, march on the Pentagon to end the Vietnam War. Primarily organized by a coalition of younger activists, the event drew a wide swath of participants from the civil rights movement, women's rights movement, and churches, as well as artists, writers, actors, and sundry pacifists. The title for *The Armies of the Night* is taken from Matthew Arnold's Victorian-era poem "Dover Beach," an elegy to fate and ebbing human faith (" ... and we are here as on a darkling plain / Swept with confused alarms of struggle and flight / Where ignorant armies clash by night"). In the book, Mailer writes about armies clashing in the jungles of Vietnam and the mayhem that erupted among the marchers and the National Guard on the Pentagon's steps. The narrative begins with an excerpt from a *Time* magazine article concerning a pre-march rally held the previous night at the Ambassador Theater in Washington, DC. *Time* describes Mailer "mumbling and spewing obscenities as he staggered about the stage—which he had commandeered by threatening to beat up the previous M.C." With typical bravado, and with a disregard for the mass media his younger counterparts largely shared, Mailer writes: "Let us leave *Time* in order to find out what happened" (Mailer 1968, 13–14). Mailer spends roughly fifty pages enhancing and justifying his harangue, much of it having been delivered in a thick, fake Southern accent. Finally, giving up the microphone, Mailer is followed by essayist Dwight Macdonald, a prominent member of the New York Intellectuals who had edited the *Partisan Review*. MacDonald reads from Rudyard Kipling's "The White Man's Burden," a poem of expansion and empire, and is followed by Robert Lowell, who reads "Waking Early Sunday Morning," a meditation on youth and memory in light of contemporary world upheaval:

> Oh to break loose like the chinook
> salmon jumping and falling back,
> nosing up to the impossible
> stone and bone-crushing waterfall

The intergenerational cracks begin to spread a little later when at the Pentagon Abbie Hoffman and the experimental rock group the Fugs, led by poets

Ed Sanders and Tuli Kupferberg, attempt to lead the marchers in a chant to levitate the building. Mailer posits, "In the air the Pentagon would then, went the presumption, turn orange and vibrate until all evil emissions had fled this levitation. At that point the War in Vietnam would end" (1968, 139).

Whether drug mania, absurd theater, or both inspired this quixotic quest, Mailer acknowledges a sea change in countercultural notions of drug tripping:

> Now, here after several years of the blandest reports from the religious explorers of LSD, vague Tibetan lama goody-goodness auras of religiosity being the only publicly announced or even rumored fruit from all trips back from the buried Atlantis of LSD, now suddenly an entire generation of acid-heads seemed to have said goodbye to easy visions of heaven, no, now the witches were here, and rites of exorcism, and black terrors of the night. (Mailer 1968, 143)

The cultural journey had turned from enlightenment to courting the fantastic as a means of fomenting revolution. But the blanket conceit the counterculture and post–World War II writers—Mailer, Macdonald, and Lowell among them—shared as they tilted at windmills is that the artist must cultivate a serious mistrust of conventional American culture. Art, in a sense, becomes a transgression. (With *Armies of the Night*, Mailer—along with contemporaries Tom Wolfe, Hunter S. Thompson, Gay Talese, and Joan Didion, among others—was well on the way to establishing the legitimacy of the New Journalism, narrative reporting that eschewed authorial distance and questioned the very notion of objective coverage.) And if the hippies took that lesson and ran with it—declaring the country sick and that inmates now were running the asylum—who could blame them in their naïveté for seeking new land, fresh dirt, alternate realities?

Openness to the fantastic in the sixties and seventies leaked into culture at large through poetry as well as music. The Beats had written openly of their experiences with hallucinogens since the fifties, but in the sixties and seventies an emphasis on the fantastic reached its apogee. Sylvia Plath's *Ariel* (1965), James Dickey's *Buckdancer's Choice* (1966), James Wright's *Shall We Gather at the River* (1967), Robert Bly's *The Light Around the Body* (1968), W. S. Merwin's *The Carrier of Ladders* (1971), Ginsberg's *Planet News* (1971), and Galway Kinnell's *The Book of Nightmares* (1973) were among the highly celebrated books that showed surrealistic influences, and in which the fantastic served as a conduit for transformation. It's worth noting that among these writers only Ginsberg, and to a lesser extent Bly, were identified with the counterculture, a fact that reflects the extent to which the fantastic had become part the era's ethos.

Bly's popular anthology, *Leaping Poetry: An Idea with Poems and Translation* (1972), is a good example of how surrealism and notions of the fantastic circa 1965 to 1975 melded. Ironically, by the time Bly published the work, many of the features he claims American poetry lacked had become widespread. Bly—a cofounder of the organization American Writers Against the Vietnam War—published the book as a reaction to what he perceived as a decline in poetry, especially American poetry, a topic he'd addressed since the late fifties and early sixties, particularly in his essay "A Wrong Turning in American Poetry" (1963). Bly largely had been responsible for introducing European and South American poets—Antonio Machado, Juan Ramón Jiménez, Federico García Lorca, and others—to American audiences in his literary magazine, which changed title with the decade, *The Fifties*, *The Sixties*, *The Seventies*. These writers had profoundly influenced Bly's National Book Award–winning *The Light Around the Body* and his other collections of Deep Image poetry. The "dwindling" he identified in *Leaping Poetry* was twofold: a loss of "associative freedom" and "psychic flight" in language and spirit. In the book's introduction, Bly takes us back to prehistory, "the time of inspiration," where the poet—as noted in the beginning of this chapter—was ascribed remarkable powers; according to Bly the "poet flew from one world to another, 'riding on dragons'" (1972, 1). What contemporary American poetry lacked was an interest in the fantastic and the tools to achieve it, a claim that more accurately characterized American poetry in the early fifties than in the early seventies.

Nonetheless, Bly's discussion of how the fantastic informed prominent European and South American writers' poetry provides a context for understanding much psychedelic music's shortcomings. For Bly, the key to reinvigorating poetry largely resided in "leaping language." While the anthology does include a few Americans—Hart Crane, Gregory Orr, Gary Snyder and, of course, Ginsberg—Bly mainly looks to poets outside of the American tradition to define "leaping poetry." For Bly the American spirit is too sodden and puritanical to fly like its old- and new-world cousins. In fact, Bly's critique of the so-called St. Mark's poets is akin to something that could have been overheard from a comparative literature student at Monterey or

Woodstock: "[They] have a leisure class mood about them; they are essentially the products of a rich country, who see nothing to fight for, and never fight. In a way, they are consumer poets. They refuse to consume cars and steaks, but they consume subtler things—like poetic pleasures" (1972, 70).

To Bly the ability to "leap" resides in the poems of Western Europe and Latin America; from European stalwarts Lorca, Rainer Maria Rilke, and Tomas Tranströmer to César Vallejo of Peru. It is virtually a secret movement:

> Freud pointed out that the dream still retained the fantastic freedom of association known to us before only from ancient art. . . . The poets then began to devote their lives to deepening the range of association in the poem, and increasing the speed of association. . . . The movement has been partly successful; after only a hundred years of effort, the psychic ability to fly has been restored. (Bly 1972, 6)

Following the connections and associations between spirit and animal worlds, other "brains," and the possibility of flight certainly reflects Bly's infatuation with the fantastic. In his chapter on "Spanish Leaping," Bly includes a poem by Vallejo, "I Have a Terrible Fear . . ." The first stanza provides a good example:

> I have a terrible fear that I may be an animal
> of white snow, who has kept his father and mother
> alive with his solitary circulation through the veins,
> and fear that on this day which is so marvelous, sunny, archbishoprical,
> (a day that stands so for night)
> this animal, like a straight line,
> will manage not to be happy, or to breathe,
> or turn into something else, or to get money. (Bly 1972, 29)

And indeed this poem does leap through its associations, using sleights of hand, unexpected detours, thwarted expectations, and punch lines. The first sign that we are in uncharted territory is the "animal" dangling at the end of the first line. A reader might expect the narrator to begin the second line with a definition of exactly what type of animal he fears it might be, or a descriptor: "this animal is the color of snow." But no, this animal *is* "white snow." We are wired to grasp for associations. Is the narrator describing a snowman? Again, no. In the third line, the pronoun morphs into the third person, from "I" to "his." The animal circulating through the veins (Whose veins? The human narrator's? The animal's? His parents'? All three?) collides with the "I" of the poem's first line and folds in on itself, creating an internal logic that is objectively illogical. The animal is and *isn't* an animal. It is and *isn't* in somebody's veins. Is the animal a metaphor for heredity? For menace?

In the fourth line, apparently, there is a reprieve: "a day which is marvelous and sunny." This is straightforward enough. However, the third adjective in the sequence, usually meant to punctuate and define the previous two, presents itself as a non sequitur, more of an *invention* than a word: "archbishoprical." The connotations of archbishoprical can be interpreted as severity or even austerity, but it complicates the image of a sunny day and tips the concrete toward the conceptual.

The sixth line, a sotto voce aside, seems like a generous explanation for the reader who has been twisted up in the poem's logic: "a day that stands so for night." At this point, we should be suspicious of matter-of-fact statements to the tune of "this day actually represents night." And yet, taken in context with the following lines, the stanza seems to be tacking toward a traditional denouement, that of the melancholy meditation: this animal "will manage not to be happy or to breathe / Or turn into something else . . ." Perhaps here a mournful "or find love, and so it goes . . ." However, the mood tips at the last moment to the sardonically humorous with "or to get money."

What exactly have we encountered? A narrator colludes with an astral narrator, describing and deconstructing, redefining, refusing to define, and then erasing definitions; the invention of vaguely familiar language. This should be nonsense. Yet there is feeling, passion, and an appealing distance. Certainly the effect is something like the fantastic. The strength of this stanza and in leaping poetry generally is the strange agreement of associations. A very difficult dance to execute: if done poorly, it merely dissolves into incoherence.

Very few rock groups of the midsixties to the seventies were immune to psychedelia's pull. Considering the breadth and cultural impact of psychedelic rock at the time, it's interesting to find a rather blasé attitude toward it today. Indeed, much of the psychedelic canon looks quaint and a bit corny; a relic of a lost era; the music of hopeless idealists and acid casualties that hasn't really held up over time. Even the Rolling Stones, who hardly took a musical misstep during the band's first two decades, did so with their most psychedelic album, *Their Satanic Majesties Request* (1967): the album is unlistenable and ill-conceived, the bad kind of weird. In psychedelia, catchphrases and token imagery began to replace the attempt at communicating the fantastic. For all of its sloganeering of "freeing your mind," taking "journeys to the center of your mind," and becoming "experienced," a sort of sentimentality—or *unearned* emotion—began to overtake the genre.

This is what Mailer was reacting to when he wrote that "vague Tibetan lama goody-goodness auras of religiosity being the only publicly announced or even rumored fruit from all trips back from the buried Atlantis of LSD." Looking back, the lyrical storytelling in much psychedelic rock often distinctly lacks the kinetic narrative power of the best "leaping poetry"— the very type of effect the genre claimed to seek. Its proponents often fell short of the transformative dynamism of blues lyrics, or the ever-changing body of Dylan's work. The Who's "Magic Bus," Jefferson Airplane's "White Rabbit," Cream's "Strange Brew," Hendrix's "Are You Experienced?": these rock narratives stop at the threshold of the experience they claim to represent, as if the event escapes language. The inability to "cross over" with language is embodied the Beatles' "Lucy In the Sky (with Diamonds)," which primarily utilizes one sense—vision—to deluge the listener with wild images, as if to compensate for its lack of narrative will and emotional engagement. In addition, previously revolutionary recording techniques became a sort of "sonic shorthand" in psychedelia: backmasking, speeding up or slowing down the recording, panning effects from side to side, sitars and rare folk instruments, a wealth of affected guitars: all these became requisite and ceased to startle the ear. The genre reached its nadir in songs like the Electric Prunes' "I Had Too Much to Dream Last Night," or the Amboy Dukes' ghastly "Journey to the Center of the Mind," featuring a young Ted Nugent, who implores the listener, "Take a ride to the land inside of your mind" to "Where fantasy is fact / So if you can, please understand / You might not come back." The song's sentiments come across as a sort of book report or poorly rendered cartoon on the pursuit of the fantastic in rock. It's not surprising that some of the most effective examples of the leaping impulse in rock narrative came from poetic song verse outside psychedelia.

Leonard Cohen began his career in Canada in the midfifties as a notable poet and novelist. As his writing stalled in the next decade, Cohen moved to New York and plied his songs on the folk scene. *Songs of Leonard Cohen* (1967) was released by Columbia Records mere months after the so-called Summer of Love and psychedelia's peak impact. After Cohen's death in 2016, his son claimed that for his father, "It's all song and it's all poetry—for him there wasn't any delineation."[3] Like Dylan, Cohen eschewed faddish sonic effects, relying on the power of literary narrative and poetic imagination. (In fact, to his dying day Cohen wrote most of his songs using the six chords a flamenco player taught him on his Spanish guitar in the 1950s.) Hence, *Songs of Leonard Cohen* has spare production that mainly focuses on his rudimentary guitar playing, augmented by female backing vocals of a more choral than soul school. The album's opener, "Suzanne," is Cohen's signature song in many ways. It was first recorded by Judy Collins in 1966 and has been covered by artists ranging from Nina Simone to Neil Diamond to Meshell Ndegeocello. Shaved down to its basic plot, "Suzanne" is about a picnic with a mentally unstable woman. However, in Cohen's hands it becomes a surreal meditation on appearances and the nature of life's journey. Like his psychedelic brethren, Cohen takes the listener on a "trip," yet he manages to reproduce a sense of revelation and wonder within the spectator. The first verse and chorus set the scene.

> Suzanne takes you down to her place near the river
> You can hear the boats go by, and you can spend the night beside her
> And you know that she's half crazy but that's why you want to be there
> And she feeds you tea and oranges that come all the way from China
> And just when you mean to tell her that you have no love to give her
> Then she gets you on her wavelength
> And she lets the river answer that you've always been her lover

Much like Vallejo's "I Have a Terrible Fear...," Cohen pivots and dodges the reader's expectations. What begins as a seemingly typical love song veers hard left ("you *know* that she's half crazy"), and then back across the median ("and that's *why* you want to be there"). The description of "tea and oranges that come all the way from China" deepens the exotic and erotic context, and we truly are at the narrative's mercy. Getting on her "wavelength" is the parlance of the era, but when combined with "She lets the river answer / That you've always been her lover," Suzanne, because she is crazy—or in spite of the fact—seems to have been ascribed supernatural powers, as she lets a body of water do her talking for her. It is a masterful displacement. The chorus continues with a wish for the conviction of faith only to flip the relationship of leader and follower in the final lines.

> And you want to travel with her, and you want to travel blind
> And you know that she will trust you
> For you've touched her perfect body with your mind

The twisting of pronouns, very much in the spirit of Vallejo, confounds traditional notions of romantic lovers and blurs the line between the sane and the mad. Thematically, the story Cohen tells is not terribly removed from that of the Amboy Dukes' "Journey to the Center of the Mind." However, substantively, aesthetically, and philosophically, they are worlds apart.

Continuing with the second verse and chorus, suddenly, Jesus appears stage left.

> And Jesus was a sailor when he walked upon the water
> And he spent a long time watching from his lonely wooden tower
> And when he knew for certain only drowning men could see him
> He said all men will be sailors then until the sea shall free them
> But he himself was broken, long before the sky would open
> Forsaken, almost human, he sank beneath your wisdom like a stone

We realize it's not the traditional, biblical Jesus. Cohen's Jesus sits in his "lonely wooden tower" like a disgruntled ancient lifeguard. The allusion to Jesus walking on the water is from Matthew 14:22–33. Out at sea, in a great storm, the disciples doubt that Jesus really is walking toward them on water to save them. Peter steps out of the boat but sinks beneath the waves, and Jesus pulls him out. "O ye of little faith," says Jesus. Peter's doubt causes him to sink. In the context of the song, Cohen inverts—or perhaps more accurately tilts—the story: Jesus is not necessarily a savior. Jesus finally speaks up once the men start to drown, declaring all men to be sailors until the sea frees them. What exactly does this mean? It is certainly not a benediction; it's almost a sort of prophecy or curse. As the verse closes, we recognize that Cohen's conception of Jesus rests on the interdependence between believer and believed. Faith, in other words, cuts both ways: toward Jesus and away from Jesus, arguably a very un-Christian concept. Thus it is possible for Jesus—and with him, grace—to disappear when our faith has fled and we have simply become rational, modern unbelievers: Our "wisdom" can unrestrainedly "sink" delicate ecosystems like belief and faith.

The third verse leaps back to Suzanne.

> Now, Suzanne takes your hand and she leads you to the river
> She's wearing rags and feathers from Salvation Army counters
> And the sun pours down like honey on our lady of the harbor
> And she shows you where to look among the garbage and the flowers
> There are heroes in the seaweed, there are children in the morning
> They are leaning out for love and they will lean that way forever
> While Suzanne holds her mirror

Back at the picnic, the song takes on an elegiac tone. Suzanne, continuing as a sort of spirit guide, carries the narrator along on a beautiful tracking shot: From the heroic seaweed waving on the ocean, to a clutch of children forever leaning out for love. In the chorus, the leader/follower dynamic is reversed again, as Suzanne touches *your* body with *her* mind.

Like all richly textured verse, "Suzanne" bears repeated attention, casting off new ribbons of meaning with each visit. But the effect is more than the sum of its words. The lyrics, married to the music, can take the listener to limits of imagination if the listener is willing to confront personal notions of how romantic love works, how faith works, how songs work. Indeed, it is an invitation to step into the numinous.

In closing this chapter, it is important to note a phenomenon at the juncture of poetry, rock, and the fantastic: rock stardom. Mass worship of musicians, artists, and entertainers is not a modern development. As we discussed earlier in the chapter, musicians and poets have been ascribed otherworldly powers since ancient times. Mississippi bluesman Robert Johnson was said to have "sold his soul to the devil at the crossroads." The great Romantic-era Italian violist Niccolò Paganini created

> untold excitement wherever he went. There was a feeling of Satanism about this tall, dark, emaciated Italian who could do undreamed of things on his Guarnerius. Musicians swarmed to his concerts trying to figure out how he achieved his effects. The public also flocked, and many of the more superstitious listeners believed him to be in league with the Devil. Paganini did nothing to dispel the notion. A great showman, he played up the diabolical quality of his concerts and did everything but come on stage wrapped in blue flame. (Schonberg 1970, 139)

Part of the phenomenon of rock stardom involves myth-making. It's noteworthy that the alluring and dangerous nature of Johnson's and Paganini's art was accounted for in their respective eras by invoking the sinister side of the supernatural, as opposed to its shamanistic or spiritual dimensions. The very same accusations were leveled in the seventies against groups like Led Zeppelin, a band deeply versed in the blues. Like Paganini, Zeppelin guitarist Jimmy Page played up satanic associations, publicly flaunting his enthusiasm for occultist Aleister Crowley's works. Heavy metal bands—including Black Sabbath (see the song "Mr. Crowley") and AC/DC—helped keep cartoonish Satanism alive in order to scandalize the parents of their primary audience, disaffected teenaged boys.

Here it's helpful to differentiate between rock stardom and pop stardom. Both rock stars and pop stars are caught up in a cyclone spun from talent, historical timing, and mass communication. From there, their paths diverge. Rock stars receive mass acclaim for appealing to society's wish to transgress and transcend. A pop star receives mass acclaim for appealing to society's wish to be entertained. Elvis began as a rock star but ended up a pop star, a beloved, bloated Las Vegas showman. Dylan started out a folk troubadour and became a rock star.

We have discussed how Ginsberg and the Beats turned to raucous performance and even rock music to amplify their message. From the sixties to the nineties, the Black Arts Movement, New York's Nuyorican Poets, and the Last Poets incorporated jazz, funk, African rhythms, and performance into their poetry. Poet Gil Scott-Heron crossed over with his brand of poetry and funk to have hits, most notably "The Revolution Will Not Be Televised." Today the work of the Black Arts Movement, the Nuyoricans, the Last Poets, and Scott-Heron are considered the bedrock of hip-hop music.

Versifiers' movement toward poetic song verse makes sense not just aesthetically but culturally. Few poets wouldn't crave the mass adulation and impact of rock musicians. On the other hand, rock stars, not content to be assembly-line products of popular culture, craved the gravitas and cultural prestige of poets. Rock stars of the sixties wanted to be taken seriously; think of Jim Morrison leaving the Doors to pursue poetry full-time in Paris. The combination of Morrison's shamanistic lyrical imagery and his debauched rock star lifestyle perfectly fit the Romantic-era ideal of the *poète maudit*: the Doomed Poet who lived fast and died young. Trafficking on the scrim between life and death, so the myth goes, allowed the *poète maudit* to communicate other worlds unavailable to the mediocre souls of the quotidian. And, for good measure, they left gorgeous corpses, arrested in perpetual youth. Morrison, Hendrix, and Joplin became the rock versions of the English Romantics Byron, Shelley, and Keats, and of the French Symbolists Baudelaire, Rimbaud, and Verlaine. As the sixties wore into the seventies, conflating rock stars with *poètes maudits* became a conscious exercise, as with Patti Smith, whose strategy seemed to be that merely mentioning Rimbaud or the Symbolist poets often enough would inevitably force a comparison. For rock stars who survived, the audience felt a compulsion to turn them into sages, mystics, or even holy fools to reflect their exalted impact. In the late sixties an ominous graffiti began to appear around London: "Clapton is God," a motto that makes Eric Clapton uncomfortable but that he's had difficulty shaking. Guitar players with great technical or natural facility were suddenly transformed into mythopoetic "guitar heroes." A pantheon of Gods and Heroes began to emerge from what merely began as reckless dance music.

To convince us that they are not mere mortals, Gods and Heroes require creation stories—myths—that chisel their sagas into the cultural landscape. Time has shown that rock stars require this too, and if they aren't willing to create their own stories, myths will be invented and applied to them, a phenomenon spoofed in Martin Scorsese's *Rolling Thunder Revue: A Bob Dylan Story* (2019), a realistically presented mock-documentary of Dylan's infamous midseventies tour. At the dawn of the decade, rock had its own Mount Rushmore of fallen stars who had blazed brightly and passed into the firmament: Jim Morrison, Jimi Hendrix, Janis, Joplin, Duane Allman, Gram Parsons, and others. Dylan, of course, already had invented his own backstory as an itinerant journeyman, very much like his hero Woody Guthrie and other assorted bluesmen. As we discussed chapter 3, artists learned to use myth and persona as a means of achieving rock stardom. David Bowie—formerly folk singer David Jones—found wild success in creating "Ziggy Stardust," an ambisexual alien who brought glam rock to Earth. New Orleans session man Mac Rebennack concocted "Dr. John," a hoodoo priest who wedded the Louisiana swamp and the New Orleans street beat with psychedelia. For decades, cosmic jazzman and big-band leader Sun Ra—who insisted he was not born in Birmingham, Alabama, in 1914, but "landed" there—proclaimed his gospel to the jazz and rock worlds: "Space is the place!" The rock star's impulse to self-mythologize is understandable. Perhaps it's a reaction to the unwieldy waves of love and adoration from a mass audience—an audience that demands that rock stars be bigger than life, better than mere mortals, incarnations of the fantastic. On the other hand, perhaps it's a means for rock star and audience to account for transformative art that issues from a murky source and leads us to the fantastic through something akin to what Leonard Cohen's favorite poet, the Spaniard Federico García Lorca, termed *duende*.[3]

> Those dark sounds are the mystery, the roots that cling to the mire that we all know, that we all ignore, but from which comes the very substance of art. "Dark sounds" said the man of the Spanish people (flamenco singer Manuel Torre), agreeing with Goethe, who in speaking of Paganini hit on a definition of the *duende*: "A mysterious force that everyone feels and no philosopher has explained."[4]

Lorca's account of music's spirit perhaps comes as close as possible to defining the fantastic and its effect on the participants: a synergy between artist, listener, and an ur-force seemingly from beyond time that at once struggles with and embraces mortality. At its best, as in Cohen and Hendrix's songs, it becomes transformative poetic song verse. Death—so uncanny and attractive to many in Paganini and Robert Johnson—sprung wholly made in the sixties and seventies with the loss of Hendrix, Morrison, Joplin, et al. Lorca writes, "Seeking the *duende*, there is neither map nor discipline. We only know it burns the blood like powdered glass, that it exhausts, rejects all the sweet geometry we understand, that it shatters styles."[5] It's as if, in the 1930s, Lorca himself foresaw rock stardom:

> With idea, sound, gesture, the *duende* delights in struggling freely with the creator on the edge of the pit . . .
> The magic power of a poem consists in it always being filled with *duende*, in its baptising all who gaze at it with dark water, since with *duende* it is easier to love, to understand, and be certain of being loved, and being understood, and this struggle for expression and the communication of that expression in poetry sometimes acquires a fatal character.[6]

Head and shoulders above the other guitar heroes, Jimi Hendrix embodies the idea of *duende*—that "mysterious force" with a "fatal character"—in his masterwork "Voodoo Chile (Slight Return)." The song closes the double album *Electric Ladyland* (1968)—the last studio album before his death—as a retooled version of "Voodoo Chile" from side two. The first version is a fourteen-plus-minute minor blues shuffle performed for an enthusiastic and responsive studio audience that revisits the familiar terrain of the supernatural in the blues, à la Robert Johnson's "Crossroads" or Muddy Waters's "Mojo Hand." The narrator is an exceptional creature, chosen by fate, and born under a dark omen (a "moon turned a fire red"). His mother takes one look at him, dies, and he's transported by mythic creatures: "Mountain lions found me there, and set me on an eagle's wings / He took me past the outskirts of infinity / And when he brought me back, he gave me Venus's witch's ring."

This is the stuff of magic and of voodoo. And yet, lyrically, it's almost as if the material confines the narrator. The sorcery, lions, eagles, and gypsies in the verse are a conflation of the blues and fantasy, but certainly not of the fantastic. The music—guitar and organ taking solo flights, an energetically rolling rhythm section—is virtuosic, but nothing unique in the rock continuum. Knowing the history of the blues, one may clinically observe that voodoo children are, indeed, delivered in this fashion.

However, with "Voodoo Chile (Slight Return)"—the last song on *Electric Ladyland* and the last official studio statement Jimi Hendrix made—the listener senses a storyteller who, having exhausted his audience over four sides of LP, surveys those hardy enough to remain at the table, rubs his hands, and says cryptically, "Now let me tell you what really happened."

There is no studio audience, no interplay between artist and listener on "Voodoo Chile (Slight Return)." The song is an act of self-will. A scratched rhythm creeps in from the silence, opening up to a wah-wah guitar melody that didn't appear in the first version, if this is, indeed, the same song. A bass drum rhythm with an implied clave beat joins the wah-wah: "Dun-duh-dun-duh / Dun-dun-dah!" alerting us that this Voodoo Chile emerges from a place beyond the deep roots of the blues, from Africa itself, before recorded time. As the band smashes in, the electric guitar threatens to bury the rhythm section entirely, howling over distant maracas with the locomotive drone of a cyclone that's upon us. The tone is deafening, even at a low volume. This is a new land, a territory known but not spoken of. Unlike the first version, the lyrics, sung in unison with the raving guitar, are blunt and effective: there's no birth story or magical archetypes; no talk of desire or making love. There's nothing, really, identifiably human. The imagery, wedded to the songs, courts the fantastic: the Voodoo Chile stands "next to a mountain" and chops "it down with the edge of [his] hand."

Unlike Bly's poets who leap *between* worlds, Voodoo Chile redux is at once a godlike destroyer and creator of these worlds. Hendrix adds humorous understatement to his gargantuan boast that he may create an island or "raise a little sand," identifying at once an act of creativity akin to the book of Genesis and an old blues trope for "making a commotion" or, more aptly, "raising hell." Hendrix continues to play diving and driving lines in an unprecedented tone that's bold, expansive, and elemental. The solo pans back and forth from one side of the stereo and back, a disorienting effect very much like being caught in an unexpected, raging storm. Cascades of razor-like notes—honed even sharper than Freddie King's—slip in and out of the ether. Then the band settles back momentarily before the last verse in which he apologizes, with gleeful understatement, for taking "up all your sweet time." But never fear: he possesses the divine power to restore time by giving it "back to you one of these days." Hendrix punctuates the line with a deliciously ironic laugh. If he doesn't see you in this world, he'll meet you on the next one—which he will presumably create—finishing with a wonderfully sarcastic exhortation from a being who can manipulate the very contours of time: "Don't be late!" Far from benevolent, this god makes powerful mischief like the Greek, Roman, or Norse deities; much more Hermes or Loki than Yahweh.

Buried deep in the guitar maelstrom that follows, Hendrix speaks parting words that are obscured, yet audible. He asserts he's a Voodoo Chile and doesn't "take no for an answer . . ." The music instructs us to hurry on to the next world, and it's more of a command than an invitation. Even if we do not seek it, the fantastic approaches, impatiently, impertinently, like death. And as with Lorca's *duende*, "there is neither map nor discipline. We only know it burns the blood like powdered glass, that it exhausts, rejects all the sweet geometry we understand."[7]

5

A New Era of Verse Composition

For many people Bob Dylan's 2016 Nobel Prize affirmed that his songs are a form of literature, yet the dismay the award caused—even among folks who admire his work—indicates a continued unease with, and even hostility toward, the blurring of traditional categories. Three years earlier, Dylan's widely publicized induction into the American Academy of Arts and Letters served as a harbinger of his Nobel award and spoke to the liminal space poetic song verse continues to occupy. In high-art circles election to the academy is considered an extremely prestigious honor. Academy members—an honor society of 250 visual artists, writers, architects, and composers—are elected for life. As members depart planet Earth—or in rare cases resign—the academicians nominate and elect new members. Virginia Dejani, the academy's executive director, said Dylan "was on a ballot with other names and he won handily."[1] However, Dejani noted that Dylan was made an honorary member—a distinction that doesn't provide him with the right to vote on potential future members—because the academy couldn't determine into which department, literature or music, he fit, perhaps an odd conclusion in retrospect, since he would be awarded the Nobel Prize in *Literature*. In his citation the organization's president, Henry N. Cobb, juggled the issue:

> For more than 50 years, defying categorization in a culture beguiled by categories, Bob Dylan has probed and prodded our psyches, recording and then changing our world and our lives through poetry made manifest in

song—creating relationships that we never imagined could exist between words, emotions and ideas.[2]

Cobb, unwittingly, helps define poetic song verse with the phrase "poetry made manifest in song." And his claim that Dylan's work has been "defying categorization" for "more than 50 years" suggests the need for naming, recognizing, and conceptualizing this new genre—especially since it's evident that though Dylan may have played *the* central role in creating poetic song verse, he certainly isn't the only artist with a superb level of achievement in it.

It's also worth repeating that we aren't claiming that splendid song lyrics didn't exist before Dylan—we've discussed the lyrical mastery of early blues artists, Chuck Berry, and others, for instance—but the widespread confluence of blues-based popular music and poetry in the sixties resulted in a concentration of artists who used voice, instrumentation, arrangement, and production to foreground richly textured lyrics. Dylan's decades-old assertion that songwriting changed because "45 records were incapable" of capturing a "new type of human existence" has proved prophetic and suggests how art forms tend to evolve. Profound changes in art seldom stem from abstract desires to experiment but grow from shifts in people's worldviews and how people experience and interpret existence. In the 1600s the novel developed out of previous genres, including epic poetry and the romance. Scientific developments spurred a greater desire for realism, and technological advances—including the printing press—created channels for distribution. Like poetic song verse, the novel was grudgingly granted status as a serious literary form.[3] In the nineteenth century, Walt Whitman's all-encompassing persona and expanding and contracting lines of symphonic free verse were inspired by a swelling immigrant nation cradled between two oceans. In the late nineteenth century Darwin's, Spencer's, and Spinoza's theories of evolution helped shape the fiction of Theodore Dreiser and other literary naturalists. In the opening decades of the twentieth century, writers' uses of stream-of-consciousness and symbolism were informed by depth psychology, especially in relation to myth, ritual, and sexuality. All of these innovations and many others were met with resistance when they first appeared.

Our consideration of poetic song verse's origins began with changes that took place in the first two decades of the twentieth century. Virginia Woolf famously claimed that "on or about December 1910, human character changed" (1924, 410). Sigmund Freud's psychological insights, Albert

Einstein's theory of special relativity, and George Frazer's views on ritual and myth had a profound influence, helping to make the teens and twenties watershed decades, as poets, novelists, and painters boldly re-evaluated art's purposes and contours. As we've discussed, at roughly the same time, over two centuries of hardship and the confluence of various African and Western musical traditions conspired to create the blues, and subsequently, blues poetry, jazz, and rock. During the sixties the media boom, the Cold War, satellite wars in Southeast Asia, and the rise of the counterculture in the United States and Europe contributed to the development of an aesthetic of disorientation that influenced forms ranging from the postmodernist novel to the creation of lyrically textured blues-based popular music replete with sometimes fantastic imagery and narratives.

The explosion of singer-songwriters in the seventies suggests the extent to which poetry had influenced rock lyrics, even in the work of artists who weren't in direct dialogue with poetry. Bruce Springsteen, Marvin Gaye, Stevie Wonder, Bonnie Raitt, Van Morrison, Curtis Mayfield, Tom Waits, Bill Withers, Gordon Lightfoot, John Prine, Carly Simon, Harry Nilsson, Joan Armatrading, Cat Stevens, Randy Newman, Jackson Browne, Joni Mitchell, Paul Simon, John Cale, Eric Andersen, Rod Stewart, Lou Reed, Carole King, Jim Dickinson, Townes Van Zandt, Tim Buckley, Bobbie Gentry, Richard Thompson, Patti Smith, Neil Young, Janis Ian, Arlo Guthrie, James Taylor, Don McLean, David Bowie, Leon Russell, Phoebe Snow, Nick Drake, Ry Cooder, Tom T. Hall, Warren Zevon, Elvis Costello, and others unveiled lyrically sophisticated albums that drew acclaim. Several of these artists—Mitchell, Browne, and Smith, for instance—continued to engage poetry, but many songwriters possessed little or no knowledge of poetry. Unlike Dylan, Lennon, McCartney, Jagger, Jim Morrison, Van Morrison, Scott-Heron, Mitchell, Cohen, and others who had self-consciously mined poetry for materials and techniques, these artists drew on musical sources that already had made the transition from entertainment to art-that-entertains. Songwriters no longer needed to draw on Beat, Symbolist, or other types of poetry for models of sophisticated verse, but could turn to the previous generation of rock artists. Roughly a decade younger than Dylan, the Beatles, the Rolling Stones, and the Doors, they were the first generation of rockers who *presumed* rich lyrical content was an important component of song and a means of self-expression.

Characteristics we detailed in chapter 1—an emphasis on a conversational style, on the personal or confessional, and the local—that served as catalysts for the confluence of blues-based popular music and poetry in the early to mid sixties informed many seventies songwriters' creative practices. An emphasis on the fantastic—our other characteristic—slowly waned but did not disappear as songwriters turned toward greater realism, but many of the changes it had inspired, especially in relation to imagery, song length, and production techniques, continued.

The differences between the Who's rock operas *Tommy* (1969) and *Quadrophenia* (1973) provide a case in point. *Tommy* tells the story of a "deaf, dumb, and blind kid" whose father goes missing during World War II, unexpectedly returns to London years later, and murders his wife's lover. Tommy's subsequent fate is conveyed through psychedelic rock songs replete with surreal imagery ("Right behind you, I see the millions / On you, I see the glory") that depict his experiences with, among other things, LSD and pinball. Like *Tommy*, *Quadrophenia* contains songs chock-full of fantastic imagery ("the cracks between the paving stones / Look like rivers of flowing veins") that range from less than a minute to over eight minutes. Both albums are elaborately produced and revolve around an adolescent protagonist's encounters with mind-altering drugs. But *Tommy* abandons a story that starts with World War II for a tale of a surreal, trippy religious cult that revolves around pinball, while *Quadrophenia* stays rooted in family dynamics and the tensions between British rockers and mods in the midsixties through the early seventies. Depictions of Jimmy's relationship to his parents, a girl he desires, and others, as well the traumas he experiences, remain realistic rather than fantastic, even as fantastic imagery is used to convey his story.

Bruce Springsteen, Marvin Gaye, and Stevie Wonder provide other prominent examples of how songwriting changed in the seventies. Like T. S. Eliot's *The Waste Land* and Dylan's *Highway 61 Revisited*, Springsteen's *Born to Run* (1975) captured the cultural zeitgeist, albeit in a less ambitious or provocative manner. The assumptions underpinning the album suggest the cataclysmic changes rock had undergone in the ten years since Dylan "went electric." On *Born to Run* Springsteen is widely quoted as wanting to create an album that sounded like "Roy Orbison singing Bob Dylan, produced by Spector." Springsteen, admittedly, had little or no familiarity with literature, art, the rural blues, or folk music until his producer and future manager, Jon Landau, began to engage him in the mid to late seventies. A junior college dropout, he notes that he "wasn't brought up in a house where there was a lot of reading and stuff. I was brought up on TV" (Marsh 1996, 24). But even in his early recordings, he was aware of lyrical content's importance:

> I was always interested in doing a *body* of work—albums that would relate to and play off of each other. And I was always concerned with doin' *albums*, instead of, like, collections of songs. I guess I started with *The Wild, the Innocent and the E Street Shuffle*, in a funny way—particularly the second side, which kind of syncs together. I was very concerned about gettin' a group of characters and followin' them through their lives a little bit.[4]

Springsteen's songwriting evolved over the decades. As his interest in reading and the arts expanded, he developed characters with wider points of view and explicitly or implicitly began to address a host of political and social issues. But his dominant lyrical technique has remained more or less the same: he creates a character who tells a story the listener is compelled to accept as realistic. This is true, even on his earliest, most romantic albums. An emphasis on the local, particularly his native New Jersey, on a conversational style, and on the personal or confessional informs his lyrics. He was unfamiliar with poetry, but he knew Dylan's work and wanted to write like him. His songs consistently rise to the level of poetic song verse because of his use of narrative, point of view, figurative language, arrangements, and other techniques, but none of these is more important than his vocal ability to inhabit characters and project their emotional states.

Springsteen's passion, his willingness to grow, and his attraction to prose—rather than poetry—are particularly striking. In interviews he comes across as thoughtful and genuine. He speaks in a heartfelt manner of his upbringing, the gaps in his education, his ambitions, and his willingness to enter therapy in order to become a better husband and father. His first three albums—*Greetings from Asbury Park, N.J.* (1973), *The Wild, the Innocent and the E Street Shuffle* (1973), and *Born to Run* (1975)—draw much of their imagery and themes from his experiences growing up in Freehold, New Jersey, where he lived next to Ducky Slattery's Sinclair Station, attended Catholic and public schools, argued with his father, and longed to escape. An indifferent student, he notes, "I didn't hang around with no crowd that was talking about William Burroughs," and claims he "was dead until I was thirteen" and bought a guitar: "The first day I can remember looking in a mirror and being able to stand what I was seeing was the day I had a guitar in my hand" (Marsh 1996, 24, 27–28).

Springsteen began playing in local bands in the midsixties. Landau observes, "For twelve years, Bruce had the time to learn to play every kind of rock and roll" because he had "roots in a place—coastal Jersey, where no record company scouts ever went" (1974, 46). When his parents moved to California in the summer of 1969, he stayed in the family home—a place he describes as "shabby"—until he was evicted in the winter and moved to Asbury Park. A loner given to dark moods—several fellow students petitioned for him to be dismissed from Ocean County Community College in 1967 because they thought him too strange—he was ambivalent about psychedelic music and embraced relatively early rock 'n' roll: Elvis, Chuck Berry, Mitch Ryder, Gary U.S. Bonds, the Rascals, the Dave Clark Five, Dylan, and the early Beatles, Stones, Who, and Animals.

Landau also favored unadorned rock—in the inaugural issue of *Rolling Stone* he'd blasted Jimi Hendrix and the psychedelic movement as pretentious. In 1974 Landau—who majored in history at Brandeis University and later became a noted collector of Italian art—penned the now famous review asserting, "I saw my rock 'n' roll past flash before my eyes. And I saw something else: I saw rock and roll future and its name is Bruce Springsteen."[5] The two formed a friendship, and Landau soon came onboard to coproduce *Born to Run*.

Born to Run showcases straightforward narratives that gain power and convey authenticity from Springsteen's compelling concrete lyrics, evocatively paced vocals, and arrangements. Whereas, say, Jagger drew on blues tropes, Beat, and Symbolist poetics to pen covert dramatic monologues from the perspective of Satan or a serial killer, Springsteen assumed the point of view of less than extraordinary characters—a lover beckoning his girl to rendezvous with him in the night, musicians competing and struggling for recognition, a desperate petty criminal looking to make a deal.

> Hey, Eddie, can you lend me a few bucks
> And tonight can you get us a ride
> Gotta make it through the tunnel
> Got a meeting with a man on the other side

In his induction speech to the Rock & Roll Hall of Fame on March 15, 1999, Springsteen singled out Dylan as "an artist whose music was a critical part of my own life." But whereas Eliot's *The Waste Land* and Dylan's albums of the midsixties had meshed disparate art forms from high and popular culture to create allusive, intentionally disjointed works that reflected the disorientation of cultures in crisis, Springsteen's early albums energetically romanticized urban America. In contrast to Eliot and Dylan's emphases on social and philosophical issues, Springsteen celebrated romantic individualism—coming-of-age stories, love, the longing to escape, the dangers and thrills of the night. Weeks after the release of *Born to Run* Greil Marcus observed that the "stories Springsteen is telling are nothing new, though no one has ever told them better or made them matter more... you've never heard anything like this before, but you understand it instantly."[6]

Released on August 25, 1975, *Born to Run* put Springsteen on the cover of *Time* and *Newsweek* by late October. The album and its creator had tapped into a new moment. The 1970 shootings at Kent State and Jackson State were in the rearview mirror. American troops had withdrawn from Vietnam in 1973, Nixon had resigned from office in August of 1974, the Arab oil embargo had ended, and the intensity of the civil rights movement had, unfortunately, diminished. Inflation, which had peaked at 12 percent, was dropping, and the economy seemed poised to move forward. Though a cauldron of domestic and international challenges continued to boil, a generation of high school and college students who weren't threatened by the draft embraced a less menacing and politically fraught environment, a dynamic captured a few years later in the teenage musical comedy *Rock 'n' Roll High School* (1979). Disco and leisure suits were entering their heyday. Springsteen and *Born to Run* offered people interested in more ambitious popular music accessible songs of high quality in the direct linage of Dylan, the Stones, the Who and other pioneers, but Springsteen had replaced "Desolation Row," Lucifer, and the Acid Queen with fast cars, guitars that flashed like switchblades, and the urge to "run away tonight and case the promised land."

"Thunder Road"—the first song on *Born to Run*—is filled with romantic longing and imagery but is laced with concrete details and qualifications that make the dramatic situation seem like less of a fantasy than a plea for bold action. The song's first verse suggests how Springsteen balances realism and romance throughout the album. The first line—"The screen door slams"—presents a realistic detail that evokes the narrator's desire for a new beginning. The verse segues into a romantic yet not extraordinary moment: Mary dancing on the porch as her dress invitingly "waves." The narrator's subsequent claim that he "can't face" himself "alone again," his acknowledgement that she's frightened and realizes they aren't "young anymore," and that she "ain't a beauty" serve as qualifications to his plea that she display a "little faith" because "there's magic in the night": he's not being unrealistic; he's asking her to take a chance.

In the second verse the narrator asks Mary to *eschew* romantic fantasy and presents himself as a realistic alternative. The narrator asserts that he's "no hero" and can only offer "redemption" through the opportunity to escape on a journey that's at once ecstatic and their final opportunity to "make it real." Heaven isn't a matter of lying beneath bedcovers, recalling old lovers, and wishing for a knight in shining armor; it involves sex in the back seat of a car on a desolate road: "trade in these wings on some wheels / Climb in back, heaven's waiting on down the tracks." Similarly, the last two verses present the narrator—armed with his guitar and car—as a realistic alternative to fantasies of past lovers. When Mary goes to the porch they are "gone on the wind," and the narrator remains the realistic alternative who is "pulling out of here to win."

Springsteen matured well beyond the postadolescent angst and exuberance that underpins most of *Born to Run*, and he came to see that album, *Darkness on the Edge of Town* (1978), and *The River* (1980) as part of a trilogy. He asserts that

> on *Born to Run*, *Darkness on the Edge of Town* and *The River*, I tried to hook things up. I guess in *Born to Run*, there's that searchin' thing; that record to me is like religiously based, in a funny kind of way. Not like orthodox religion, but it's about basic things, you know? That searchin', and faith, and the idea of hope. And then on *Darkness*, it was kind of like a collision that happens between this guy and the real world. He ends up very alone and real stripped down. Then, on *The River*, there was always that thing of the guy attemptin' to come back, to find some sort of community.[7]

In the late seventies and early eighties, his relationship with Landau led to his increasing awareness of rock as an artistic medium. Ambitious movies—particularly those by John Ford and Sergio Leone, as well as Terrence Malick's *Badlands*—and prose—Steinbeck's novels, Flannery O'Connor's stories ("The River" is the title of an O'Connor story), and biographies of Woody Guthrie and Elvis—became fonts of inspiration. Before embarking on his first European tour, he read Henry Steele Commager's and Allan Nevins's

A Pocket History of the United States (1981, 7th ed.) and began referring to it in preambles to songs during live performances. In Paris he announced, "I just started to read *History of the United States* and the thing about it is that I started to learn about how things got to be the way they are today, how you end up a victim without even knowing it, and how people get old, and just die after not having hardly a day's satisfaction or peace of mind in their lives." In Brussels, he added: "I was reading this book, it was called the *History of the United States* and in it you find out, I found out how I ended up where I was and how the chances of me breaking out of that kind of life, or anybody breaking out of that kind of life get slimmer and slimmer every day." In Rotterdam he asserted, "I read this book the *History of the United States* and in it I found out where I came from and how I ended up, where I was and how easy it is to be a victim of things that you don't even know exist and you don't even know are there 'cause I go back and I see my friends at home and there's a lot of people there that had strong hearts and force and power inside them that just got crushed."[8] In 2007 he noted another history that was important to him during that period:

> Howard Zinn's *A People's History of the United States* had an enormous impact on me. It set me down in a place that I recognized and felt I had a claim to. It made me feel that I was a player in this moment in history, as we all are, and that this moment in history was mine, somehow, to do with whatever I could. It gave me a sense of myself in the context of this huge American experience and empowered me to feel that in my small way, I had something to say, I could do something. It made me feel a part of history, and gave me life as a participant.[9]

Springsteen's evolving sense of the contrast between the ideas on which the United States had been founded and the country in which he found himself heavily influenced *Nebraska* (1982)—a solo acoustic album—and *Born in the U.S.A.* (1984).[10] In the eighties his comments in interviews and onstage became increasingly political. After George Will and Ronald Reagan infamously misconstrued and misappropriated the song "Born in the U.S.A.," he corrected them and remarked that Reagan's tactic amounted to a "manipulation" that was emblematic of his "mythic" presidency. On *Nebraska* and *Born in the U.S.A.* he approached the questions "Where is the real thing? Where is the real America?"—lines of inquiry that in many ways continue to inform his songwriting.[11] On "Born in the U.S.A." he presents the perspective of a man forced into military service because of a "hometown jam" and then sent to off to "kill the yellow man." He returns from the Vietnam War to find himself an outcast and unemployable, but the song's overarching point is summed up in the first verse. The speaker was born into a situation in which the odds were stacked against him: "Born down in a dead man's town / The first kick I took was when I hit the ground / You end up like a dog that's been beat too much."

Like Springsteen, in the early seventies Marvin Gaye and Stevie Wonder drew on previous musicians' practices, rather than on poetry, for lyrical content. All three men had spotty formal educations and scant interests in art other than music during their youth, but whereas Springsteen cut his chops in relative obscurity, Gaye worked with Bo Diddley and Chuck Berry (he sang background on "Back in the U.S.A." and "Almost Grown") as a teenager, and Wonder signed with Motown at age eleven.

Gaye and Wonder arrived at Motown at roughly the same time. They both released hit singles in the early sixties and were part of the fabled traveling troupe called the Motown Revue. Gaye had been born and raised in the housing projects of Washington, DC, where he battled with his father, who'd retreated from his role as a preacher in the radically fundamentalist denomination the House of God into a life of seclusion, alcoholism, and occasional cross-dressing. He beat his wife and children and had an especially contentious relationship with Marvin, whom he viewed as a competitor for his wife's attention and of whose success he was deeply envious. Despite their acrimony Marvin shared his father's religious fervor, as well as his penchant for addiction and violence. He battled stage fright, was notorious for missing performances, and suffered from severe mood swings and sexual insecurities. On April 1, 1984, the elder Gaye shot and killed his son after Marvin—who was deeply depressed and paranoid—pummeled him for verbally abusing his mother. Marvin's father was sentenced to five days of incarceration and two years of probation.

Like *Born to Run*, Gaye's *What's Going On* (1971) is a landmark album, but whereas Springsteen's record embraced a youthful romantic ethos, Gaye's is the work of a sophisticated and mature artist. In the forties and fifties Gaye had been weaned on the rhythmic, love-soaked spiritual harmonies of mid-century African American groups—the Orioles, the Drifters, the Capris—as well as the instrumental genius of Miles Davis and the vocals of

Billie Holiday, Perry Como, Ray Charles, and Frank Sinatra. Gaye, whose oft-stated goal was to become the "black Sinatra," signed with Motown in 1960; he soon became Smokey Robinson's drummer and cut his first album, *The Soulful Moods of Marvin Gaye* (1961). He enjoyed a string of hits—including "Hitch Hike" and "Pride and Joy"—in the early sixties, and in 1963 married Motown owner Berry Gordy's sister, Anna, a savvy businesswoman seventeen years his senior. During the sixties he recorded sixteen albums, including popular duets with Mary Wells, Kim Weston, and Tammi Terrell. His version of "I Heard It through the Grapevine" topped the R&B and pop charts in 1968 and made him an international star, but throughout his career his staple audience consisted of women, to whom he pandered in concert and whose adoration he needed and resented. In the late sixties he grew a beard and stopped wearing fashionable outfits in favor of sweats, athletic wear, and tennis shoes. He fantasized about becoming a professional athlete, played baseball with the Detroit Tigers' Willie Horton, and skated with the Chicago Blackhawks' Gordie Howe. He trained for a tryout with the Detroit Lions football team but was rebuffed due to concerns he'd get hurt. Dismayed, he claimed that "singing to 20,000 women, all of them screaming and grabbing for a piece of your hide" was far "more frightening" than getting "popped by some defensive end" (Ritz 1991, 135).

Gaye also yearned to be respected as a serious artist. He had watched RCA Victor release Sam Cooke's "A Change Is Gonna Come" (1964), a song motivated by Dylan's "Blowin' in the Wind"—Cooke believed it was important that a Black artist record an anthem for the civil rights movement. But Berry Gordy had become rich selling Black music to white audiences, which he believed required keeping lyrical content on a noncontroversial level, a policy that limited and stalled many Motown artists' development as lyricists. Gaye bristled at being restrained and later complained that "sometimes I felt like the shuffle-and-jive n-----s of old, steppin' and fetchin' for the white folks" (Ritz 1991, 106). But despite Gordy's reluctance, Motown artists gradually inched toward making socially relevant records. Edwin Starr's funk-propelled version of Norman Whitfield's and Barrett Strong's "War" shot to the top of the charts in 1970:

War has caused unrest
Within the younger generation
Induction then destruction
Who wants to die?

In the early seventies Gaye—inspired by sources as diverse as Carlos Castaneda's *The Teaching of Don Juan*, Woodstock, Isaac Hayes's *Hot Buttered Soul* (1969), and his brother's trenchant stories after returning from combat duty in Vietnam—decided "it was time to stop playing games" (Ritz 1991, 140). He later reflected that "white kids wanted a different kind of music. They wanted to hear about something besides love. They were smoking weed and dropping acid and I went along with them. I loved the hippies. They were rebels, like me, and they did this country a world of good" (119). Accordingly, Gaye turned, temporarily, from Eros to Ethos.

Gaye's self-produced masterpiece, *What's Going On*, was the first concept album by a rhythm and blues artist. Like most poetic song verse, it's set in a specific place and time, is profoundly personal, and is threaded with evocative, imagistic, conversational language. Told from the point of view of a returning Vietnam vet, the album only saw daylight after Gaye threatened to leave Motown. Gaye's brother, Frankie, reports that his brother told him Gordy had called it "the worst record I've ever heard." When the record vaulted to the top of the charts, Gordy was "shaken with the record's success. He had prided himself on knowing the business, and being able to predict what would sell and what wouldn't" (Gaye 2003, 83–84).

It's no surprise that Gaye's vocals on the album are superb, but what raises the songs to the level of stellar poetic song verse are his ambitious lyrics, use of point of view, and extraordinary arrangements. Like several other post–*Sgt. Pepper* concept albums, *What's Going On* employed multi-track vocals, an orchestra, classical music arrangements, and a variety of sound effects to create a cohesive song cycle. Gaye's compositional method was unusual: he'd start with the seed for a song—sometimes furnished by others—and sit at the recording console, scat singing or humming into the microphone, stopping and starting as the lyrics, the melody, and the arrangement developed. He became highly skilled at singing and mixing his own lead and background vocals, weaving his falsetto and tenor in ways one reviewer likened to "dots from a Seurat landscape."[12] Backed by the Funk Brothers, Motown's fabulous session players, with David Van DePitte conducting and arranging the orchestra, Gaye recorded most of the album over ten days (the title track was recorded several months earlier and had been released as a single). The album was released in May 1971, and the cultural stage was set for a work that asked, "What's going on?" In January Charles Manson and his "family" had been convicted of murder; in February South Vietnamese troops backed by US firepower invaded Laos; in March the Weather Underground ignited a bomb in the US Capitol and Lieutenant William Calley was convicted of twenty-two murders in the My Lai massacre; in April half a million people marched on Washington protesting the war; in May police arrested roughly twelve thousand anti-war militants attempting to disrupt the government in Washington. The moment was more than ripe, and *What's Going On* quickly soared to number one on the R&B and number six on the pop charts. In 2003 and in 2012 *Rolling Stone* listed it as the number six album of all time, and in 2020 ranked it number one.

Gaye designed the album to work on three interrelated levels: familial/personal, political/topical, and spiritual/metaphysical. The record starts with the voices of several men (including Lem Barney and Mel Farr of the Detroit Lions and members of the Miracles) greeting one another. Their greetings—"Hey, what's happening?"; "Hey, brother, what's happening?"; "Everything is everything. What's your name?"—at a party are echoed throughout the album. Though the greetings are colloquial and casual, they also suggest questions that are raised as the album unfolds. "Hey, what's happening?" queries a war-riven nation facing a multitude of challenges; "Hey brother, what's happening?" summons Gaye's intense family dynamic; and "Everything is everything. What's your name?" invokes the essence of self and its relationship to God.

A fluid saxophone bridges the conversational greeting, and Gaye starts to sing. His invocation "Mother," "Brother," and "Father" and a background chorus of "sister, sister" in the first three verses reflect the Gaye family dynamic and address a country whose families, like Gaye's, were fragmented by war. The second verse protests the war and presents a plea to Marvin's contentious father ("Father, father, we don't need to escalate"). Gaye's multi-track vocals meld in and out of the foreground and background, reflecting the song's and the album's tapestry of themes and the need for spiritual love to serve as a healing and unifying element.

> Mother, mother
> There's too many of you crying
> Brother, brother, brother
> There's too many of you dying
> You know we've got to find a way
> To bring some loving here today

> Father, father
> We don't need to escalate
> You see, war is not the answer
> For only love can conquer hate
> You know we've got to find a way
> To bring some loving here today

During the chorus fingers snap rhythmically, as Gaye sings "Picket lines (sister) and picket signs (sister) / Don't punish me with brutality (sister) / Talk to me (sister), so you can see (sister)" and weaves in his background vocals, represented here in parentheses. His enunciation of sharp "p," "k," and "t" sounds plays off the sounds of the fingers snapping, and the vocal shifts from "ahhh" to an invocation of "sister, sister" before seguing to "What's going on?" The returning veteran then asks the forces repealing protestors to engage in conversation rather than oppression. Voices from the party scene that opens the record reappear, with the phrase "Right on!" punctuating and reinforcing the narrator's plea in a manner that suggests a congregation's response to a sermon. Gaye's scat singing ("Haa Haa y yay a yay a ya ... bep bep bep"), the Funk Brothers' propelling rhythm, and the soaring symphony strike a tone of spiritual yearning.

In the penultimate verse the narrator amplifies his sentiments to encompass much of the nation's youth, the hippies Gaye admired, with the assertion,

> Mother, mother
> Who are they to judge us
> Simply because out hair is long?
> Oh you know, we've got to find a way
> To bring some understanding here today

Again, the scat singing, conversation, deep rhythm, and orchestra weave in and out, raising various themes' resonance and creating crescendo after crescendo of emotional impact. The song returns to the chorus—this time addressed to "brother"—and stresses the need for dialogue, asking that establishment forces "tell me what's going on" so he can reciprocate: "I'll tell you what's going on."

After a slight pause the second track, "What's Happening Brother," picks up with the narrator announcing "I'm just getting back ... / War is hell, when will it end." The narrator laments that he can't find a job and asks about the baseball pennant races and other matters, "cause I'm slightly behind the time." The sequence segues and slows into "Flyin' High (in the Friendly Sky)," a song about alienation, despondency, and escape via heroin: "And I go to the place where the good feelin' awaits me / Self-destruction in my hand." "Save the Children" follows and seamlessly moves between recitation and singing; it protests selfishness and cynicism and links saving children to saving the planet. After a sweep of the piano keys, the pace quickens and the narrator turns preacher, proclaiming "God is my friend" and that "all He asks of us is we give each other love." Again references to family evoke personal, cultural, and spiritual dimensions:

> Love your mother, she bore you
> Love your father, he works for you
> Love your sister, she's good to you
> Love your brother, your brother

After pleas for God's mercy, the suite swings into "Mercy Mercy Me (the Ecology)," a song that, like the title track, was a top-ten single. It touches on air pollution, mercury in the seas, and radiation in an "overcrowded land / How much more abuse from man can she stand?" The album concludes with three songs—"Right On," "Wholy Holy," and "Inner City Blues (Make Me Wanna Holler)"—that echo the work's themes and loop back to phrases and sounds in previous songs, culminating with a repetition of lines from the title track:

> Mother, Mother
> Everybody thinks we're wrong
> Who are they to judge us
> Simply cause we wear our hair long

Gaye later asserted, "When I was struggling for the right of the Motown artist to express himself, Stevie knew I was also struggling for him. He gained from that fight, and the world gains from his genius... as it turned out, Stevie's really a preacher like the rest of us" (Ritz 1991, 153). Gaye's comment reflects the lyrical turn many of Wonder's songs took in the seventies. Born two months premature in Saginaw, Michigan, on May 13, 1950, Steveland Morris—or Steveland Judkins—was placed in an incubator, where he developed

ROP (retinopathy of prematurity), then a poorly understood condition. Blind at birth, he played bongos in his cribs, banged pots and pans with spoons, and became proficient on the drums, harmonica, and keyboards as a child.

Like many African Americans during the first half of the twentieth century, Stevie's parents were southerners who'd migrated north looking for work. In 1953 his family trekked from Saginaw to Detroit and moved into what Stevie later described as an "upper lower middle class" setting. Though his violent and drunken behavior caused a good deal of anguish, Calvin Judkins loved music and occasionally bought Stevie instruments. The Baptist church choir, his mother's penchant for playing blues on the radio, and singing and playing music with his siblings fed his seemingly insatiable appetite for harmony and rhythm. When WCHB hit the radio airwaves in 1956, a Sunday evening show called *Sundown* helped him connect the dots between gospel, Delta blues, jazz, and R&B. Motown, which Gordy had famously founded at 2648 West Grand Boulevard in Detroit in 1959, signed him after Stevie and his friend John Glover (who became a songwriter for the company) attracted attention as street musicians. Glover's cousin, Ronnie White of Smokey Robinson and the Miracles, brought the duo to the studio for an audition after he and fellow Miracle Bobby Rogers listened to them. (They were bemused when Stevie announced he could "sing badder than Smokey" and offered advice on how the Miracles could improve [Ribowsky 2010, 41–42].)

Motown became Stevie's second home. Producer Mickey Stevenson remarks, "You couldn't get him to go home. He wouldn't leave Motown. You'd almost have to drag him out" (Ribowsky 2010, 63). At the studio, Stevie bounced from instrument to instrument, sometimes annoying people with his relentless energy and his tendency to barge in on others' recording sessions unannounced. Veteran bluesman Clarence Paul guided his early recordings, and he formed friendships with Gaye, Smokey Robinson, Martha Reeves, and other luminaries. He jammed with the Funk Brothers and in the sixties had various hits, including "Fingertips (Part 2)," "Uptight (Everything Is Alright)," "I Was Made to Love Her," "Shoo-Be-Doo-Be-Doo," "For Once in My Life," and "My Cherie Amour." He also recorded movie soundtracks, appeared in beach movies alongside Frankie Avalon and Annette Funicello, and made albums that ranged from jazz to surfer music to soul.

Gaye's *What's Going On* was released eight days after Wonder turned twenty-one and could opt out of his contract with Motown. While his lawyer negotiated a new deal—one that would allow him much greater creative autonomy—Wonder set up shop in New York City, where he quickly pursued his desire for more ambitious lyrical content and sonic variety. Influences as varied as Dylan (Wonder had recorded "Mr. Tambourine Man" and had a top-ten hit with "Blowin' in the Wind"), Sly Stone's funk, the guitar licks of Beck, Clapton, and Duane Allman (with whom he'd played at King Curtis's funeral in August of 1971), sounds from Senegal and Ghana, and the Beatles' harmonies and sound effects would contribute to his seventies masterpieces. Perhaps most importantly, after hearing their album *Zero Time*, he showed up at Malcolm Cecil's and Bob Margouleff's New York studio, where they had built a massive polyphonic analogue synthesizer dubbed TONTO (The Original New Timbral Orchestra). Cecil, Margouleff, and their synthesizer would make a vital contribution to Wonder's transitional album *Music of My Mind* (1972), as well as to his masterpieces *Talking Book* (1972), *Innervisions* (1973), and *Fullfillingness' First Finale* (1974). Cecil—who went on to work with the Isley Brothers, James Taylor, Quincy Jones, Weather Report, and many other artists—notes that "all [the lyrics] of [Stevie's] songs before us were written by his girlfriends or wives, or other people. On the albums we did with him, most are only credited to him. And those are the best songs he did. Why? Because we never let him slide. We wouldn't stand for crap" (Ribowsky 2010, 203). At times Wonder consented to being locked in a room until his lyrics attained poignancy, a quality that, when wedded to his extraordinary vocals and arrangements, resulted in compelling poetic song verse.

At age twenty-two Wonder released *Talking Book*, his fifteenth album, and took home two Grammy awards. Over the next five years he would win fourteen Grammy awards, including three for Album of the Year. Two hit singles from *Talking Book*, "You Are the Sunshine of My Life" and "Superstition," characterize the polarities in his recordings of the seventies. Like many of his songs, "You Are the Sunshine of My Life" has a beautiful melody, but the lyrics are little more than a vehicle for his impressive vocal talents. "Superstition," on the other hand, is lyrically ambitious and moves between enigmatic imagery—"Thirteen-month-old baby, broke the looking glass"—and pointed commentary concerning a country mired in a perplexing foreign war and political intrigue: "When you believe in things that you don't understand / Then you suffer / Superstition ain't the way."

"Living for the City," a single from *Innervisions*, describes the plight of a rural Black teen who moves from Mississippi to New York City looking for work. Unlike the allusive, imagistic emphasis of "Superstition," the song presents a family portrait, and a tightly constructed narrative, complete with dialogue and sound effects, including the voices of actual Long Island police for the arrest interlude at the song's midpoint. After the interlude Wonder roughens his vocals to reflect the young man's transition from innocence to experience:

> His hair is long, his feet are hard and gritty
> He spends his life walkin' the streets of New York City
> He's almost dead from breathin' in air pollution
> He tried to vote but to him there's no solution

Struggles like the ones Gaye and Wonder experienced to take control of their career paths and write the songs they wanted to write are commonplace among musicians, and the situation for people of color and for women often has been and remains more difficult. As we suggested in this book's introduction, the sociological phenomena discussed in dozens of relatively recent academic studies concerning race and gender in popular music have been evident to musicians—and to many aficionados—since blues-based music first was recorded. Gaye and Wonder were enormously successful by any measure, but it's certain that many talented songwriters' work never made it into the recording studio due to some combination of racism, sexism, greed, and market forces, as well as the contours of individual lives. As Gayle Wald makes clear in *Shout, Sister, Shout: The Untold Story of Rock-and-Roll Trailblazer Sister Rosetta Tharpe* (2007), a mixture of all these things led to Tharpe's disappearance from the public spotlight, though many well-known musicians—including Little Richard, Carl Perkins, Jerry Lee Lewis, Ray Charles, Johnny Cash, and Keith Richards—admired her and cited her as an influence, leading to her long overdue induction into the Rock & Roll Hall of Fame in 2018.

In the late seventies and early eighties iconoclasts Bobbie Gentry and Bill Withers both unceremoniously bid the music business adieu in early middle age. They didn't even stop to say goodbye. They were just . . . gone. Of course, nothing had happened to them physically. Yet neither artist performed or recorded for decades after their success. Examining Gentry's and Withers's works suggests how and why this happened and helps one gain a better understanding of the depth and breadth of their individual achievements.

In the fall of 1967 Bobbie Gentry's album *Ode to Billie Joe* knocked the Beatles' *Sgt. Pepper's Lonely Hearts Club Band* out of the number one slot after its fifteen-week reign. Written almost entirely by the twenty-five-year-old Mississippi-born Gentry, the album was an innovative hybrid of country, soul, folk, and rock. The press honed in on Gentry's dusky voice, dark good looks, and bluesy acoustic picking. Critics also noted the "Southern Gothic" mise-en-scène she rendered in her compositions, particularly the title track, the chorus of which is "Billie Joe Macallister jumped off the Tallahatchee Bridge" (not an obvious sentiment for a chart-burner).

Characteristics that often underpin poetic song verse—a conversational tone, an emphasis on the personal and the local—are evident. On the surface, the song involves a young woman's description of her family's chatter over Sunday supper. Their conversation strings together a cast of small-town Mississippi Delta characters, including the narrator, her family, the local preacher, and Billie Joe himself. Details are scant and the tone is offhand and gossipy: "And Papa said to Mama, as he passed around the black-eyed peas / Well, Billie Joe never had a lick of sense; pass the biscuits, please." The presumed events of the story are never explicitly enumerated, besides the stark fact of Macallister's suicide. Was his death a result of the relationship between himself and the narrator? What did they throw off the Tallahatchee Bridge before Billie Joe killed himself? Who saw? Who knew? What actually happened?

It's hard to understand how ubiquitous "Ode to Billie Joe" was in its time. The song was covered by dozens of artists—from contemporary mainstays the Fifth Dimension to soul jazz great Lou Donaldson—and even inspired a 1976 movie of the same name, except that "Billie" was changed to "Billy." For me, Mike Mattison, it was a song of my youth; nothing to obsess over, just ever present, like curious wallpaper. Yet the song's dark, intriguing shadow endures (unlike its sentimental, even maudlin countrypolitan cousins of the era, number ones like Eddy Arnold's "Turn the World Around" or Jack Greene's "All the Time"). It should be noted that Gentry's "country" album topped the pop and country charts simultaneously in October of 1967, while Glen Campbell, famously admired for his dual-chart success with *Gentle on My Mind*, did not manage the same feat until the title track was re-released in 1968, perhaps using the success of "Ode" as its crossover template. In any case, the pair's careers indelibly were crossed when they made an album together, *Glen Campbell & Bobbie Gentry* (1968), and she became a fixture on his television show. A televised Gentry performance is a reel of contradictions. She is attractive and presented as such—high brunette beehive, stylishly tailored polyester suits, and extra-long false eyelashes. But she is seated—not go-going about—and she plays her own guitar. Her ability and her earnestness are what command attention. The fact that she's dolled up in accordance with the time is almost a distraction.

The song opens with Gentry gently plucking an acoustic guitar, pedaling on a D-major 7 chord. This is a jazz chord, positively *un*-country, being applied with something approaching a samba rhythm. We are beyond *Hee Haw*'s mandate. The only other instrument is a pizzicato stand-up bass. Stark instrumentation at the introduction usually foreshadows the arrival of additional instruments as the song expands and resonates. But the drums and piano never arrive. Instead, strings are applied in languorously chilling strokes, as if from a Hitchcock film or a horror soundtrack—the antithesis of the treacly orchestrations coming out of Nashville at the time. The song is a basic agreement between voice, guitar, and bass, with strings cryptically commenting: no pedal steel guitar, no fiddle, and no harmonica, nothing to place us "down home." As the verse unfolds, Gentry veers lazily up to the fourth—oh, I see, a blues!—only to return to the tonic, and back again to the fourth. Well, apparently, this is *not* a blues. It's just a pattern. The song is a "mood" wedded to a simple form. The perfect framework on which to hang a compelling yarn.

Gentry's rhythm guitar drives the song, ebbing and flowing in a natural and satisfying manner with her voice, a sure sign that she is performing "live" in the studio (meaning, without overdubbing vocals), perhaps with the bassist (which, indeed, she was). In this sense, the pulse originates and is maintained by Gentry herself. The washes of strings seem to have been added later as mood enhancers. According to arranger, Jimmie Haskell, he asked the producer, "What do you want me to do?" [The producer] said, 'Just put some strings on it so we won't be embarrassed. No one will ever hear it anyway.'"[13] Critics have pointed out that the guitar lick on "Ode" recurs on multiple tracks throughout the album, perhaps implying that Gentry's guitar playing is limited or that she lacked compositional imagination. A better explanation is that Gentry used this lick as a musical marker, a narrative throughline, presaging song suites on the horizon like Gaye's *What's Goin' On*, which is, harmonically speaking, an entire album of "variations on a theme," or in the vernacular, "the same song, except different." (Did Gentry understand this when she named her next album *The Delta Sweete*?) Musically, "Ode to Billie

Joe" certainly is a more subtle and deft *concept* album than the record she unseated at number one, *Sgt. Pepper's*. Her experimentation relied on thematic intention rather than technological virtuosity and otherworldly insight.

The song "Ode to Billie Joe" is an ode in the technical sense; it's sung in metered and rhymed verse. However, in the poetic sense, while the song contends with matters of life and death, it is quite unlike the tragedies the Greeks rendered so agelessly in that it doesn't employ exalted or elevated language. No person or thing is glorified in "Ode to Billie Joe." Quite the opposite. Traditionally, multiple choruses sang a Greek ode across the stage and back—strophe, antistrophe, and epode—mimicking an epic journey. The scale of Gentry's "Ode" is much smaller, localized, a splash that doesn't ripple. And yet "Ode to Billie Joe" was a commercial and artistic triumph, a wonderful example of poetic song verse, largely because of Gentry's use of literary suggestion.

Listeners actively discussed the song's opaque clues, trying to piece together the mystery. *What is happening in this story, and why do we care?* To my childhood mind, "Ode" was *Twin Peaks* before its time: It meant everything...It meant nothing. Gentry actually collaborated on the script for the 1976 motion picture based on her song (starring Robby Benson, just beginning his ascent to the heights of teen heartthrob-dom). But the film, like any nuanced work whittled down to Hollywood formulas, failed to capture the spirit of the original or even an audience. "Everybody has a different guess about what was thrown off the bridge," Gentry said, "flowers, a ring, even a baby. Anyone who hears the song can think what they want, but the real message of the song, if there must be a message, revolves around the nonchalant way the family talks about the suicide."[14]

Greek odes usually involve a tragedy. Gentry scored an enduring hit by venturing to explore a tragedy's aftermath: How do we talk about what we aren't supposed to talk about? How does gossip mask and distort the realities it is born of, which are hiding in plain sight, maybe even seated at our dinner table? Nuance—the *implied*—properly rendered as an artistic strategy turned popular culture on its ear for a moment. Gentry bent the popular and country mediums to her will, critiquing American middle-class mores with an impact the counterculture's rock could only dream of. This was the gift of her "Ode."

On one hand, distinct voices in popular music drive the genre forward. On the other, unique talents are much more difficult for the mainstream to comprehend, market, and absorb. Throughout the sixties and seventies, one finds women singer-songwriters straining at the assumptions that bind them; from the salability of their attractiveness to the idea that "chick singers" are merely ornamental delivery devices for professionally written songs, and that they should pick an appropriate lane and stay in it. Looking back, it would be impossible to define Joni Mitchell as a folk chanteuse, or Laura Nyro or Carole King as mere Brill Building songsters. They had to fight to find space as individual voices. Roberta Flack, Aretha Franklin, and Nina Simone, while seldom crossing over as songwriters themselves, owned their material so wholly that the popular assumption was that they had written the bulk of it. Nevertheless, that wasn't enough to get more than a handful of their self-penned songs onto records. A cursory knowledge of cultural and business norms at the time should stand to explain why this is so. None of this is news. The music industry has been and will continue to be exploitative, cynical, exclusionary, and often plain criminal. Fredric Dannen's *Hit Men: Power Brokers and Fast Money Inside the Music Business* (1990) is an excellent resource on this topic. Or, as veteran record producer John Snyder once told Mike Mattison regarding the industry, "I can to teach you how to bob and weave, but you *will* get hit." As we discuss poetic song verse we must keep in mind that the process of writing, recording, and releasing one's own material to a mass market has always been a minefield of obstacles and barriers—intentional and unintentional—through which only the most ardent, talented, and sometimes lucky, are able to maneuver. The fact that we have these women's songs and performances at all is a miracle to a certain degree. It's no revelation, for example, that Etta James's autobiography is called *Rage to Survive.*

Nina Simone should be counted among The Missing—that is, those who in today's parlance "ghosted" the music business. Her pioneering blend of jazz, soul, blues, and folk proved too eclectic and advanced to pigeonhole. Perhaps it was her near-tenor voice, often mistaken for a man's, with its unsparing vibrato. Or her classical- and jazz-trained ear for improvising on—and often over and through—popular melodies, revealing entirely new melodic strata beneath (one is reminded of her piano solo on Billie Holiday's signature, "Love Me or Leave Me," transforming it into a swinging, two-handed Goldberg Variation). Or her reputation as one of the mid-twentieth century's premier song interpreters, mining so recklessly into the rawness of the material's subtext that even the most jazz-hardened felt ripples of discomfort. Aretha

Franklin had already been crowned "the Queen," so they dubbed Simone "the High Priestess of Soul." A cultural polymath, she was close friends with James Baldwin and Lorraine Hansberry (in whose memory she cowrote in 1969 "To Be Young, Gifted and Black," also the title of a posthumous play based on Hansberry's writings released the previous year), and her unabashed political stances, particularly regarding race, were far ahead of their time (she recounts in her autobiography, *I Put a Spell on You*, an evening attempting to initiate an affair with Congolese nationalist Patrice Lumumba). Simone scaled these artistic heights while harried by severe bipolar disorder, a struggle poignantly portrayed in the documentary *What Happened, Miss Simone?* (2015). In the 1970s, she retreated from music to live in the Caribbean and Africa. Thankfully, she experienced a career renaissance toward the end of her life in the late eighties and nineties, touring and recording mostly in Europe, the continent that reliably welcomed twentieth-century Black cultural homesteaders.

Also of note is Betty Davis, the funk pioneer who struggled to have her own voice recognized outside the long shadow of her former husband, Miles Davis. The former Betty Mabry kept her married name as a performer, perhaps conflating herself with the apogee of Hollywood's femme fatales. The author of such anthems as "Nasty Gal" and "Anti-Love Song," Davis was an innovator of the first order. In the liner notes to the 2007 reissue of her album *Betty Davis* (1973), Carlos Santana claimed, "She was the first Madonna, but Madonna is more like Marie Osmond compared to Betty Davis." She authored or cowrote of all of her songs. Her fearlessness and outlandishness in dress, subject matter, and performance ran neck and neck with African American contemporaries like Funkadelic, and she wedded minimalist grooves to heavy guitar rock, presaging Prince. Her music was an indispensable expression of—and soundtrack to—Black female social, sexual, and political empowerment, although her oeuvre generally didn't strive for the lyrical dynamism that typifies poetic song verse. Davis's lyrics were plain talk, more manifesto than anything; hard funk statements of the New Values in a voice that ranged from righteous screaming to whispered come-on to a sort of proto-rap. When she sang, "He was a biiiiig freak / I used to beat him with a turquoise chain!" believability was paramount. That song and "Don't Call Her No Tramp" prompted the NAACP to ask Black radio stations to boycott her music. Davis later retorted, "They're for the Negro advancement of colored people, and they were stopping my advancement by banning my music."[15] She produced three albums between 1973 and 1975 and then walked away from music. At the time of this writing, she lives quietly in Homestead, Pennsylvania.

In the 2009 documentary *Still Bill*, Bill Withers comments on the process of songwriting. He notes that you're "searching through your feelings and your vulnerabilities and your strengths and your weaknesses. You're already loaded up enough with the burden of just trying to *find* those feelings. And so here come a bunch of guys trying to tell you what to do with all of their goofy suggestions" (Baker and Vlack 2009). And that's the nice way of putting it.

Withers was born in Slab Fork, West Virginia, the youngest of thirteen children and the grandson of a former slave. He was a navy veteran working a job fabricating toilets for airplanes when, untrained at singing and really even playing, he landed a record contract at the ripe age of thirty-two. Withers didn't strictly play funk, blues, jazz, or R&B, the styles proscribed for the Black entertainer. Neither did, say, Ray Charles, but by his example, one had to be immensely talented and nimble to chart a course between the Scylla of the Industry and the Charybdis of Black Genre. One had to be an innovator. Again, from *Still Bill*: "[Record companies] didn't want me to do anything quiet. They had this rhythm and blues syndrome in their mind, with the horns and the three chicks and the gold *lamé* suit, you know" (Baker and Vlack 2009).

Withers combined a folk-blues sensibility with the modern idea of a sensitive male singer-songwriter; simple acoustic strumming with top contemporary studio players. Down-home but up-to-date. Like Gentry's "Ode," Withers's music combines the minimalism of the acoustic guitar with orchestral lushness. If white American pop had Glen Campbell and the Wrecking Crew—a talented cast of LA studio musicians who performed on nearly every big sixties and seventies pop hit—Withers had the interracial rock/soul version of the Legion of Doom: Booker T. Jones (Booker T. & the MGs) on keyboards and production, Jim Keltner (Joe Cocker, Eric Clapton) and Al Jackson Jr. (Booker T. & the MGs, Al Green) on drums, Donald "Duck" Dunn (Booker T. again) on bass, and Stephen Stills on guitar.

The title of Withers's debut, *Just as I Am* (1971), underscores his lack of pretension and his commitment to communicating directly and effectively. In fact, in the middle of the album's jazzy vamp, "Do It Good," Withers takes a moment to directly address the listener in his speaking voice: "If you read the album cover by now you know that my name is what my name is. When I came in here to try and ... *do this*—something I've never done before—Mr.

Jones, Booker T., said to me, 'Don't worry about it. Just do what you do. And do it good.'" The moment is disarming, like an actor in a play taking a moment to thank the audience for coming and sharing a bit of his process. Who comes out and literally says, on a debut album, "I've never done this before"? Withers wasn't just innovating, he was breaking down walls between genres, between listener and musician, perhaps between people.

"Ain't No Sunshine," a minor blues lament, was the surprise hit single of Withers's debut. But "Grandma's Hands" is the album's standout track, a stellar example of how imagery can inform poetic song verse by serving as a cynosure for the local and the personal conveyed through intense yet accessible language. The idea behind the song is simple, as Withers stated: "Instead of singing about romantic love all the time, you make a love song about your grandma." The danger here is what gospel scholar Anthony Heilbut identified as "mama songs," compositions that sentimentally idealize the long-suffering mother/grandmother figure. Heilbut notes a twinge of cynicism in the creation of "mama songs": "tributes to Mother's goodness and reminders of children's ingratitude always reach the guilt-stricken record buyer" (1972, 184).

However, Withers wisely grounds "Grandma's Hands" in a single image that thwarts the lure of the sentimental: we can imagine the gnarls and veins of a grandparent's hands, the wisdom and the history in them, what they did and didn't accomplish in their work, and what they held (mostly, you).

> Grandma's hands clapped in church on Sunday morning
> Grandma's hand played a tambourine so well
> Grandma's hands used to issue out a warning
> She'd say "Billy don't you run so fast
> Might fall on a piece of glass
> Might be snakes there in that grass"
> Grandma's hands

Like Gentry's "Ode to Billie Joe," "Grandma's Hands" is built on a simple acoustic riff. It is not so much a blues as a proto-gospel song, a minor chant à la "Wade in the Water," which is appropriate, since the first line describes Grandma's hands clapping in church on Sunday morning. The phrase "Grandma's hands" is restated at the beginning of the first three lines, methodically, rhythmically, providing the central image, focus, and refrain. It's almost as if these hands are disembodied, flying around issuing out warnings and hitting tambourines, until the turn of phrase at the end of the first verse grounds the image and author's intention: "She'd say, 'Billy don't you run too fast.'" And it dawns on the listener: "This is actually *Bill Withers's* grandma!" The use of "Billy" localizes Grandma's hands in an unanticipated fashion. The specificity of Withers identifying himself in the song causes us to listen more closely.

In the second verse, the drums, which have been keeping simple time on the hi-hat, come in full kit. A tension is released and the song begins to gallop. We settle in to hear more of Withers's experiences with his grandma's hands, only to have the point of focalization shift abruptly. Grandma's hands are involved in soothing a local unwed mother. The breadth of Grandma's careful eye includes far more than her own grandchild, even her own family. Grandma's largesse applies to their community's desperate outcasts, in this case a pregnant teen. Grandma's hands aren't prudish by any means.

> Grandma's hands soothed a local unwed mother
> Grandma's hands used to ache sometimes and swell
> Grandma's hands used to lift her face and tell her
> She'd say "Baby, grandma understands
> That you really love that man
> Put yourself in Jesus' hands"

The third verse swings its focus back to the author as a young boy:

> Grandma's hands used to hand me a piece of candy
> Grandma's hands picked me up each time I fell
> Grandma's hands, boy they really came in handy
> She'd say, "Mattie don't you whip that boy
> What do you want to spank him for?
> He didn't drop no apple core"
> But I don't have Grandma anymore
> If I get to heaven I'll look for
> Grandma's hands

Again, the use of a proper name, "Mattie"—presumably Withers's mother—and the phrase "don't you whip that boy" is strangely intimate. The listener feels he is eavesdropping on a very private multigenerational family argument. Grandma's hands intervene between a mother and child, sparing the rod. But the song ends with a lament that carries a dual implication: "But I don't have Grandma anymore." Grandma has passed away. The song is a dirge and a memorial. At the same time, Grandma's hands can no longer intervene on Withers's behalf. He is grown, and the watchful eye, the kindness, the justice embodied in Grandma's hands can no longer help in the wider world. Life can seem cruel without the buffer of Grandma's hands.

In *Still Bill* there's a clip of Withers performing "Just the Two of Us" on *American Bandstand* in 1981. Dressed in a brown leisure suit, he stands artlessly with his arms at his side, not a whiff of The Entertainer about him. He obviously is uncomfortable, with a thousand-yard "what am I doing here?" stare. Is it the fact that after all of his songwriting triumphs, he finds himself singing someone else's song (Grover Washington Jr.'s, about romantic love, no less)? His mien might not faze successive generations whose baked-in disdain for the "Business of Show" eventually became the norm, but at the time, it was weird to watch. The reasons behind his attitude are clear. As he says in *Still Bill*, "The Fame Game was kicking my ass."

An audience believes they know an artist, and that on some level their feelings are returned. The artist, while grateful, understands that his primary duty is to make art. So when artists disappear, we must suspect that something about their art and its making is afoot. For Gentry and Withers, was their disappearance a defiant gesture or courageous act? Was it neither? A way of cowering, finally, out of the limelight, away from overzealous fans on the one hand, and accountants, record men, managers, and lawyers on the other? Or did the artist never really need the spotlight in the first place, and walking away was like walking out of a grocery store? Did they disappear because the next generation was urgently shoving them aside? The questions mount.

Tillie Olsen wrote an entire book about the "silences" that visit writers and their output. She writes of artists of a certain "class, sex, color still marginal in literature, and whose coming to written voice at all against complex odds is an exhausting achievement" (1978, 146). All of this to say that we should be mindful of artists' real-world experiences, particularly of those who have been systematically marginalized—or even systematically marginalized and then "allowed in." The disappointed fan, the casual cynic, and the music industry executive may share a point of view: "The artists got what they wanted. What are they complaining about?" But from the artists' perspective the casual cynic never truly was listening, and the disappointed fan and the music industry executive must understand that they got what they wanted, too, without having to do any of the creative or emotional work. Where commerce meets art, all of us—artists, fans, cynics, business executives, and critics—should recognize the Faustian twist, the fairy-tale sleight of hand that accompanies wish-granting: It's possible to get what you want before you understand the nature of what you want. Grasping this analytically is one thing; it's another thing entirely to live it. The road to popular success is littered with the creative corpses of legions of Gentrys, Witherses, Simones, Davises, and Flacks about whom we'll never hear a word. Or a note.

★ ★ ★

The closing decades of the twentieth century and the opening decades of the twenty-first have witnessed a continuation of poetic song verse in rock and other modes. Green Day, Titus Andronicus, the Mountain Goats, the Avett Brothers, Anaïs Mitchell, Janelle Monáe, the Drive-by Truckers, and other relatively recent well-known acts have made lyrically ambitious albums in the twenty-first century, but several of the most successful recent ventures into poetic song verse have come from lesser-known bands, like AmeriCamera (it's worth recalling the blues' humble origins and that literary modernism sprang from a small coterie of young artists publishing in little magazines in the 1920s).[16] Jim Carroll, who first gained widespread recognition for his autobiographical memoir, *The Basketball Diaries* (1978), was active until his death in 2009, recording six poetry-inflected punk albums. In the *New York Times* music critic Stephen Holden characterized him as "not so much a singer as an incantatory rock-and-roll poet, whose style of speech-song echoes the vocal inflections of Mick Jagger, Lou Reed, Jimi Hendrix and Patti Smith."[17] In addition to her own recordings, Ursula Rucker has contributed verse to albums and live performances with the Roots and 4hero. On *The Inevitable Rise and Liberation of Niggy Tardust* (2007)—an allusion to David Bowie's *The Rise and Fall of Ziggy Stardust and the Spiders from Mars* (1972)—poet and hip-hop artist Saul Williams combines music and lyrics drawn from his book of poetry, *The Dead Emcee Scrolls: The Lost Teachings of Hip Hop* (2006).

Punk, rap, and hip-hop challenged and extended rock and poetic song verse. Part of our case for poetic song verse as a genre is the emergence of rock as pastiche, the combining of disparate materials, forms and genres, often without regard to their individual rules of usage. Thus poetic song verse is boundary-hopping. Or perhaps more accurately, boundary-leveling.

Almost any art form's success depends on understanding—whether intuitively or intentionally—one's historical moment: when exactly to ignore or break the rules. But what happens when an established genre encounters its rebellious progeny? The dynamic between Bruce Springsteen and Joe Strummer of the Clash is emblematic of this phenomenon and suggests how punk defied and sometimes reconstituted poetic song verse.

As we've discussed, Springsteen's verse often expressed a concern for—and with—the existential temperature of the working-class individual. While Springsteen sometimes addressed the overtly political in his songwriting and storytelling in the 1980s and after, his point of view mostly involves artistic empathy rather than polemics. He took the old writing workshop adage to heart: "Show, don't tell." Starting out as a Dylan wannabe (a good thing in Springsteen's case), he evolved over several records into a songwriter of cinematic vision, often using techniques, tropes, and even whole narratives from cinema. Because of his artistic abilities, on first listen, one might miss the deep anti-war sentiments and rage-fueled irony of "Born in the U.S.A." (as George Will and Ronald Reagan did). Part of Springsteen's accomplishment, like that of any great artist, are the layers of meaning revealed with repeated listening. Employing poetic song verse, he became "The Boss," a champion of the American Everyman. A fine regionalist, he mined his small square of the map—suburban New Jersey—to evoke larger, more universal themes. He was a rock star, but he belonged to "the folks."

Unlike Springsteen, his acolyte Joe Strummer started out as a political populist, using his music to battle class and racial barriers. The Clash became the standard-bearer of the first generation of punk, or as the group's record company put it, "The Only Band That Matter[ed]." Punk was, above all, a reaction to the state of rock in the midseventies. Rock had matured and, like much of its audience, had become everything many associated with it claimed to despise: wealthy, older, comfortable, safe. Perhaps inevitably, Pete Townshend's cry "Hope I die before I get old!" no longer appealed to *his* generation. Much rock music had begun to value facility over emotion and instinct. Consider the advent of the guitar hero, "Clapton is God," stadium spectacle, Learjets, designer drugs, the baroque clamor of prog rock, and the bombastic theatrics of heavy metal. For many upstart musicians the rebellion was gone, leaving a decadent imposter in its place. Punk rockers took up Harlan Howard's summation of country music as their new battle cry: "Three chords and the truth."

Many strains and iterations of punk seemed to simultaneously metastasize in the midseventies in New York (the Ramones, the Dictators), Los Angeles (X, the Germs), and London (the Sex Pistols, the Damned, the Clash). While the Sex Pistols perhaps were the most notorious and well-remembered punk phenomenon, the Ramones are generally acknowledged as the American group that brought the spark to England. As rock critic Lester Bangs wrote, covering the Clash in 1977, "I mean, it's easy to forget that just a little over a year ago there was only one thing: the first Ramones album" (Bangs and Marcus 2003, 225). Of course the seeds of punk lie even further back in the mid to late sixties, with the willful primitivism of the Velvet Underground, Iggy and the Stooges, and the Modern Lovers; the Stones-derived junkie rock of the New York Dolls and the Heartbreakers; the garage-band-meets-Beat poetry of Patti Smith; and others too numerous to name. The Ramones were the perfect iteration of punk: three-chord, two-minute tunes, played loud, fast, and inexpertly. They were delinquents, ostensibly idiots, who dressed in indistinguishable black biker jackets and wore brunette bowl-cuts. Their songs were about sniffing glue, self-sedation, and prayers for frontal lobotomies and shock treatment. It was hard to tell if they were joking or not. And that was a large part of their appeal.

Besides being a snot-nosed reaction to the state of rock, punk—especially in its British incarnation—also was a sophisticated cultural critique, an intentional, intellectual prank of the most annoying order. In *Lipstick Traces: A Secret History of the 20th Century* (1989), Greil Marcus deftly sketches the history of cultural movements like Dadaism and Situationism, and how they were resuscitated in Malcolm McLaren's and Vivienne West's "Sex" boutique in Soho, London. McLaren, looking for a vehicle for his ideas, formed and managed the Sex Pistols in 1976. The band was a very intentional creation, a preconceived reaction to the state of the world—nihilism and anarchy were promoted as the hallmarks of punk. As Marcus writes of the Sex Pistols and the bands they inspired, "there was a reversal of perspective, of values: a sense that anything was possible, a truth that could be proven only in the negative" (1989, 67).

Many punk bands deliberately avoided anything that resembled poetic song verse, but the Clash was cut from a slightly different cloth, and they made forays into it. The band came to punk via the hardscrabble lanes of pub rock, a kind of proto-punk that was a signature in working-class English pubs in the early to mid seventies, with practitioners like Graham Parker,

Dr. Feelgood, and Rockpile (featuring Nick Lowe and Dave Edmunds). Pub rock was rough-hewn, a nod to country, R&B, and Britain's own "skiffle," featuring caustic, ironic, and knowing lyrics. Leftist working-class politics were its foundation. Many of pub rock's practitioners and progeny would feed the punk revolution and later come to fame under a post-punk genre, New Wave. Elvis Costello, Ian Dury and the Blockheads, and others would be the angry young men of Stiff Records. Strummer graduated from pub rockers the 101ers in the midseventies, and he saw punk as the vehicle for his musical and political ideas. He joined forces with guitarist Mick Jones and bassist Paul Simonon, and the Clash was born.

Strummer's deep affinity for Springsteen—perhaps the premier rock star of the seventies and early eighties—is shocking on some level, but it helps explain the lyrical power of the Clash's *London Calling* (1980). Springsteen ostensibly was what the punks were against, so it makes sense that Strummer's deep affinity for the American songwriter was never part of the official band bio. Yet Strummer—formerly John "Woody" Mellor, middle-class son of a career British diplomat—changed his name in honor of Springsteen's chugging workmanlike rhythm guitar. In a nod to his influence, Strummer played the same model guitar as Springsteen: a blonde Fender Telecaster (iconically pictured on the cover of *Born to Run*). What did Strummer see in Springsteen that he wanted to become? According to Strummer biographer Chris Salewicz,

> On November 18, 1975, Joe Strummer saw the first of two shows at the Hammersmith Odeon by Bruce Springsteen. Springsteen, who had never played in London before, was promoting his *Born to Run* album, his third LP, a landmark record that saw him touted as the "future of rock and roll." "When Strummer went to see Springsteen his head was turned," said Clive Timperley. "The whole idea of Springsteen doing full-on three-hour concerts, Strummer thought, 'That's the way to do it!'... Joe even bought an excessively long guitar lead, allowing him to wander at will about the stage and even into the audience—just like Springsteen." (Salewicz 2005, 137)

It should be noted that in that fateful November of 1975, another band had its first shows in London: the Sex Pistols. Strummer was there, too. Part of punk's thrill was enforced stupidity. Even if you *could* play your instrument, you pretended like you couldn't. Punks hobbled their talent for the collective's sake. Punk was self-limiting, but because it never sought to achieve mastery—whether technically or artistically—it opened the doors of popular music to legions of *imperfectionists*. It was base populism. A whole new strata of opportunity arose because rules were canceled and boundaries leveled. Depending on one's perspective, the chances of developing an art of any depth or seriousness became either nil or limitless.

Punk of the 1970s also smashed sociological barriers. The distance between performer and audience was erased, with the audience often joining the band onstage, or the band leaping into the audience. "Pogoing," jumping up and down in place, was the antithesis of any sort of recreational dancing that preceded it, and it was soon replaced in popularity by slam dancing—throwing oneself into fellow dancers—as a sort of violent self-critique of the very concept of dance. Audiences showed their approval and disapproval by "gobbing" or spitting at the band and each other. It was trashy and it was gross—the antithesis of poetic song verse. Punk attempted to drag songwriting and public performance back to prehistory.

The Clash grasped the punk movement's power but eschewed its practiced nihilism. The band, particularly Strummer, took "three chords and the truth" to its logical political conclusion. In the seventies England was rife with recession, unemployment, national strikes, and race riots. The Clash, rather than dabbling in the high- and low-brow mockery of the establishment like the Sex Pistols and their punk peers, reached back for the mantle of folk music's ethos of populist political outrage. If Woody Guthrie's acoustic guitar was a machine that could kill fascists, imagine what a punk rock band could do.

The Clash's eponymous debut appeared in 1977. The album cover is telling in its contrasts: a black-and-white photo of the boys standing in a Soho alleyway, hands in pockets, looking petulant and tough; they are wearing armbands with indistinguishable slogans, and bass player Paul Simonon has a patch of the Union Jack on his breast. The photo's frayed edges imply that it has been torn hastily, like a posted handbill from a work site. The background is martial, military green, offset by the band's name in hot pink. It's an advertisement for a new type of army.

The opening track, "Clash City Rockers," is a manifesto. Its introductory bar chords—chopped out on the Springsteenian Telecaster—are a slight reworking of the Who's midsixties mod anthem "Can't Explain." Except this song is not a rumination on teenage angst; it's a call to arms. Against what, exactly, remains unclear. Every element of the song is used to enhance the lyrics. Strummer snarls:

> I want to move the town to the clash city rockers
> You need a little jump of electrical shockers
> You better leave town if you only want to knock us
> Nothing stands the pressure of the clash city rockers

> See them as they come down the escalator
> Now listen to the tube train accelerator
> Then ya realize that you've gotta have a purpose
> Or this place is gonna knock you out sooner or later

The tribal tom-tom beat of the verse straightens into a vaguely doo-wopish chorus. Here the Clash puts the onus of this opaque revolution on the listener; the band is merely the messenger. They invite their listeners to make a move or "shut their mouths" and enjoy their treatment.

> So don't complain about your useless unemployment
> Jack it in forever tonight
> Or shut your mouth and pretend you enjoy it
> Think of all the money you've got

In essence, he wants the Clash to wake up people from their perceived apathy

> I want to liquefy everybody gone dry
> Or plug into the aerials that poke up in the sky
> Or burn down the suburbs with the half-closed eyes
> You won't succeed unless you try

The jackhammer delivery belies the rough-hewn ambition of the songwriting. While adhering to punk's prescriptions for anger, guitars, and brevity, the song has two separate musical codas, which is a great deal of information to pack into three and half minutes. The first coda reveals the revolutionary matter at hand: Over an entirely different chord progression, with church bells chiming in the background (a nod, perhaps, not only to the lyric, but to the production style of Phil Spector's famous recording of "The Bells of St. Mary"), Strummer sings of bells chiming out for David Bowie, Gary Glitter, and Prince Far I.

> You owe me a move say the bells of St. Groove
> Come on and show me say the bells of Old Bowie
> When I am fitter say the bells of Gary Glitter
> No one but you and I say the bells of Prince Far I
> No one but you and I say the bells of Prince Far I

Rock music—presumably punk rock music—is an invitation not only to dance, but to action. In fact, the listener owes it to the music, which should be your church; nay, your religion! The gender-bending outrageousness of David Bowie's glam rock was a subversive guidepost as well as a gauntlet thrown to punk: "Show me!" The next line is a snide aside to the corpulent and self-indulgently decadent glam artist Gary Glitter (author of "Rock and Roll Parts 1 & 2," which went on to become a popular crowd anthem at soccer matches). Glitter was the wrong kind of glam, a dead end. But the most pressing invitation rings out from Prince Far I. How the hell did the listener suddenly find himself a coreligionist with Rastafarians?

Rastafarianism began as a religious movement in colonial Jamaica. Prince Far I is Ras Tafari Makonnen, or Ethopian emperor Haile Selassie (crowned in 1930), whom adherents of Rastafarianism revere as the living God who would return the slave diaspora's descendants back to Africa. Rastafarianism mirrored pan-African political movements, including Marcus Garvey's Universal Negro Improvement Association, of the same era. Rastafarianism's dreadlocked adherents saw themselves as living in a fallen, decadent "Babylon" of white colonial rule. In the late sixties and early seventies reggae performers, most notably Bob Marley, began spreading the tenets of Rastafarianism internationally with their music.

Strummer equates the punk movement with Black Rastafarians straining to find redemption in fallen Babylon. The fervor, he seems to say, should be religious. This comparison is not as far-fetched as it seems. The "Suedehead" movement of the early seventies was closely aligned with pub rock, which developed into punk. An almost entirely white working-class subculture enamored with reggae, Suedeheads dressed in dandyish suits. They were an offshoot of the anti-racist skinheads of the 1960s. On the one hand, their musical proclivities were a gesture of solidarity and welcome to the massive wave of Caribbean migrants who came to England in the 1950s after the islands gained independence. On the other hand, Suedeheads' love of reggae was a rejection of traditional white working-class racism. That is to say, Suedeheads adapted reggae as a populist political gesture, promoting class solidarity across racial lines. The Clash locked on to this.

Strummer suggests that white, Black, punk, and whoever need to heed the tolling bells of this new quasi-religious movement: punk, like Rastafarianism, looks for believers to enact its tenets. "White Riot," off the the Clash's debut album, is more explicit in its admiration of the archetypal rebellious Jamaican immigrant. Singing about the race riots of 1977, Strummer applauds the bravery of the Black rioters: "Black people gotta lot a problems / But they don't mind throwing a brick." Whereas white people do "Just what they're told to / An' nobody wants to go to jail!" On the chorus, Strummer wonders why white punks aren't in the business of starting riots. There could be a revolution, if punks moved beyond pogoing in place and spitting on each other. It's a brazen call for violence in the streets, yet it is phrased in a petulant and cheeky manner, self-aware in its childishness. Somewhat ahead of his time, Strummer understood the dangers of what today we might call "cultural appropriation."

"(White Man) in Hammersmith Palais" is an attempt at reggae, played inexpertly as per the unwritten protocols of punk. Obviously, these guys are no Rastafarians. The band escapes self-parody by the earnestness of their delivery and the strength of the lyrics, which are a nuanced consideration of a young white kid trafficking in another culture, namely reggae night at London's Hammersmith Palais:

> I'm the all-night drug-prowling wolf
> Who looks so sick in the sun
> I'm the white man in the Palais
> Just lookin' for fun

It is a tough line for the narrator to walk; a mix of admiration and jealousy. He is seeking access to the Jamaicans' "realness," a quest that recalls Norman Mailer's ideas of "authenticity" and "hip," which he sketched with problematic success in his 1957 essay "The White Negro." But for the narrator, the real disappointment isn't that he is unwelcome; it's that there is no revolution: no "roots rock reggae," the dangerous kind, the Rastafarian kind—just the pop reggae stylings of artists like Ken Boothe. The white man in Hammersmith Palais realizes Blackness itself isn't a rebellion, and that simply wanting to feel Black isn't enough. With these performances, the Clash all but admit that the band's dabbling in reggae only could be an homage, a borrowing. The record's other reggae song, a shabbily conscientious cover of Junior Murvin's "Police and Thieves," is a testament to this too. They represent themselves as Rastas in spirit, somehow hoping to merge the spirit of rebellion on both sides of the color line.

One could be forgiven for glossing over the band's cover of rockabilly legend Eddie Cochran's "I Fought the Law"; it fits snugly into the record's theme of general lawlessness. But the song and its pedigree, along with the band's reggae fixation, are a clue to the Clash's sources of inspiration. The rockabilly stylings of Eddie Cochran and Gene Vincent, a favorite of Strummer, were the pure strain of what Elvis jump-started and eventually abandoned: greaser worldview, ducktails, drag racing, teenage delinquency, rebels without causes, stiffing the system, prelapsarian rock.

After the band's debut, the Clash was hailed as music's—and perhaps society's—savior. The press picked up on the group's record company's sell line: "The Only Band That Matters" (echoes of the Springsteen's tagline, "The Future of Rock and Roll"). The Clash reluctantly embraced its place at the vanguard of the punk revolution, even though what the band was articulating and whom it was leading remained unclear. It's revealing to watch film of the Clash's performances in 1977. The band members tend to dress as they did on their debut album cover. Every player has an individual performance style. Mick Jones's toy soldier routine possesses a bit of dance-worthy swagger, while Strummer pitches such a shit fit when hammering his guitar that his leg shakes involuntarily, as if he's being electrocuted. This isn't Elvis's shimmy. It is chaotic and disjointed, a reflection of the music. Trying to righteously wage revolution is a tall order. When one considers every righteous point of view, politics can quickly devolve into squabbling cadres. Punk nihilists and hard-core leftists accused the Clash of selling out, while many in the rock establishment reviled the band. Was it possible to be all things to everybody? One imagines John Reed among the bickering cadres after the October Revolution in *Ten Days that Shook the World*. The mob might begin as anarchy and freedom, but it eventually dictates the limits of its own freedom. Hence, almost immediately the punk debate devolved into the question, Who was a real punk and who was a "poseur"? Who was righteous and who was a sellout? In spite of themselves, the Clash became victims of the polemics that underpinned their work. Lester Bangs, in his long-form review of the Clash's first British tour, wrote,

> When the Clash come on in Coventry, Joe [Strummer] repeats a little speech he first tried out in Birmingham: "Listen—before we play anything, we'd like to ask you one favor: please don't spit on us. We're just trying to do something good up here and it throws us off our stride." I was glad to hear it, because what gobbing really represents to me, besides nausea, is *people doing what they think is expected of them rather than whatever it is they might really want to do.* (Bangs and Marcus 2003, 257)

The Clash's second album, *Give 'Em Enough Rope* (1978), continues in the vein of its debut. The album's opener, "Safe European Home," starts with a snare drum hit so drenched in reverb it sounds like a gunshot. It's another call to arms. The guitars rip a Chuck Berry–worthy riff, and Strummer picks up where he left off, mocking white Europeans who are upset when actual Third World problems disrupt their tropical vacations:

> I went to the place where every white face
> Is an invitation to robbery
> And sitting here in my safe European home
> Don't want to go back there again

The album rocked, but the band seemed hamstrung by its choice of subject matter: anti-war screeds ("Tommy Gun"), inner-city turmoil ("Drug Stabbing Time"), general critiques of consumer culture (in every song), and intra-punk squabbling "All the Young Punks (New Boots and Contracts)." Querulous punks balked at the rich, professional production by Sandy Pearlman, whose main claim to fame was producing the decidedly un-punk Blue Öyster Cult. We'd note that the artistic problem wasn't that the Clash allowed itself to be sanitized; it's that the band merely was giving more of the same. In art, polemics, once heard, usually don't bear repeating.

The Clash's third album, *London Calling*, in many ways is a love letter to the wider world, and arguably when the band came to poetic song verse fully. It is a celebration of Caribbean and American music, culture, and themes through a British punk lens. It also serves as a dismissal of the punk cadre's claustrophobia. The album leveled the fantasy of punk solidarity and celebrated its freedom. Springsteen went local to go wide; the Clash shed its locality, opened itself globally, and created a masterpiece.

The album cover's font and coloring—"London" in pink down the left side, "Calling" in green across the bottom—directly imitates Elvis Presley's debut album. However, the picture is not the iconic black-and-white image of Presley in full-throated swoon with his guitar; it's the now equally iconic picture of Paul Simonon in mid–hatchet swing, smashing his bass on the stage, à la Pete Townshend splintering his guitar a decade earlier. The Clash claimed its place in the continuum even as the band bashed the tradition.

The opening track, "London Calling," typifies the entire album. During World War II the BBC World Service began its broadcasts to occupied territories with "This is London calling...". It was a signal to those living behind enemy lines that they were not forgotten or abandoned: a beacon of hope, a lifeline, the opposite of cynicism. "London Calling," cowritten by Jones and Strummer, was inspired by the so-called nuclear error at Three Mile Island (which occurred just months before the song was recorded) and, according to Jones, by a newspaper headline "warning that the North Sea might rise and push up the Thames, flooding the city. We flipped. To us, the headline was just another example of how everything was coming undone."[18] Thus, rather than issuing a lifeline, the song decries apathy during a time the Clash detected impending doom (the single's B side was "Armagideon Time").

Sonically, "London Calling" is not your typical punk song. It is not particularly unique either; it's a fairly obvious lift of the introduction to Creedence Clearwater Revival's "Walk on Water." A similar straight 4/4 beat kicked off the Sex Pistols' debut, "Holiday in the Sun." But the Sex Pistols intentionally invoked martial parading, going so far as to sync goose-stepping sounds to the bass drum. The Clash, however, implies a 6/8 feel over the 4/4 beat, swinging it ever so slightly. This effect mainly comes from Simonon's ingenious bass line and can be heard in drummer Topper Headon's hi-hat pattern and snare drum fills. This polyrhythmic stratagem served as a warning to punk purists that the old rules don't apply: we're punks, but we're also musicians.

Strummer, the primary lyricist, quickly puts aside a polemical cry to arms and evokes atmospheres and moods, changes that propel the verse toward blunt, resonant imagery and textures.

London calling to the faraway towns
Now war is declared and battle come down
London calling to the underworld
Come out of the cupboard, you boys and girls
London calling now don't look to us
Phony Beatlemania has bitten the dust
London calling, see we ain't got no swing
Except for the ring of that truncheon thing

The first four lines signal a trademark Clash call to action, but then the verse pivots: the band abdicates its leadership role in punk; denigrates its own fame, the "phony Beatlemania" applied to them by the press (ironically, the single would sell more than five million copies worldwide); and renounces its political responsibilities, which seem futile in a city where "swing" signifies police pummeling people with truncheons.

The chorus and the next verse present a phantasmagoric picture of London in full apocalypse:

The ice age is coming, the sun is zooming in
Meltdown expected, the wheat is growing thin
Engines stop running, but I have no fear
Because London is drowning
And I live by the river

London calling to the imitation zone
Forget it, brother, you can go it alone
London calling to the zombies of death
Quit holding out and draw another breath
London calling and I don't want to shout
But while we were talking I saw you nodding out
London calling, see we ain't got no high
Except for the one with the yellow eyes

An ice age looms, followed by extreme heat, famine, industrial collapse, and floods. The Clash no longer wants to provide an illusory outlet for people—"zombies of death"—who continue to ignore impending catastrophe.

"London is drowning," Strummer sings, but "I live by the river," circumstances that point to threatening floods and the determination ("I have no fear") to survive and strike out on his own. The band's warnings have been, and will continue to be, ignored by drug-addled, jaundiced-eyed, soporific punks who are "nodding out" as calamity encroaches. Hence the Clash will go its own way, politically and musically.

On *London Calling* the surprises keep rolling in, song after song. A pop sensibility threads even the most esoteric pieces. Hooky melodies are shamelessly, gleefully at the forefront of the songwriting, a poke in the eye to punk primitivists. Yet the righteous political anger is ever present. There is uplift *and* world-weary fatalism. Curiously, these opposing throughlines don't negate each other. Rather, from a slight distance, they seem to clasp the whole together like veins in igneous rock. Much of this is due to producer Guy Stevens, who expanded the Clash's sonic pallet via instrumentation, guitar and vocal effects, orchestration, and well-chosen ambient noise. For all the evident contrasts between *London Calling* and the Clash's earlier work, the sonic pallet is consistent from song to song, creating an album with its own internal logic, like drawing with thirty-two Crayolas instead of sixteen. The story of making *London Calling* is an epic in itself. Stevens, a music industry vet and a notoriously unstable alcoholic, forced the band out of its normal working routine, pushing and goading it to new creative heights, occasionally using not-so-veiled threats of violence. But in the end, the Clash and Stevens tapped into such a vital wellspring that *London Calling* became a double album containing nineteen songs, many of which reach lyrical and sonic mastery. The album was exhilarating in its genre-bending and rule-breaking; a wild-spirited thing; a devil-may-care kiss-off to punk orthodoxy that evokes the expansive, heart-soaring spirit of Springsteen's Jersey-scapes of the 1970s, if not always sonically, then in essence. One had to rethink what punk was, what rock music was. It emphasized the sense that you are free, and that anything is possible if you'll only trust your soul to rock 'n' roll's mercurial hands.

The Clash continued to employ pastiche in album making during the 1980s. *Sandinista!* (1980) was a triple album, heavily indebted to reggae and dub with splashes of Motown. *Combat Rock* (1982)—which contained the garage-rock pièce de résistance "Should I Stay or Should I Go?"—established the group's obsession with funk and the burgeoning underground genres of rap and hip-hop. But in the mideighties drug abuse and infighting led to the band's disintegration, and after years of flirting with reconstituting the Clash, in 2002 Strummer died of a heart condition. That year, for the Grammy Awards' In Memoriam segment, Springsteen and his lead guitarist Little Steven Van Zandt led a band consisting of multiple generations of punk acolytes—Elvis Costello, Dave Grohl, and the rhythm section from California ska/punks No Doubt—in a raw and riveting version of "London Calling." The band kicked into the iconic opening stomp in front of a screen flashing scenes of World War I aerial dogfights. Springsteen called out, simply, "This is for Joe!"

In the early eighties Strummer and the Clash had recognized the similarities of rap and hip-hop to punk and to the band's populist politics. Similar to the ways punk often de-emphasized individual instrumental virtuosity in favor of bluntly conveying a message, rap and hip-hop—and a decade later spoken word verse—straddled the line between singing and recitation and eschewed emphasizing each band member's instrumental prowess. And like punk, rap and hip-hop often were greeted with a lack of enthusiasm by their progenitors. For instance, Snoop Dogg, Chuck D, Eminem, Kanye West, and others credit Gil Scott-Heron as an inspiration. But reminiscent of Langston Hughes and bebop musicians, who were less than enthusiastic about Beat and San Francisco Renaissance poetry, Scott-Heron rejected the moniker "father of rap and hip-hop" and insisted that he considered himself a "bluesologist" who blended poetry, blues, jazz, soul, and funk. He declared that rap and hip-hop artists needed to "study music" and that he "couldn't be blamed" for the forms.[19] In the preface to his book of poetry, *Now and Then* (2000), he mused, "If there was any individual initiative that I was responsible for it might have been that there was music in certain poems of mine, with complete progression and repeating 'hooks,' which made them more like songs than just recitations with percussion" (xiv). He called his lyrics "blessings" and his songs "spirituals." Nonetheless, his recordings inspired internationally popular blends of music and incantatory verse that have led to a bevy of critical studies, including Tricia Rose's *Black Noise: Rap Music and Black Culture in Contemporary America* (1994) and *The Hip Hop Wars* (2008), Jim Fricke's *Yes Yes Y'all: The Experience Music Project Oral History of Hip Hop's First Decade* (2002), Jeff Chang's *Can't Stop Won't Stop: A History of the Hip-Hop Generation* (2005), Adam Bradley's *Book of Rhymes: The Poetics of Hip Hop* (2009), Sujatha Fernandes's *Close to the Edge: In Search of the Global Hip Hop Generation* (2011), Fernando Orejuela's *Rap and Hip Hop Culture*

(2015), Jessica Nydia Pabón-Colón's *Graffiti Grrlz: Performing Feminism in the Hip Hop Diaspora* (2018), and Mark Katz's *Build: The Power of Hip Hop Diplomacy in a Divided World* (2019) .

In the late seventies and early eighties, rap primarily was the province of underground parties in New York, specifically the Bronx. Disc jockeys developed techniques to extend drum breaks on disco and funk records—eventually known as break beats—over which they could talk to the audience or "rap." In Jamaican music this was known as "toasting." The DJ would use the prescribed musical space they'd created to improvise, rhyme, and entertain the dancers. The message usually was one of self-promotion, with DJs asserting their superiority over rivals. Rap was party music, trifling but communal and fun.

Ever attuned to the new sounds coming from the street, in 1981 the Clash had rap pioneers Grandmaster Flash and the Furious Five open for them in New York City, although the underground innovators fell on deaf ears with the punk crowd. In July Grandmaster Flash had released "The Message," a recording that would forever change the face of hip-hop and American popular music. The song's subject matter was groundbreaking, pivoting from early rap's obsession with parties and self-promotion to tales of urban blight and inner-city despair in the tradition of relatively recent socially conscious soul anthems like Scott-Heron's "Whitey's on the Moon," Gaye's "What's Going On" and "Inner City Blues," Curtis Mayfield's "People Get Ready," and Stevie Wonder's "Living for the City" and "Higher Ground." "The Message" announced that rap *had* a message and could be poetic song verse in its unsparing portrayal of contemporary urban (read "Black") life. Woven between a refrain of "It's like a jungle / Sometimes it makes me wonder / How I keep from going under," rapper Melle Mel—trading verses with MC Duke Bootee—fused poetry, reportage, and social consciousness in a track that declared rap's new self-seriousness. We should note that the record was cowritten and produced by Sylvia Robinson, a former R&B singer-songwriter who, in launching Sugar Hill Records with her husband in the late seventies, transformed herself into a rap pioneer. An earlier Robinson production, the Sugar Hill Gang's 1979 smash "Rapper's Delight," was arguably the first major crossover rap hit.

The underlying sonic track played an important role in making "The Message" surpass even "Rapper's Delight." People hadn't heard anything quite like it. The band employed a minimalist programmed beat and bass line overlaid with washes of synthesizer that shimmer, swell, and decline. Random bleeps, computerized squiggles, and intermittent stabs of percussion give the song a futuristic ambience. But the beat is everything; it's utterly relentless and heavy. The overall effect is akin to the physical environment the song evokes: urban and mechanized; dissociated, alienated, and alienating.

The term *flow* has come to mean a rapper's delivery style or cadence. Rap is not, after all, merely *speaking*. In ways it's lyrically closer to poetry than rock 'n' roll because it's not wedded to melody. Rappers elevate their language with their "flow," but the words are never sung. The sound is akin to the African American preaching tradition, where individual words and phrases *almost* take off into melody, but stay grounded in rhetoric; musical, but never quite music. It's the sound of moral authority.

Melle Mel and Duke Bootee's focus on narrative and evocative wordplay helped make "The Message" relatable to listeners outside the Bronx community. Beginning with the chorus, almost meditatively, Mel raps, "It's like a jungle sometimes / It makes me wonder how I keep from going under." Next we are unceremoniously and unsentimentally tossed into the song's brutal landscape with the sound of a smashed bottle:

> Broken glass everywhere!
> People pissing on the stairs you know they just don't care
> I can't take the smell, can't take the noise
> Got no money to move out
> I guess I got no choice
> Rats in the front room
> Roaches in the back
> Junkies in the alley with a baseball bat
> I tried to get away, but I couldn't get far
> Because a man with a tow truck repossessed my car

He evokes the smells and sounds, the chaos of merely walking out of one's front door in the inner city. The general atmosphere is one of paranoia and harassment. But one of the song's most intriguing aspects is how the narrator—a point of view that is essentially shared by Melle Mel and Duke Bootee—slowly weaves in the experiences of his extended family and members of the community.

Standing on the front stoop, hanging out the window
Watching all the cars go by, roaring as the breezes blow
A crazy lady living in a bag
Eating out of garbage pails
Used to be a fag hag
Said she'll dance the tango, skip the light fandango
A zircon princess, seemed to lost her senses
Down at the peep show watching all the creeps
So she can tell stories to the girls back home
She went to the city and got so, so saditty
She had to get a pimp, she couldn't make it on her own

Don't push me 'cause I'm close to the edge
I'm trying not to lose my head
Ah-huh-huh-huh-huh
It's like a jungle sometimes
It makes me wonder how I keep from going under

My brother's doing bad, stole my mother's TV
Says she watches too much, it just not healthy
All My Children in the daytime, *Dallas* at night
Can't even see the game or the Sugar Ray fight
The bill collectors, they ring my phone
And scare my wife when I'm not home
Got a bum education, double-digit inflation
Can't take the train to the job, there's a strike at the station
Neon King Kong standing on my back
Can't stop to turn around, broke my sacroiliac
A mid-range migraine, cancered membrane
Sometimes I think I'm going insane
I swear I might hijack a plane

The narrator's brother is concerned that their mother is becoming a television addict. However, the brother, an actual junkie, employing the addict's logic, steals the television not simply to promote his own habit, but to help *her*: "It's just not healthy." Bill collectors harass and frighten the narrator's wife when he's at work. His son is already cynical. He's so fed up with school that he's considering dropping out to become a street sweeper. Even as a boy, he understands an elemental American reality: "You've got to have a con / In this land of milk and honey"—sentiments that recall Chuck Berry's "Too Much Monkey Business" and Bob Dylan's "Subterranean Homesick Blues."

The characters despair under constant pressure. When Mel raps, "Don't push me, cause I'm close to the edge / I'm trying not to lose my head," he exaggeratedly staggers the words against the beat, wobbling on the edge of the rhythm, *this close* to toppling off the musical precipice. In a later verse the narrator ironically muses that, medicine being what it is, a girl's arm can be sewn back on if she's pushed in front of a subway train. A man can get a transplant and start over if stabbed in the heart. It's an idea that Gil Scott-Heron addressed in his proto-rap of a nearly a decade earlier, "Whitey's on the Moon": "A rat done bit my sister Nell / And whitey's on the moon." It's the absurdity of poverty in an advanced nation awash in plenty. "The Message" deepens to indict poverty, modernity, and the anxiety they produce: The "neon King Kong standing on my back." The last verse of the song records the image of a wannabe "stick up kid" hanging dead in his jail cell. The song concludes with a casual street corner conversation among the band members—shades of the introduction to Gaye's "What's Goin' On" when partygoers greet each other—but it plays out like the breakdown in Stevie Wonder's "Living for the City," with a police car pulling up and arresting everyone—the eventual fate, it seems, for even the innocent in their neighborhood.

"The Message" was a hit. The song was pivotal in bringing rap out of the underground and set it on equal footing with rock, R&B, jazz, and country. Grandmaster Flash and the Furious Five put a legitimizing stamp on the new genre, commanding respect and critical regard for its poetics, and the many hip-hop innovations set to come.

Perhaps it's appropriate to conclude our discussion of more recent artists with Lucinda Williams, a Grammy-winning songwriter and the daughter of poet Miller Williams. She provides a robust example of how poetic song verse evolved for artists in the post-Dylan generation. Williams was born in Lake Charles, Louisiana, in 1953, and the many places she's lived are practically a catalog of cities mentioned in her songs: Macon, Atlanta, Jackson, Vicksburg, Baton Rouge, New Orleans, Austin, and Nashville. During her childhood, her father took temporary appointments at various universities before settling at the University of Arkansas in 1970, where he helped start the University of Arkansas Press and gained distinction as a poet and critic. He enjoyed widespread attention when President Clinton asked him to compose and read a poem for his inauguration in 1997. Writers frequently visited their home, and Lucinda began composing poetry and stories almost as soon as she could write. She credits Miller's friend, poet James Dickey, for encouraging her songwriting, and she adored Bob Dylan and wanted to be Joan Baez. As a youngster she began diary entries "Dear Dylan," addressing her favorite songwriter. In the 1960s her father's graduate students would drop by and play albums. Lucinda notes,

> The advantage was that I was turned on to quite a bit of music from these people who were in their 20s, turning me on to Dylan and the Doors. This guy set the album [*Highway 61 Revisited*] down and I put it on and listened to it. Even though I was only 12 1/2 and I didn't understand all the lyrics, it didn't matter. What struck me was the blend of traditional folk music and these lyrics that seemed to come from both of those worlds: my dad's world of creative writing and the folk music world I had been steeped in through people like Peter, Paul & Mary, Gordon Lightfoot, the traditional folk songs.[20]

Williams felt that Dylan "was the first artist who actually managed to incorporate both of the worlds I came out of, which was the more traditional folk music of America and the poetic, literary world. That's when I decided what I wanted to achieve."[21] Other musical influences spanned from Robert Johnson to John Lee Hooker to Neil Young to the Allman Brothers Band. Various poets, especially Emily Dickinson, had a profound impact on her work, but her father—with whom she performed concerts, alternating acoustic versions of her songs with her father reading his poetry—was her most consistent mentor:

> I grew up around poets and novelists and my dad wrote poems about everything—from a cat sleeping in a window to a car wreck he passed on the highway. I learned not to censor myself: that was one of things I learned in my apprenticeship, my creative-writing apprenticeship with my dad. I didn't study creative writing formally, but I learned as much as you could just by watching him, and sitting in on his workshops at the house, and hearing him teach, and all of that. He taught me about not censoring myself. He taught me about the economics of writing and editing. He's a great editor.[22]

Miller Williams, who died in 2015, described Lucinda as a "late bloomer." He observed that his "poetry and her songs—you could say they both have dirt under the fingernails. In my writing, I try to get down to the nuts and bolts of living, and there's no question that Lucinda does that, too. Her music is not abstract. There's real sweat in every song."[23] Lucinda traveled incessantly throughout the seventies and eighties, playing small venues and honing her craft. She feels that for years she "fell through the cracks between rock and country . . . there was no 'Americana' back then."[24] That she's won Grammy awards in the folk and rock categories reflects her range. In 1989 *Rolling Stone* characterized her as a "veteran singer and songwriter who released two albums on the Folkways label, but since then has played mostly to smart folk- and country-inclined listeners who've frequented the right clubs in Houston, Austin, Louisiana, New York, and for the past several years, Los Angeles."[25] Williams spent nearly another ten years writing, recording, and performing before *Car Wheels on a Gravel Road* (1998)—an album five years in the making—resulted in a national audience and a Grammy for Best Contemporary Folk Album.

Like her father's poetry, much of her verse assumes a conversational tone and emphasizes the personal and the local, characteristics that marked the blues and contemporary poetry. Before the release of *Car Wheels* she performed the title track at Nashville's legendary Bluebird Cafe, where musicians often sharpen songs for recording. Miller was in attendance and in the song recognized scenes of Lucinda's childhood traumas, many of which stemmed from his contentious relationship with Lucinda's mother, a concert pianist who suffered from mental illness. When the show ended he hugged Lucinda and told her he was "sorry." After the album's release, Lucinda declared, "You can't be afraid to deal with your demons. You've got to go there to be able to write."[26]

Williams's intermingling of folk, blues, rock, and ambitious verse typifies post-Dylan artists ranging from Steve Earle (who played on and helped produce *Car Wheels*) and James McMurtry to Robert Cray and Jonny Lang to Jeff Lynne and Sarah McLachlan to the metal bands Alice in Chains and Rage Against the Machine to the blues rock groups the Tedeschi Trucks Band, the North Mississippi Allstars, and Larkin Poe. The song "Car Wheels on a Gravel Road" mixes an adult's and a child's perspectives. The title forms the song's refrain and is associated with fragments of memories concerning constantly moving. The memories' elliptical qualities accrue around the wheels' sound and suggest an adult's anxieties and a child's partial understanding of events.

> Low hum of voices in the front seat
> Stories nobody knows
> Got folks in Jackson we're going to meet
> Car wheels on a gravel road

Another song from the album, "2 Kool 2 B 4-Gotten," is a good example of how blues, folk, and poetry blend for Williams. The song's compressed, elliptical qualities are reflected by its title and suggest, as she told Ernest Suarez in conversation, Emily Dickinson's influence. The narrator sits in a bar, and images ranging from signs on the wall ("No dope smoking no beer sold after 12 o'clock") to Robert Johnson playing the blues filter through her mind. The bar's ambience and the narrator's blues—"I had a lover / I thought he was mine"—merge to create a lyric that's historically evocative ("Rosedale Mississippi Magic City Juke Joint") and intensely personal ("He asked me baby would you jump into the water with me / I told him no way baby that's your own death you see").

* * *

In chapter 1 we discussed how music influenced poetry during the first half of the twentieth century, but noted that poetry had little influence on music during that period. In subsequent chapters we examined how the situation changed in the sixties as poetry invigorated rock and helped turn it into a more ambitious art form, eventually resulting in the literary genre we call poetic song verse. On the evening Dylan was inducted (he didn't show up) into the American Academy of Arts and Letters, novelist Michael Chabon delivered the plenary address, which he titled "Rock 'n' Roll," despite the fact the other inductees were novelist Justin Ward and visual artists Richard Tuttle and Terry Winters. Obviously, Dylan's and rock's status were on Chabon's mind. He drew distinctions between poetry and song lyrics but came to the conclusion that

> the question of whether or not Dylan's lyrics are poetry feels irrelevant. Dylan's lyrics are *writing*, and as writing they have influenced my own writing

as much as if not more than the work of any poet apart from O'Hara and maybe Edgar Allan Poe. In fact, song lyrics in general have arguably mattered to and shaped me more, as a writer, than novels or short stories written by any but the most crucial of my literary heroes....

I don't think I could have learned more about the joy and sensuous appeal of alliteration, assonance, and consonance from any poem of Gerard Manley Hopkins than I did from Warren Zevon's wonderful line in "Werewolves of London": "*Little old lady got mutilated late last night*"; more about elliptical storytelling from Raymond Carver than from "Ode to Billie Joe" (Bobbie Gentry is another underrated writer); more about unreliable narrators from Poe or Nabokov than from Steely Dan (*passim*). And yet while songwriters are given the opportunity, often enough, to cite their literary influences, no one has ever thought to ask me about the songwriters who have shaped my work, any more than I have asked myself, until now. I'm not sure why. Maybe it's the *sha-la-la-las* and the *wo-o-wo-os*. Maybe it's the fact that so many lyrics are nothing but clichés strung like costume jewelry beads on a string of backbeat.[27]

Chabon's ruminations concerning why songwriters often are asked about literary influences, but other writers are seldom asked about songwriters' influences, speaks to poetic song verse's status as an art form, but not in a manner one might suppose. Chabon speculates that there may be too many clichéd rock songs, but we'll note that there's not a shortage of clichéd poems, plays, novels, or operas, either. It's also true that musical instruments and singers' vocals are central to most lyrically rich rock songs, though why that would curtail recognition of artistic achievement is difficult to understand. As Chabon acknowledges, the fact remains that exceptional song lyrics are a form of verse composition that moves people and influences artists working in different mediums.

Before returning to Chabon, let's consider another event that honors writers. In 2012, at the John F. Kennedy Library in Boston, PEN New England, the nation's oldest literary organization, named Chuck Berry and Leonard Cohen as the first recipients of the Song Lyrics of Literary Excellence award. Judges for the award consisted of a mix of poets, novelists, and songwriters, including Bono, Rosanne Cash, Elvis Costello, Paul Muldoon, Smokey Robinson, Salman Rushdie, and Paul Simon. Caroline Kennedy opened the ceremony, addressing a packed house that included Keith Richards and other celebrities by quoting her father's speech dedicating the Robert Frost Library:

"I see little that is more important to our country and our civilization than full recognition of the place of the artist. In serving his vision of the truth, the artist best serves the nation." Dylan sent congratulatory remarks, calling Berry "the Shakespeare of rock and roll."[28] When Cohen took the stage, he compared Berry's "Roll Over, Beethoven" to Walt Whitman's "barbaric yawp" from *Leaves of Grass*.

The tendency—even among musicians—to laud songwriters by comparing them to poets seems to reflect an assumption that, to be taken seriously, popular songs must be validated by poetry, a sentiment we reject. Perhaps the answer to Chabon's inquiry is partially related to the relatively short period—about sixty years—that poetic song verse has existed. It might also have to do with blues-based popular music's almost unmatched ability to combine popular and high culture in reaching mass audiences—can something so widely embraced be great art? Perhaps it concerns overexposure to clichéd pop songs—it's much easier to avoid bad poetry, fiction, or drama than music. Or perhaps the answer resides in this book's central premise: rock's roots in the blues helped open it to poetry's influence, resulting in a new literary genre consisting of songs that combine sonics with semantically rich verbal techniques. This transformation resulted in Dylan, the Rolling Stones, the Beatles, the Doors, Jimi Hendrix, Leonard Cohen, Joni Mitchell, Van Morrison, Lou Reed, Marvin Gaye, Bruce Springsteen, and other lyrically ambitious artists changing music and verse composition across continents, and it has helped make poetic song verse a powerful art form with a relatively young, but extraordinary legacy.

Over the last several decades poetic song verse has become an international phenomenon. Songwriters from the United States and other English-speaking countries led the way in the sixties, primarily thanks to the blues and subsequent forms of blues-based popular music, but today there are lyrically ambitious songwriters working in rock and other modes in China, Japan, Korea, Russia, Africa, Eastern and Western Europe, Scandinavia, and throughout the world. Nevertheless, the story of poetic song verse remains uniquely American. The racially inflected borrowings and imitations in blues-based music have served large functions in American art and race relations, with various motifs of progress, irony, and tragedy woven into the tapestry. The progress embodied in white and Black musicians so publicly involved in a common enterprise (which they all did not see as such); the irony of Black blues musicians expressing their pain and fury in the 1920s and 1930s, and then as singers of pain and fury becoming idols to young white musicians in the United States, Britain, and beyond; the tragedy of Black musical styles appropriated and used to enrich white musicians, producers, and record companies; and the creativity, lure, and destructiveness involved in celebrity are all part of this heritage. Poetic song verse reflects how American culture zealously mixes racial identities, ethnicities, the highbrow and the lowbrow, the rhetorical and the colloquial, the popular and the refined. Walt Whitman called for an American art that blended the vernacular with traditions that had been inherited from Europe; how remarkable that rock sprang from the blues, assimilated poetry, and broadcast poetic song verse to the world.

Appendix of Songs and Poems Discussed

Below is a list of songs and poems discussed in each chapter. Costs for permissions prohibit us from quoting every song more fully in the book, but it's very helpful to know their contents, including the songs' full use of sonics. We have listed songs and poems separately, but in each case the order in which they appear below roughly reflects the order in which they are discussed in the book. An asterisk accompanies the titles for which we obtained permission to quote more fully. We also assembled a playlist of songs on Spotify that reflects the general order in which we discuss them in the book: https://open.spotify.com/playlist/4emRCtg3eCWDdp36aFtf6m?si=NuWr-VrLQoqOLN46FXHuoQ.

Introduction

Songs

The Beatles: "She Loves You," "Norwegian Wood"
Chuck Berry: "Brown Eyed Handsome Man"
Bob Dylan: "Blowin' in the Wind"
Bruce Springsteen: "Born to Run"

Chapter 1

Songs

W. C. Handy: "St. Louis Blues"
Langston Hughes (with Charles Mingus and Leonard Feather): *The Weary Blues*
Dizzy Gillespie and Charlie Parker: *Town Hall, New York City, June 22, 1945*; *Bird and Diz*
Bo Diddley: "Bo Diddley"
Lead Belly: "Lining Track"
Fred McDowell: *I Do Not Play No Rock and Roll Y'all*

Appendix of Songs and Poems Discussed

Bessie Smith: "Down Hearted Blues"
Muddy Waters: "Mannish Boy"
Hound Dog Taylor: *Have Some Fun*
Skip James: "22–20," "Crow Jane"
Furry Lewis: "Furry's Blues"
Alberta Hunter: "Empty Bed Blues"
Charley Patton: "34 Blues," "High Water Everywhere"
Robert Johnson: "Crossroads," "Hellhound on My Trail"
Ma Rainey: "Black Dust Blues"

Poetry

Langston Hughes: "The Weary Blues," "Jazzonia," "Negro Dancers," "Dream Boogie"
Sterling Brown: "Ma Rainey," "New St. Louis Blues"
Margaret Walker: "Bad-Man Stagolee"
Robert Creeley: "I Know a Man"*
Robert Lowell: "Memories of West Street and Lepke"
Allen Ginsberg: "Kaddish"
Anne Sexton: "Double Image"
James Wright: "Autumn Begins in Martins Ferry, Ohio," "A Blessing"
Frank O'Hara: "A Step Away from Them"
Robert Bly: "Waking from Sleep"
Sylvia Plath: "Lady Lazarus"
James Dickey: "The Sheep Child"

Chapter 2

Songs

Bob Dylan: "Nobel Prize Acceptance Speech," *Bob Dylan*, *The Freewheelin' Bob Dylan*, *The Times They Are a-Changin'*, *Another Side of Dylan*, *Bringing It All Back Home*, *Highway 61 Revisited*, *Blonde on Blonde* (lyrics are available at BobDylan.com).
Little Richard: "Tutti Frutti"
Chuck Berry" "Maybellene," "Roll Over Beethoven," "School Days," "Brown Eyed Handsome Man," "Promised Land," "Too Much Monkey Business"
Mississippi John Hurt: "Avalon Blues"
Bo Diddley: "Who Do You Love?"
Crosby, Stills & Nash: "Helplessly Hoping"*
Joni Mitchell: "Both Sides Now"

Chapter 3

Songs

The Beatles: "Nowhere Man," "Tomorrow Never Knows," "Eleanor Rigby," *Sgt. Pepper's Lonely Hearts Club Band* (especially "A Day in the Life"*)

The Rolling Stones: "Monkey Man," "Satisfaction," "Mother's Little Helper," "Sympathy for the Devil," "Gimme Shelter," "Midnight Rambler,"* "Brown Sugar"
The Doors: "Moonlight Drive," "The End,"* "Celebration of the Lizard," "L.A. Woman"

Poetry

Allen Ginsberg: "Howl," "A Supermarket in California," "Sunflower Sutra," "Consulting the I Ching Smoking Pot Listening to the Fugs Sing Blake," "Portland Coliseum," "Beginning of a Poem of These States," "First Party at Ken Kesey's with Hell's Angels," "Bayonne Turnpike to Tuscarora"
Walt Whitman: *Song of Myself* sections 1–6

Chapter 4

Songs

Bob Dylan: "Subterranean Homesick Blues," "Like a Rolling Stone"*
The Who: "Magic Bus"
The Grateful Dead: "Truckin'"
Jimi Hendrix: "Are You Experienced?," "Voodoo Chile," "Voodoo Chile (Slight Return)"
Jefferson Airplane: "White Rabbit"
Amboy Dukes: "Journey to the Center of the Mind" (apologies for suggesting this, but negative examples can be useful)
Leonard Cohen: "Suzanne"*
Gil Scott-Heron: "The Revolution Will Not Be Televised"

Poetry

Robert Lowell: "Waking Early Sunday Morning"
César Vallejo: "I Have a Terrible Fear . . ."

Chapter 5

Songs

The Who: *Tommy* and *Quadrophenia*
Bruce Springsteen: "Meeting Across the River," "Thunder Road," "Born in the U.S.A."
Marvin Gaye: *What's Going On*
Sam Cooke: "A Change Is Gonna Come"
Edwin Starr: "War"
Stevie Wonder: "You Are the Sunshine of My Life," "Superstition," "Living for the City"
Bobbie Gentry: "Ode to Billie Joe"
Betty Davis: "He Was a Big Freak"
Bill Withers: "Grandma's Hands"*
The Clash: "Clash City Rockers,"* "White Riot," "White Man in Hammersmith Palais," "Safe European Home," "London Calling"*

Gil Scott-Heron: "Whitey's on the Moon"
Grandmaster Flash: "The Message"*
Lucinda Williams: "Car Wheels on a Gravel Road," "2 Kool 2 B 4-Gotten"*
Warren Zevon: "Werewolves of London"

Notes

Introduction

1. John Hollander's *The Untuning of the Sky: Ideas of Music in English Poetry, 1500–1700* (Princeton University Press, 1961) remains an evocative consideration of the relationship between music and poetry.

2. Jack Hamilton's *Just Around Midnight: Rock and Roll and the Racial Imagination* (2016), Kevin Young's magnificent *The Grey Album: On the Blackness of Blackness* (2012), Michael J. Kramer's *The Republic of Rock: Music and Citizenship in the Sixties Counterculture* (2013), Karl Hagstrom Miller's *Segregating Sound: Inventing Folk and Pop Music in the Age of Jim Crow* (2010), Josh Kun's *Audiotopia: Music, Race, and America* (2005), Ronald Radono's *Lying Up a Nation: Race and Black Music* (2003), Maureen Mahon's *Right to Rock: The Black Coalition and the Cultural Politics of Race* (2004), and Angela Y. Davis's *Blues Legacies and Black Feminism* (1998) are among the eruption of sociologically oriented academic books that discuss the politics of race, gender, fame, and money in popular music. Emily J. Lordi's approach in *Black Resonance: Iconic Women Singers and African American Literature* (2013) is closer to ours in some ways. Lordi emphasizes the relationship between vocal performance by canonical singers and literature by canonical writers. Her focus isn't on songwriting but on demonstrating that "black women singers are not just muses for writers but innovative artists whose expressive breakthroughs illuminate literary works, which in turn reattune us to music" (1). She embarks on a "theoretical revaluation of the relationship between music and writing in black expressive culture by staging singers and writers as collaborators in the creations of twentieth-century black aesthetics" (8). Our study focuses on songwriters who were influenced by literature, especially poetry, but who recorded the songs they wrote.

3. Bradley uses the term *pop* to encompass a wide range of popular music, including soul, rhythm and blues, and rock.

Chapter 1

1. Studies concerning the influence of jazz and blues on poetry reach back to the 1950s. Relatively recent works by Bolden (*Afro-Blue: Improvisations in African American Poetry*

and Culture, 2003), Anderson (*Notes to Make the Sound Come Right: Four Innovations of Jazz Poetry*, 2004), Feinstein (*Jazz Poetry from the 1920s to the Present*, 1997), and Yaffe (*Fascinating Rhythm: Reading Jazz in American Writing*, 2006) examine improvisation in music and poetry. Books published during the twenty-first century by Filene (*Public Memory & American Roots Music*, 2000), Davis (*The History of the Blues: The Roots, The Music, The People*, 2003), and others analyze the history and cultural impact of American roots music, extending the work of Palmer, Marcus, and Lomax (see bibliography). Marcus (*A History of Rock 'n' Roll in Ten Songs*, 2014) also explores rock 'n' roll history by considering multiple versions of ten songs.

2. Quoted in *The Literary Digest*, October 20, 1917, 26, http://www.oldmagazinearticles.com/article-summary/african-american-art_reviewed_by_james-weldon-johnson#.YFDDLZ1KhPY.

3. Sascha Feinstein's *Jazz Poetry: From the 1920s to the Present* provides an extended discussion of poetry and jazz.

4. Afro-Cuban sounds had made their way into American music in the 1800s. Musicians often took the twice-a-day ferry from New Orleans to Havana and performed in both cities.

5. On Davis's LP *Move*, "Move" is on the A side. "Boplicity" is on the "reverse side." Parker recorded "Cheryl" and "Chasin' the Bird" in 1947.

6. "The Cool, Cool Bards," *Time*, December, 2, 1957, 71.

7. Herb Caen, "Pocketful of Notes," *San Francisco Chronicle*, April 2, 1958, https://www.sfgate.com/news/article/Pocketful-of-Notes-2855259.php.

8. The McGraw-Hill Book Company published the first edition of Murray's *Stomping the Blues* in 1976. We reference the University of Minnesota Press's fortieth anniversary edition (2017).

9. In a review of Baraka's book, Ellison challenged Baraka's premises for "ignoring the intricate network of connections which binds Negroes to the larger society." The review, titled "Blues People," appeared in the *New York Times* on February 6, 1964, and was collected in *Shadow and Act* (1965).

10. From an unpublished personal interview with Mike Mattison recorded in September 2008.

11. "Hound Dog" was written by Jerry Leiber and Mike Stoller; it was originally recorded by Willie Mae "Big Mama" Thornton and released as a single in 1953. Elvis's version was released in 1956.

12. By the new American poetry we primarily mean poetry associated with the Beat, Black Mountain, New York School, Confessional, Deep Image, and Black Arts movements.

13. For a detailed description of the musical and racial scene in New Orleans in the early part of the twentieth century, see Thomas Brothers, *Louis Armstrong's New Orleans* (New York: W.W. Norton, 2006).

14. Since the 1980s James Breslin (*From Modern to Contemporary: American Poetry 1945–1965*

[Chicago: University of Chicago Press, 1985]), Lynn Keller (*Remaking It New: Contemporary American Poetry and the Modernist Tradition* [Cambridge: Cambridge University Press, 1987]), and others have explored the formation of poetic movements after World War II and documented the transition from modern to contemporary poetry.

15. Ginsberg's, O'Hara's, and Sexton's poetry was influenced by blues-based popular music. In 1967 Sexton formed a band—Anne Sexton and Her Kind—that toured and recorded. Robert Penn Warren became one of the first literary critics to acknowledge the blues' poetic power, and the first to include a section on song verse in a literary anthology,

instead of reprinting, say, lyrics by Dylan or Lennon and McCartney as a type of "popular poetry." See *American Literature: The Makers and the Making* (New York: St. Martin's Press, 1973), coedited by Cleanth Brooks, R. W. B. Lewis, and Robert Penn Warren. Lewis told Ernest Suarez that the section on song verse was "all Warren." In the introduction to that section, Warren noted that the blues "represent a body of poetic art unique and powerful" and that "much of the poetry recognized as 'literature,' white or black, seems tepid beside it."

16. Stephen C. LaVere, Eric Clapton, and Keith Richards, liner notes to *Robert Johnson: The Complete Recordings* (New York: Columbia Records, 1990).

17. In chapter 4 we distinguish between surrealism as an artistic practice associated with a movement and the fantastic. We use "surrealistic" as an adjective in the sentence associated with this note and throughout the book.

18. A use of the fantastic marked much of the era's most celebrated poetry. Dickey's *Buckdancer's Choice* (1966), Bly's *The Light Around the Body* (1968), John Berryman's *His Toy, His Dream, His Rest* (1969), Frank O'Hara's *The Collected Works of Frank O'Hara* (1972), and Ginsberg's *The Fall of America* (1974) were National Book Award winners that displayed surrealistic influences. Similarly, Louis Simpson's *At the End of the Open Road* (1964), John Berryman's *77 Dream Songs* (1965), W. S. Merwin's *The Carrier of Ladders* (1971), and James Wright's *Collected Poems* (1972) won Pulitzer Prizes.

Chapter 2

1. The acceptance speech Patti Smith read for Dylan can be accessed via Maya Rhodan, "Read Bob Dylan's Novel Prize Acceptance Speech: 'I Realize I Am in Very Rare Company,'" *Time*, December 10, 2016, http://time.com/4597291/bob-dylan-nobel-prize-speech/?xid=homepage. Smith's performance of "A Hard Rain's a-Gonna Fall" at the ceremony can be accessed at Emma Stefansky, "Patti Smith Emotionally Accepts Bob Dylan's Nobel Prize in Literature," *Vanity Fair*, December 11, 2016, https://www.vanityfair.com/culture/2016/12/patti-smith-accepts-bob-dylan-nobel-prize.

2. Dylan's Nobel Prize recording can be accessed at https://www.nobelprize.org/prizes/literature/2016/dylan/lecture.

3. "The Rock Is Solid," *Time*, November 4, 1957, 48.

4. For a full discussion of opposition to rock 'n' roll, see Linda Martin and Kerry Segrave, *Anti-Rock: The Opposition to Rock 'n' Roll* (Cambridge, MA: Da Capo, 1993) and Glenn C. Altschuler, *All Shook Up: How Rock 'n' Roll Changed America* (New York: Oxford University Press, 2003).

5. In subsequent decades films and TV shows set in the fifties, from *Back to the Future* and *Forrest Gump* to *Happy Days* and *Laverne and Shirley*, and movies depicting fifties rock 'n' roll culture, like *Crazy Mama*, reinforced this narrative. Even *American Graffiti*, a more ambitious film set in 1962, associates a waning rock 'n' roll era with a loss of innocence.

6. See Steven C. Tracy, *Hot Music, Ragmentation, and the Bluing of American Literature* (Tuscaloosa: University of Alabama Press, 2015), for a discussion of how "hot" music influenced American literature and culture during the twenties and more widely.

7. Payola is the illegal practice of bribing a commercial radio station to play a song without disclosing it as sponsored airtime.

8. See Charles White, *The Life and Times of Little Richard* (London: Omnibus Press, 2003), 55, 82–83. In 1956 producer Robert "Bumps" Blackwell famously hired Dorothy LaBostrie to

rewrite the homoerotic lyrics to Little Richard's "Tutti Frutti" from "Tutti Frutti, good booty / If it don't fit, don't force it / You can grease it, make it easy" to "Tutti Frutti, aw rooty! Tutti Frutti, aw rooty." In 1958 Little Richard abruptly abandoned rock 'n' roll to study theology at Oakwood College in Huntsville, Alabama, and formed the Little Richard Evangelistic Team. After several years of preaching and recording gospel music, in 1962 he returned to rock 'n' roll, donning even more makeup and flaunting his sexual ambiguity during performances.

8. Bob Dylan, liner notes to *Biograph* (New York: Columbia Records, 1985).

9. "I Am My Words," *Newsweek*, November 4, 1963, 94–95.

10. Rock 'n' roll's influence on sixties songwriters would re-emerge later in the decade and remain potent. Cohen has stated, "All of us are footnotes to the words of Chuck Berry." Mitchell cites Berry's "Harlem in Havana" and "Johnny B. Goode" in a list of eighteen songs that most "matter to her." Berry is the only artist to have more than one song on her list. Paul McCartney, who idolized Berry as a teenager, has called him "one of the greatest poets America has ever produced." It should be noted that when McCartney, Willie Dixon, and others call Berry a "poet," a distinction should be made. Berry is a poet in the sense that he employed vivid imagery and figurative language, and penned superb rhyming, rhythmic condensed-verse narratives. But he did not possess detailed knowledge of poetic techniques or traditions. In other words, he wasn't engaged with poetry in the way Dylan, Mitchell, McCartney, Jagger, Lennon, Van Morrison, Jim Morrison, or Gil Scott-Heron would be. However, it's clear his verse practices influenced these songwriters and many others, helping open them to song lyrics' poetic possibilities.

11. Dylan, liner notes to *Biograph*. In the quote Dylan is clearly referring to late 1963 or early 1964, when he had begun to leave the folk scene behind; there's no mention of Guthrie or of his fellow folkies.

12. Mick Jagger, "Mick Jagger Remembers" (interview with Jann S. Wenner), *Rolling Stone*, December 14, 1995, https://www.rollingstone.com/feature/mick-jagger-remembers-92946/. Many links in the endnotes to RollingStone.com are from the magazine's wonderful archive, which is accessible by subscription.

13. Paul Zollo, "Leonard Cohen, Paul Simon and More on Bob Dylan," *American Songwriter*, February 14, 2012, https://americansongwriter.com/many-artists-on-dylan/.

14. Stephen Holden, "Pop: Carroll's Anthem Eulogizes Peers." *New York Times*, May 31, 1982, Arts.

15. Taped interview with Ernest Suarez for the article "Little Honey," *Washington Post*, February 27, 2009, Weekend. Miller Williams wrote the inaugural poem for the induction ceremony celebrating President Clinton's second term.

16. Dylan, Mitchell, McCartney, Cohen, Lennon, Morrison, Reed, Scott-Heron, and Robert Hunter are among the era's many songwriters who also published poetry, albeit little that is compelling.

17. We consider Joni Mitchell among the very finest lyricists of our time. We hoped to quote from her songs more fully and made repeated attempts over several months to purchase permissions, but her representatives never responded.

Chapter 3

1. "The History of The Rolling Stones and the Announcement of the No Filter Tour Dates," *Record World*, accessed March 18, 2021, http://www.recordworldmagazine.com/blog/the-history-of-the-rolling-stones-and-the-announcement-of-the-no-filter-tour-dates/.

2. Artists' emphasis on creating extravagant fictional selves sometimes led them to modify characteristics, especially a stress on the personal or confessional, that had led to the confluence of blues and poetry in the verse of Dylan, Stills, Mitchell, Van Morrison, and others, a trend that, as we discuss in chapter 5, reversed itself as psychedelia waned in the seventies.

3. These trends have continued to proliferate over time, of course, and have influenced other forms of blues-based popular music, including rap, hip-hop, and spoken-word verse, as well as the ways in which music is distributed and consumed.

4. During the summer of 1955 Ginsberg attempted to capture a greater sense of openness in his poetry. He emulated Kerouac's spontaneous prose style and considered how blues lyrics combined conversational language, repetition, and rhythms. Significantly, both types of writing were not based on traditional meters.

5. In the fifties San Francisco Renaissance and Beat writers formed a jazz poetry axis between the Bay Area and New York City that stirred the public's imagination. In 1955 Ginsberg moved from New York to Berkeley, and Lawrence Ferlinghetti opened City Lights Bookshop and City Lights Books (a publishing house) in San Francisco. On October 7, Kenneth Rexroth hosted a reading by Ginsberg, Gary Snyder, and others at Six Gallery in San Francisco. Earlier in 1955 *New World Writing*, a publication devoted to avant-garde artists, had featured an excerpt titled "Jazz of the Beat Generation" from Kerouac's novel *On the Road*.

6. See Tom Clark's interview with Ginsberg in the *Paris Review* (Spring 1966). In this and other interviews Ginsberg claimed that he had been suffering from depression because of a love affair gone awry with a fellow Beat, Neal Cassady, and that his direct communication with William Blake, who died in 1827, precipitated a metaphysical experience that lasted several days, during which he wandered around New York City and realized the sentience and interconnectedness of all things. Yet Ginsberg, who was keeping detailed journals at the time, didn't mention the incident in his journals or in his lengthy—and highly personal—correspondence with friends. William Morgan's biography indicates that in the months immediately following the alleged experience, he was undergoing psychotherapy and seeking a more conventional lifestyle. He took a job as an office boy at the *New Jersey Labor Herald*, and his letters to Kerouac claim that he had been "cured" of homosexuality and fallen in love with a woman. However, he later mythologized the "Blakean vision" in several poems and often stated that one of the reasons he used drugs was to recapture the experience.

7. In 1956 City Lights Books released *Howl and Other Poems*, and the book catapulted to fame when the US Customs Office leveled pornography charges against Ferlinghetti for publishing it. Ferlinghetti was arrested and the ACLU defended him. The trial drew national publicity, and Ferlinghetti later "recommended a medal be made for Collector MacPhee, since his action was already rendering the book famous. But police were soon to take over this advertising account and do a much better job—10,000 copies of *Howl* were in print by the time they finished with it." Lawrence Ferlinghetti, "Horn on *Howl*," in *On the Poetry of Allen Ginsberg*, ed. Lewis Hyde (Ann Arbor: University of Michigan Press, 1984), 43.

8. In the years before the Beat poets' climb to fame and the explosion of rock's popularity, Welshman Dylan Thomas served as a kind model, tantalizing American audiences with robust, boozy performances on four tours and dozens of radio broadcasts. Thomas's biographer, Andrew Lycett, points out that the poet "exhibited the excesses and experienced the adulation which would later be associated with rock stars. . . . Until Dylan's appearance, American poetry had been a modest, staid, and introverted affair . . . he anticipated the beat poets with his sense of theater and 'happening'" (Lycett 2004, 286).

9. See Berry Miles, *The Zapple Diaries: The Rise and Fall of the Last Beatles Label* (London: Peter Owen Publishers, 2015). In 1996 Ginsberg, McCartney, Philip Glass, and Lenny Kayne collaborated on *The Ballad of the Skeletons*, an audio CD (Mercury Records) of Ginsberg's poems set to music.

10. Matt Diehl, "It's a Joni Mitchell Concert, sans Joni," *Los Angeles Times*, April 22, 2010, https://www.latimes.com/archives/la-xpm-2010-apr-22-la-et-jonimitchell-20100422-story.html.

11. The Stones' image was, at least in part, a fabrication. Keith Richards, Charlie Watts, and Bill Wyman came from working-class families, but Brian Jones, the band's leader during in its early years, was the child of an aeronautical engineer, and his mother led their church choir. Mick Jagger was from a solidly middle-class family; his father was a teacher, and his mother was an active member of the Conservative Party. Jagger was a gifted student who briefly attended the London School of Economics.

12. See David Sheff, *All We Are Saying: The Last Major Interview with John Lennon and Yoko Ono* (New York: St. Martin's Griffin, 2000).

13. Paul and Linda McCartney, interview by Joan Goodman, *Playboy*, December 1984, http://www.beatlesinterviews.org/dbpm.int2.html.

14. McCartney, *Playboy* interview.

15. Jagger, *Rolling Stone* interview.

16. Keith Richards, "The Rolling Stones' Keith Richards Looks Back on 40 Years of Making Music," *Guitar World*, October 2002, https://www.guitarworld.com/gw-archive/rolling-stones-keith-richards-looks-back-40-years-music-gimme-shelter-interview.

17. Jagger, *Rolling Stone* interview.

18. While appealing the charges, the Stones recorded the single "We Love You," which opens with the sound of a prison door closing.

19. Ben Fong-Torres, "Jim Morrison's Got the Blues," *Rolling Stone*, August 5, 1971, https://archives.waiting-forthe-sun.net/Pages/Players/Personal/mcclure_recalls.html.

20. Howard Smith, "The *Village Voice* Interview with Jim Morrison," *Village Voice*, November 1970, https://archives.waiting-forthe-sun.net/Pages/Interviews/JimInterviews/village_voice.html.

Chapter 4

1. André Breton, "Manifesto of Surrealism" (1924), https://www.ubu.com/papers/breton_surrealism_manifesto.html

2. Bob Dylan, interviewed by Nat Hentoff, *Playboy*, March 1966. The interview was conducted in February 1966 and collected in Jonathan Cott, ed., *Dylan on Dylan: The Essential Interviews* (New York: Wenner Media, 2006). It can be found online at https://www.interferenza.net/bcs/interw/66-jan.htm.

3. Scott Timberg, "Romance, Regrets and Notebooks in the Freezer: Leonard Cohen's Son on His Father's Final Poems," *The Guardian*, September 28, 2018, https://www.theguardian.com/books/2018/sep/28/leonard-cohen-poetry-the-flame-adam-cohen-interview.

4. Timberg, "Romance, Regrets and Notebooks."

5. Federico García Lorca, "Theory and Play of the *Duende*," http://www.poetryintranslation.com/pitbr/Spanish/LorcaDuende.htm.

6. Lorca, "Theory and Play of the *Duende*."

7. Lorca, "Theory and Play of the *Duende*."

8. Lorca, "Theory and Play of the *Duende*."

Chapter 5

1. Reuters, "Bob Dylan Named Honorary Member of the American Academy of Arts and Letters," May 16, 2013.

2. John Clarke, "Bob Dylan Inducted into the American Academy of Arts and Letters," *Rolling Stone*, May 16, 2013, https://www.rollingstone.com/music/music-news/bob-dylan-inducted-into-american-academy-of-arts-and-letters-243564.

3. The French scholar and cleric Pierre Daniel Huet is widely credited for having advanced the case for the novel as literature in his treatise *Traitte de l'origine des romans* (1670). There are many works on the novel's development, including the following: Margaret Doody, *The True Story of the Novel* (New Brunswick, NJ: Rutgers University Press, 1996); Michael McKeon, *The Origins of the English Novel, 1600–1740* (Baltimore: Johns Hopkins University Press, 1987); Michael Schmidt, *The Novel: A Biography* (Cambridge, MA: Belknap Press, 2014); William B. Warner, *Literary to a Cultural History of the Early Novel* (Berkeley: University of California Press, 1998); Ian Watt, *The Rise of the Novel: Studies in Defoe, Richardson, and Fielding* (Berkeley: University of California Press, 1957).

4. Kurt Loder, "The *Rolling Stone* Interview: Bruce Springsteen on 'Born in the U.S.A.,'" *Rolling Stone*, December 6, 1984, https://www.rollingstone.com/music/music-news/the-rolling-stone-interview-bruce-springsteen-on-born-in-the-u-s-a-184690/.

5. Jon Landau, "Growing Young with Rock and Roll," *Real Paper*, May 22, 1974, http://www.brucespringsteen.it/Other/real.htm.

6. Greil Marcus, "Bruce Springsteen: Born to Run," *Rolling Stone*, October 9, 1975, https://www.rollingstone.com/music/music-album-reviews/born-to-run-87675/.

7. Loder, "*Rolling Stone* Interview."

8. Louis P. Masur, "Bruce Springsteen and American History," History News Network, https://historynewsnetwork.org/article/115729. Also see Masur's *Runaway Dream: Born to Run and Bruce Springsteen's American Vision* (London: Bloomsbury Press, 2010).

9. Joe Levy, "Bruce Springsteen: The *Rolling Stone* Interview," *Rolling Stone*, November 15, 2007, https://www.rollingstone.com/music/music-news/bruce-springsteen-the-rolling-stone-interview-238478/.

10. Springsteen notes that "half of the *Born in the U.S.A.* album was recorded at the time of *Nebraska*. When we initially went in the studio to try to record *Nebraska* with the band, we recorded the first side of *Born in the U.S.A.*, and the rest of the time I spent tryin' to come up with the second side—'Bobby Jean,' 'My Hometown,' almost all those songs. So if you look at the material, particularly on the first side, it's actually written very much like *Nebraska*—the characters and the stories, the style of writing—except it's just in the rock-band setting" (*Rolling Stone*, December 6, 1984). The title track from *Nebraska* draws on Malick's film (based on Charles Starkweather and his girlfriend's 1958 killing spree) and O'Connor's story "A Good Man is Hard to Find." The song's last line "Well sir I guess there's just a meanness in this world"—echoes O'Connor's villain, the "Misfit": "it's nothing for you to do but enjoy the few minutes you got left the best way you can—by killing somebody or burning down his house or doing some other meanness to him."

11. Mikal Gilmore, "The *Rolling Stone* 20th Anniversary Interview: Bruce Springsteen," *Rolling Stone*, November 5, 1987, https://www.rollingstone.com/music/music-news/the-rolling-stone-20th-anniversary-interview-bruce-springsteen-2-231800/.

12. "Music: Motown Beatitudes," *Time*, October 11, 1971, http://content.time.com/time/subscriber/article/0,33009,903183-1,00.html.

13. Lydia Hutchinson, "Bobbie Gentry's 'Ode To Billie Joe,'" *Performing Songwriter*, July 27, 2013, http://performingsongwriter.com/bobbie-gentry-ode-billie-joe.

14. Hutchinson, "Bobbie Gentry's 'Ode To Billie Joe.'"

15. Scott Mervis, "Betty Davis, a Funk Icon Living in Homestead," *Pittsburg Post-Gazette*, July 22, 2019, https://www.post-gazette.com/ae/music/2019/07/22/Betty-Davis-interview-funk-legend-Homestead-Miles-A-Little-Bit-Hot-Tonight/stories/201907220086.

16. The brainchild of poet T. R. Hummer and veteran musician Billy Cioffi, AmeriCamera explores Americana by probing the synergy between poetry and blues-based rock. Hummer, a multi-instrumentalist who has published nine books of poetry and edited the *Kenyon Review* and the *Georgia Review*, claims that reading Robert Penn Warren's essay "Pure and Impure Poetry" provided him with a strategy for amalgamating his interests in music, literature, criticism, philosophy, history, and myth. Cioffi, a professional musician with deep literary interests, has toured and played guitar with Bo Diddley, Chuck Berry, Del Shannon, and Ben E. King, and recorded with George Harrison, Jeff Lynne, Tom Petty, and others. *Highminded* consists of interrelated songs and poetic vignettes that form an homage to Walt Whitman, Emily Dickinson, T. S. Eliot, Elvis Presley, Robert Johnson, Chuck Berry, Richard Hugo, Otis Redding, Bob Dylan, Sam Cooke, Gram Parsons, and others. The recording's structure echoes the blues' dominant verse form. Hummer asserts that he and Cioffi strove to "capitalize on the possibility of the various traditions of what (mostly) text-based poetry might become in a call-and-response relationship with the traditions of American popular music, particularly the family of musics generally lumped together under the marketing label 'rock.'" See Hummer and Cioffi's essay on creating *Highminded*: "Call and Response," *Five Points* 15, no. 3 (Fall 2013): 182–98.

17. Holden, "Pop: Carroll's Anthem Eulogizes Peers."

18. Marc Myers, "The Sound of Going to Pieces," *Wall Street Journal*, August 29, 2013, https://www.wsj.com/articles/the-sound-of-going-to-pieces-1377812079.

19. Andy Gensler, "The *Daily Swarm* Interview with Gil Scott-Heron—The Revolution Will Not Be Blogged," March 10, 2010, http://www.thedailyswarm.com/swarm/daily-swarm-interviewgil-scott-heron-revolution-will-not-be-blogged.

20. "Lucinda Williams on Discovering Bob Dylan: 'This Is What I Want to Do,'" *Los Angeles Times Music Blog*, January 20, 2012, https://latimesblogs.latimes.com/music_blog/2012/01/lucinda-williams-bob-dylan-tribute-chimes-of-freedom-amnesty-international.html.

21. "Miller and Lucinda Williams: All in the Family," Poets.org, February 19, 2014, https://poets.org/text/miller-lucinda-williams-all-family.

22. Madeleine Schwartz, "An Interview with Lucinda Williams," *The Believer*, July 1, 2012, https://believermag.com/an-interview-with-lucinda-williams.

23. Williams, "All in the Family."

24. Schwartz, "An Interview with Lucinda Williams."

25. Steve Pond, "Lucinda Williams," *Rolling Stone*, January 26, 1989, 46.

26. Chris Mundy, "Lucinda Williams' Home-Grown Masterpiece," *Rolling Stone*, August 6, 1998, https://www.rollingstone.com/music/music-news/lucinda-williams-home-grown-masterpiece-79686/.

27. The address was published in Michael Chabon, "Let It Rock," *New York Review of Books*, July 11, 2013, https://www.nybooks.com/articles/2013/07/11/let-it-rock/.

28. James Sullivan, "Chuck Berry, Leonard Cohen Get First PEN Songwriting Awards," *Rolling Stone*, February 27, 2012, https://www.rollingstone.com/music/music-news/chuck-berry-leonard-cohen-get-first-pen-songwriting-awards-106279/.

Works Cited and Consulted

Altschuler, Glenn C. 2003. *All Shook Up: How Rock 'n' Roll Changed America.* New York: Oxford University Press.
Amburn, Ellis. 1999. *Subterranean Kerouac: The Hidden Life of Jack Kerouac.* New York: MacMillan.
Anderson, T. J., III. 2004. *Notes to Make the Sound Come Right: Four Innovations of Jazz Poetry.* Fayetteville: University of Arkansas Press.
Appleford, Steve. 1997. *The Rolling Stones: The Stories behind the Biggest Songs.* London: Carlton Books Limited.
Aronowitz, Al. 1995. "The Blacklisted Journalist." http://www.johnlennon.it/al-aronowitz-eng.htm.
Baker, Damani, and Alex Vlack, dirs. 2009. *Still Bill.* Late Night and Weekends Productions.
Baker, Houston A., Jr. 1987. *Modernism and the Harlem Renaissance.* Chicago: University of Chicago Press.
Bangs, Lester, and Greil Marcus, eds. 2003. *Psychotic Reactions and Carburetor Dung.* New York: Anchor Books.
Baraka, Amiri. 1963. *Blues People: Negro Music in White America.* New York: William Morrow.
Barnett, Lashonda Katice. 2007. *I Got Thunder: Black Women Songwriters on Their Craft.* New York: Thunder's Mouth Press.
Benét, Stephen Vincent. 1942. Foreword to *For My People,* by Margaret Walker. New Haven, CT: Yale University Press.
Berry, Chuck. 1987. *Chuck Berry: The Autobiography.* New York: Harmony Books.
Bertrand, Michael T. 2005. *Race, Rock, and Elvis.* Champaign: University of Illinois Press.
Bloom, Harold. 1973. *The Anxiety of Influence: A Theory of Poetry.* New York: Oxford University Press.
Bloomfield, Mike. 1999. *Big Joe and Me.* San Francisco: Re/Search Publications.
Bly, Robert. 1959. "On English and American Poetry." *The Fifties,* no. 2.
Bly, Robert. 1962. *Silence in the Snowy Fields.* Middletown, CT: Wesleyan University Press.
Bly, Robert. 1972. *Leaping Poetry: An Idea with Poems and Translation.* Madison, WI: Seventies Press.
Bolden, Tony. 2003. *Afro-Blue: Improvisations in African American Poetry and Culture.* Champaign: University of Illinois Press.

Bradley, Adam. 2009. *Book of Rhymes: The Poetics of Hip Hop*. New York: Basic Civitas Books.
Bradley, Adam. 2017. *The Poetry of Pop*. New Haven: Yale University Press.
Breslin, James E. B. 1985. *From Modern to Contemporary: American Poetry 1945–1965*. Chicago: University of Chicago Press.
Brinnin, John Malcolm. 2000. *Dylan Thomas in America*. London: Prion Lost Treasures.
Brooks, Cleanth, R. W. B. Lewis, and Robert Penn Warren. 1973. *American Literature: The Makers and the Making*. Vol. 2. New York: St. Martin's Press.
Brothers, Thomas. 2006. *Louis Armstrong's New Orleans*. New York: W.W. Norton.
Brown, Sterling A. 1989. *The Collected Poems of Sterling Brown*. Edited by Michael S. Harper. Evanston, IL: TriQuarterly Press.
Burger, Jeff. 2018. *Dylan on Dylan: Interviews and Encounters*. Chicago: Chicago Review Press.
Callois, Roger. 1965. *Au coeur du fantastique*. Paris: Gallimard, 1965.
Calt, Stephen. 1994. *I'd Rather Be the Devil: Skip James and the Blues*. Chicago: Chicago Review Press.
Chabon, Michael. 2013. "Let It Rock." *New York Review of Books*, July, 11, 2013: 26–27.
Charters, Ann. 1992. *The Portable Beat Reader*. New York: Viking Press.
Charters, Samuel. 1959. *The Country Blues*. New York: Rinehart and Company.
Charters, Samuel. 1963. *The Poetry of the Blues*. New York: Oak Publications.
Clark, Tom. 1966. "Allen Ginsberg, The Art of Poetry No. 8." *The Paris Review* 10, no. 37 (Spring 1966): 13–55.
Cook, Bruce. 1971. *The Beat Generation: The Tumultuous '50s and Its Impact on Today*. New York: Charles Scribner's Sons.
Cott, Jonathan, ed. 2006. *Dylan on Dylan: The Essential Interviews*. New York: Wenner Media.
Coupe, Laurence. 2007. *Beat Sound, Beat Vision: The Beat Spirit and Popular Song*. Manchester, UK: University of Manchester Press.
Creeley, Robert. 2008. *Selected Poems: 1945–2005*. Berkeley: University of California Press.
Dannen, Fredric. 1990. *Hit Men: Power Brokers and Fast Money inside the Music Business*. New York: Vintage Books.
Davis, Angela Y. 1998. *Blues Legacies and Black Feminism*. New York: Vintage Books.
Davis, Francis. 2003. *The History of the Blues: The Roots, the Music, the People*. Cambridge, MA: Da Capo Press.
Densmore, John. 1990. *Riders on the Storm: My Life with Jim Morrison and the Doors*. New York: Delta.
Dickey, James. 1965. "Barnstorming for Poetry." *New York Times Book Review*, January 3, 1965, https://archive.nytimes.com/www.nytimes.com/books/98/08/30/specials/dickey-barnstorming.html.
Dickey, James. 1967. *Poems, 1957–1967*. Middletown, CT: Wesleyan University Press.
Dickey, James. 1971. *Sorties*. New York: Doubleday.
Dickinson, Jim. 2017. *I'm Just Dead, I'm Not Gone*. Edited by Ernest Suarez. Jackson: University Press of Mississippi.
Doors, the. 1978. *The Complete Lyrics*. Compiled by Danny Sugerman. New York: Delta.
Doors, the, with Ben Fong-Torres. 2006. *The Doors*. New York: Hyperion.
Dylan, Bob. 2004. *Chronicles: Volume One*. New York: Simon and Schuster.
Edwards, Honeyboy. 1997. *The World Don't Owe Me Nothing: The Life and Times of Delta Bluesman Honeyboy Edwards*. Chicago: Chicago Review Press.
Ellison, Ralph. 1945. "Richard Wright's Blues." *Antioch Review* 5, no. 2 (Summer 1945): 198–211.

Ellison, Ralph. 1964. *Shadow and Act*. New York: Random House.
Eliot, T. S. 1921. "Tradition and the Individual Talent." In *The Sacred Wood: Essays on Poetry and Criticism*, 42–53. New York: Alfred A. Knopf.
Fahey, John. 2000. *How Bluegrass Music Destroyed My Life*. Chicago: Drag City.
Farley, Christopher John. 2004. "Elvis Rocks. But He's Not the First." *Time*, December 6, 2004, Entertainment section.
Feinstein, Sascha. 1997. *Jazz Poetry: From the 1920s to the Present*. Westport, CT: Praeger Publishers.
Feinstein, Sascha. 2007. *Ask Me Now: Conversations on Jazz and Literature*. Bloomington: Indiana University Press.
Ferlinghetti, Lawrence. 1957. "Horn on Howl." *Evergreen Review* 1, no. 4 (1957): 145–58.
Fernandes, Sujatha. 2011. *Close to the Edge: In Search of the Global Hip Hop Generation*. New York: Verso.
Filene, Benjamin. 2000. *Public Memory and American Roots Music*. Chapel Hill: University of North Carolina Press.
Flanagan, Bill. 1987. *Written in My Soul: Conversations with Rock's Great Songwriters*. Chicago: Contemporary Books.
Fowlie, Wallace. 1994. *Rimbaud and Jim Morrison: Two Rebel Poets*. Durham, NC: Duke University Press.
Fricke, David. 1989. "Lou Reed: The Rolling Stone Interview." *Rolling Stone*, May 4, 1989, https://www.rollingstone.com/music/music-news/lou-reed-the-rolling-stone-interview-2-174015/.
Gaye, Frankie, with Fred Basten. 2003. *Marvin Gaye, My Brother*. Guilford, CT: Backbeat Books.
Ginsberg, Allen. 1974. *Allen Verbatim: Lectures on Poetry, Politics, Consciousness*. Edited by Gordon Ball. New York: McGraw-Hill.
Ginsberg, Allen. 2006. *Collected Poems 1947–1997*. New York: HarperCollins.
Gray, Michael. 2000. *Song and Dance Man III: The Art of Bob Dylan*. New York: St. Martin's Press.
Greenfield, Robert. 2011. *The Last Sultan: The Life and Times of Ahmet Ertegun*. New York: Simon and Schuster.
Grualnick, Peter. 1994. *Last Train to Memphis*. New York: Bay Back Books.
Guthrie, Woody. 1943. *Bound for Glory*. New York: E. P. Dutton.
Hajdu, David. 2001. *Positively 4th Street: The Lives and Times of Joan Baez, Bob Dylan, Mimi Baez Farina, and Richard Farina*. New York: Farrar, Straus and Giroux.
Hamilton, Jack. 2016. *Just Around Midnight: Rock and Roll and the Racial Imagination*. Cambridge, MA: Harvard University Press.
Handy, W. C. 1969. *Father of the Blues: An Autobiography*. Cambridge, MA: Da Capo Press. First published in 1941 by Macmillan, with an introduction by Arna Bontemps.
Hartman, Charles O. 1991. *Jazz Text: Voice and Improvisation in Poetry, Jazz, and Song*. Princeton, NJ: Princeton University Press.
Heilbut, Anthony. 1972. *The Gospel Sound: Good News in Bad Times*. Guilford, CT: Limelight.
Henderson, Stephen. 1973. *Understanding the New Black Poetry: Black Speech and Black Music*. New York: William Morrow.
Hepworth, David. 2016. *Never a Dull Moment: 1971; The Year that Rock Exploded*. New York: St. Martin's Griffin.

Hollander, John. 1961. *The Untuning of the Sky: Ideas of Music in English Poetry, 1500–1700*. Princeton, NJ: Princeton University Press.
Hopkins, Jerry. 1992. *The Lizard King: The Essential Jim Morrison*. New York: Charles Scribner's Sons.
Hopkins, Jerry, and Danny Sugerman. 1980. *No One Gets Out of Here Alive*. New York: Barnes and Noble Books.
Hughes, Langston. 1940. *The Big Sea: An Autobiography*. New York: Hill and Wang.
Hughes, Langston. 1995. *The Collected Poems of Langston Hughes*. London: Vintage Classics.
Hummer, T. R. 2019. "'On a Jet to the Promised Land': Riding the Lyric Turbine." *Five Points: A Journal of Literature and Art* 19, no. 2 (Summer 2019): 132–40.
Hummer, T. R., and Billy Cioffi. 2013. "Call and Response: How Humans Live, Love, Create, Get Ten Dollars for a Cup of Coffee, and by Extension How We Wrote *Highminded*." *Five Points: A Journal of Literature and Art* 15, no. 3 (Fall 2013): 182–98.
Hyde, Lewis. 1998. *Trickster Makes This World*. New York: Farrar, Strauss and Giroux.
Jackson, Andrew Grant. 2015. *1965: The Most Revolutionary Year in Music*. New York: Thomas Dunne Books.
Jackson, John. 1991. *Big Beat Heat: Alan Freed and the Early Years of Rock and Roll*. New York: Schirmer Books.
Johnson, James Weldon. 1917. "The Negro's Contributions to American Art." *The Literary Digest*, October 20, 1917.
Johnson, James Weldon. 1922. *The Book of American Negro Poetry*. New York: Harcourt, Brace and Company.
Johnson, James Weldon. 1932. Preface to *Southern Road*, by Sterling A. Brown. San Diego: Harcourt Brace.
Keller, Lynn. 1987. *Remaking It New: Contemporary American Poetry and the Modernist Tradition*. Cambridge: Cambridge University Press.
Kelly, Robert. 1961. "Notes on the Poetry of Deep Image." *Trobar* 2 (1961): 14–16.
Kerouac, Jack. 1958. *The Dharma Bums*. New York: Viking Press.
Kramer, Michael J. 2013. *The Republic of Rock: Music and Citizenship in the Sixties Counterculture*. New York: Oxford University Press.
Kubik, Gerhard. 1999. *Africa and the Blues*. Jackson: University Press of Mississippi.
Kun, Josh. 2005. *Audiotopia: Music, Race, and America*. Berkeley: University of California Press.
Lait, Jack, and Lee Mortimer. 1952. *USA Confidential*. New York: Crown Publishers.
Lauterbach, Preston. 2011. *The Chitlin' Circuit and the Road to Rock 'n' Roll*. New York: W.W. Norton.
Lomax, Alan. 2002. *The Land Where the Blues Began*. New York: New Press.
Lordi, Emily J. 2013. *Black Resonance: Iconic Women Singers and African American Literature*. New Brunswick, NJ: Rutgers University Press.
Lowell, Robert. 1959. *Life Studies*. New York: Farrar, Straus and Giroux.
Lycett, Andrew. 2004. *Dylan Thomas: A New Life*. New York: Overlook Press.
MacLowry, Randall, dir. 2001. *American Experience*. "Stephen Foster." Aired April 23, 2001, on PBS. http://www.pbs.org/wgbh/amex/foster/sfeature/sf_minstrelsy_10.html.
Mahon, Maureen. 2004. *Right to Rock: The Black Coalition and the Cultural Politics of Race*. Durham, NC: Duke University Press.
Mailer, Norman. 1968. *Armies of the Night: History as a Novel, the Novel as History*. New York: Signet.
Manzarek, Ray. 1998. *Light My Fire: My Life with The Doors*. New York: G. P. Putnam's Sons.

Marcus, Greil. 1989. *Lipstick Traces: A Secret History of the Twentieth Century*. Cambridge, MA: Harvard University Press.
Marcus, Greil. 1998. *Invisible Republic: Bob Dylan's Basement Tapes*. New York: Picador.
Marquesee, Mark. 2005. *Wicked Messenger: Bob Dylan and the 1960s*. New York: Seven Stories Press.
Marsh, Dave. 1996. *Born to Run: The Bruce Springsteen Story*. New York: Thunder's Mouth Press.
Martin, Linda, and Kerry Segrave. 1993. *Anti-Rock: The Opposition to Rock 'n' Roll*. Cambridge, MA: Da Capo Press.
Masur, Louis P. 2010. *Runaway Dream: Born to Run and Bruce Springsteen's American Vision*. London: Bloomsbury Press.
Middlebrook, Diane Wood. 1992. *Anne Sexton: A Biography*. New York: Vintage Books.
Miles, Berry. 2015. *The Zapple Diaries: The Rise and Fall of the Last Beatles Label*. London: Peter Owen Publishers.
Miller, James. 1999. *Flowers in the Dustbin: The Rise of Rock and Roll, 1947–1977*. New York: Simon and Schuster.
Miller, Karl Hagstrom. 2010. *Segregating Sound: Inventing Folk and Pop Music in the Age of Jim Crow*. Durham, NC: Duke University Press.
Morgan, Bill. 2006. *I Celebrate Myself: The Somewhat Private Life of Allen Ginsberg*. New York: Penguin Books.
Murray, Albert. 2017. *Stomping the Blues*. Minneapolis: University of Minnesota Press.
Murray, Albert. 2020. *Omni-Americans: Some Alternatives to the Folklore of White Supremacy*. With a foreword by Henry Louis Gates. New York: Library of America.
Nelson, Cary. 1981. *Our Last First Poets: Vision and History in Contemporary American Poetry*. Champaign: University of Illinois Press.
Nielsen, Aldon Lynn. 1997. *Black Chant: Languages of African-American Postmodernism*. Cambridge: Cambridge University Press.
O'Hara, Frank. 1964. *Lunch Poems*. San Francisco: City Lights Pocket Series.
Olsen, Tillie. 1978. *Silences*. New York: Feminist Press at CUNY.
Olson, Charles, and Ezra Pound. 1991. *An Encounter at St. Elizabeths*. Edited by Catherine Seelye. New York: Paragon House.
Palladino, Grace. 1996. *Teenagers: An American History*. New York: Basic Books.
Palmer, Robert. 1981. *Deep Blues*. New York: Penguin Books.
Pegg, Bruce. 2002. *Brown Eyed Handsome Man: The Life and Hard Times of Chuck Berry*. London: Routledge.
Pence, Charlotte, ed. 2012. *The Poetics of American Song Lyrics*. Jackson: University Press of Mississippi.
Pennebaker, D. A., dir. 1967. *Don't Look Back*. N.p.: Leacock-Pennebaker Inc.
Plath, Sylvia. 1965. *Ariel: Poems*. London: Faber Poetry.
Radono, Ronald. 2003. *Lying Up a Nation: Race and Black Music*. Chicago: University of Chicago Press.
Rampersad, Arnold. 1995. Introduction to *The Collected Poems of Langston Hughes*. London: Vintage Classics.
Ramsey, Guthrie P., Jr. 2003. *Race Music: Black Cultures from Bebop to Hip-Hop*. Berkeley: University of California Press.
Ratliff, Ben. 2013. "Lou Reed, 1942–2013: Outsider Whose Dark, Lyrical Vision Helped Shape Rock 'n' Roll." *New York Times*, October 27, 2013, https://www.nytimes.com/2013/10/28/arts/music/lou-reed-dies-at-71.html.

Ribowsky, Mark. 2010. *Signed, Sealed, and Delivered: The Soulful Journey of Stevie Wonder*. New York: Wiley.
Richards, Keith. 2010. *Life*. Boston: Little, Brown and Company.
Ricks, Christopher. 2004. *Dylan's Visions of Sin*. New York: Ecco Press.
Ritz, David. 1991. *Divided Soul: The Life of Marvin Gaye*. Cambridge, MA: Da Capo Press.
Romine, Scott. 2008. *The Real South: Southern Narrative in the Age of Cultural Reproduction*. Baton Rouge: Louisiana State University Press.
Rose, Tricia. 1994. *Black Noise: Rap Music and Black Culture in Contemporary America*. Middletown, CT: Wesleyan University Press.
Rose, Tricia. 2008. *The Hip Hop Wars: What We Talk About When We Talk About Hip Hop—and Why It Matters*. New York: Civitas Books.
Rotolo, Suze. 2008. *A Freewheelin' Time: A Memoir of Greenwich Village in the Sixties*. New York: Broadway Books.
Russell, Ethan A. 2009. *Let It Bleed: The Rolling Stones, Altamont, and the End of the Sixties*. New York: Springboard Press.
Salewicz, Chris. 2005. *Redemption Song: The Definitive Biography of Joe Strummer*. New York: HarperCollins.
Schonberg, Harold C. 1970. *The Lives of Five Great Composers*. New York: W.W. Norton.
Scorsese, Martin, dir. 2005. *No Direction Home*. Los Angeles: Paramount Pictures.
Scorsese, Martin, dir. 2019. *Rolling Thunder Revue: A Bob Dylan Story*. Netflix.
Segrest, James, and Mark Hoffman. 2005. *Moanin' at Midnight: The Life and Times of Howlin' Wolf*. Cambridge, MA: Da Capo Press.
Sheff, David. 2000. *All We Are Saying: The Last Major Interview with John Lennon and Yoko Ono*. New York: St. Martin's Griffin.
Shelton, Robert. 1997. *No Direction Home: The Life and Music of Bob Dylan*. Cambridge, MA: Da Capo Press.
Siff, Stephen. 2008. "Henry Luce's Strange Trip: Coverage of LSD in *Time* and *Life*, 1954–1968." *Journalism History* 34, no. 3 (2008): 126–34.
Smith, Harry Everett, ed. 1952. *Anthology of American Folk Music*. Folkways Records SFW40090, 6 compact discs.
Solt, Andrew, dir. 1995. *The History of Rock 'n' Roll*. "Rock 'n' Roll Explodes." Aired March 6, 1995, on PBS.
Sornberger, Lisa and John. 2013. *Gathered Light: The Poetry of Joni Mitchell's Songs*. Toronto: Three O'Clock Press.
Spitz, Bob. 2005. *The Beatles: The Biography*. Boston: Little, Brown and Company.
Stone, Robert. 2007. *Prime Green: Remembering the Sixties*. New York: Ecco Press.
Suarez, Ernest. 1999. *Southbound: Interviews with Southern Poets*. Columbia: University of Missouri Press.
Szatmary, David. 1996. *A Time to Rock: A Social History of Rock 'n' Roll*. New York: Schirmer Books.
Todorov, Tzvetan. 1973. *The Fantastic: A Structural Approach to a Literary Genre*. Ithica, NY: Cornell University Press.
Tosches, Nick. 1999. *Unsung Heroes of Rock 'n' Roll*. Cambridge, MA: Da Capo Press.
Tracy, Steven C. 2001. *Langston Hughes and the Blues*. Champaign: University of Illinois Press.
Tracy, Steven C. 2015. *Hot Music, Ragmentation, and the Bluing of American Literature*. Tuscaloosa: University of Alabama Press.

Van Ronk, Dave, with Elijah Wald. 2005. *The Mayor of MacDougal Street: A Memoir*. Cambridge, MA: Da Capo Press.
Von Hallberg, Robert. 1985. *American Poetry and Culture, 1945–1980*. Cambridge, MA: Harvard University Press.
Wald, Elijah. 2004. *Escaping the Delta: Robert Johnson and the Invention of the Blues*. New York: Amistad.
Wald, Gayle. 2007. *Shout, Sister, Shout: The Untold Story of Rock-and-Roll Trailblazer Sister Rosetta Tharpe*. Boston: Beacon Press.
Walser, Robert. 1998. "The Rock and Roll Era." In *The Cambridge History of American Music*. Cambridge: Cambridge University Press.
Warner, Simon. 2013. *Text and Drugs and Rock 'n' Roll: The Beats and Rock Culture*. London: Bloomsbury Press.
Warren, Robert Penn. 1957. "The Art of Fiction No. 18." Interview by Ralph Ellison and Eugene Walter. *Paris Review*, no. 16 (Spring/Summer 1957): 112–40.
White, Charles. 1984. *The Life and Times of Little Richard: The Quasar of Rock*. New York: Harmony.
White, Charles. 2003. *The Life and Times Of Little Richard: The Authorized Press*. London: Omnibus Press.
Woolf, Virginia. 1924. "Character in Fiction." *The Criterion* 2, no. 8 (July 1924): 409–30.
Yaffe, David. 2006. *Fascinating Rhythm: Reading Jazz in American Writing*. Princeton, NJ: Princeton University Press.
Yaffe, David. 2011. *Bob Dylan: Like a Complete Unknown*. New Haven: Yale University Press.
Yaffe, David. 2017. *Reckless Daughter: A Portrait of Joni Mitchell*. New York: Sarah Crichton Books.
Young, Kevin. 2012. *The Grey Album On the Blackness of Blackness*. Minneapolis: Graywolf Press.

Credits

"Elvis and Eliot" from *Highminded*. © Americamera. Reprinted by permission.
Robert Creeley, excerpts from "I Know a Man," from *The Collected Poems of Robert Creeley 1945–1975*. Copyright © 1962 by Robert Creeley. Reprinted with the permission of the Permissions Company, LLC, on behalf of Penelope Creeley.
"Like a Rolling Stone," written by Bob Dylan. Copyright © 1965 by Warner Bros. Inc.; renewed 1993 by Special Rider Music. All rights reserved. International copyright secured. Reprinted by permission.
"Motorpsycho Nitemare," written by Bob Dylan. Copyright © 1964 by Warner Bros. Inc.; renewed 1992 by Special Rider Music. All rights reserved. International copyright secured. Reprinted by permission.
"Midnight Rambler," written by Mick Jagger and Keith Richards. Published by ABKCO Music, Inc. Used by permission. All rights reserved.
"Helplessly Hoping," words and music by Stephen Stills. Copyright © 1969 Gold Hill Music, Inc. Copyright renewed. All rights reserved. Used by permission. *Reprinted by permission of Hal Leonard LLC.*
"The End," words and music by John Densmore, Robby Krieger, Ray Manzarek, and Jim Morrison. Copyright © 1967 Doors Music Company, LLC. Copyright renewed. All rights administered by Wixen Music Publishing, Inc. All rights reserved. Used by permission. *Reprinted by permission of Hal Leonard LLC.*
"The Message," words and music by Edward Fletcher, Clifton Chase, Sylvia Robinson, and Melvin Glover. Copyright © 1982 Sugar Hill Music Publishing Ltd. and Twenty Nine Black Music. All rights controlled and administered by Songs of Universal, Inc. All rights reserved. Used by permission. *Reprinted by permission of Hal Leonard LLC.*
"Suzanne," words and music by Leonard Cohen. Copyright © 1967, 1995 Sony/ATV Music Publishing LLC. Copyright renewed. All rights administered by Sony/ATV Music Publishing LLC, 424 Church Street, Suite 1200, Nashville, TN 37219. International copyright secured. All rights reserved. *Reprinted by permission of Hal Leonard LLC.*
"Grandma's Hands," words and music by Bill Withers. Copyright © 1971 Interior Music Corp. Copyright renewed. All rights controlled and administered by Songs of Universal, Inc. All rights reserved. Used by permission. *Reprinted by permission of Hal Leonard LLC.*

"London Calling," words and music by Joe Strummer, Mick Jones, Paul Simonon, and Topper Headon. Copyright © 1979 Nineden Ltd. All rights in the US and Canada controlled and administered by Universal–Polygram International Publishing, Inc. All rights reserved. Used by permission. *Reprinted by permission of Hal Leonard LLC.*

"Clash City Rockers," words and music by Joe Strummer, Mick Jones, Paul Simonon, and Topper Headon. Copyright © 1979 Nineden Ltd. All rights in the US and Canada controlled and administered by Universal–Polygram International Publishing, Inc. All rights reserved. Used by permission. *Reprinted by permission of Hal Leonard LLC.*

"A Day In the Life," words and music by John Lennon and Paul McCartney. Copyright © 1967 Sony/ATV Music Publishing LLC. Copyright renewed. All rights administered by Sony/ATV Music Publishing LLC, 424 Church Street, Suite 1200, Nashville, TN 37219. International copyright secured. All rights reserved. *Reprinted by permission of Hal Leonard LLC.*

"What's Going On," words and music by Renaldo Benson, Alfred Cleveland, and Marvin Gaye. Copyright © 1970 Jobete Music Co., Inc., MGIII Music, NMG Music, and FCG Music. Copyright renewed. All rights administered by Sony/ATV Music Publishing LLC on behalf of Stone Agate Music (a division of Jobete Music Co., Inc.), 424 Church Street, Suite 1200, Nashville, TN 37219. International copyright secured. All rights reserved. *Reprinted by permission of Hal Leonard LLC.*

"You Say You Want a Revolution: The Blues, Poetry and Rock," by Mike Mattison and Ernest Suarez. Authors retain all copyrights. *Five Points: A Journal of Literature and Art* 15, no. 3 (2013): 145–67.

Bob Dylan at piano (image 86204288), Elliot Landy/Redferns photographer, permissions supplied via Getty Images.

Chuck Berry/Keith Richards (image #1088202125), Terry O'Neill photographer, Iconic Images Collection, permissions supplied via Getty Images.

Index

Abramson, Herb, 48
"Addict, The," 99
Adventures of Ozzie and Harriet, The, 47
aesthetic of disorientation, 46, 63, 68, 70, 72, 76–77, 90, 96, 109, 124, 128, 147, 151
Africa and the Blues, 37
Aftermath, 99
"Ain't No Sunshine," 169
Alice in Wonderland, 129
Allen, Donald, 105
Alligator Records, 34
"All I Really Want to Do," 70
Allman, Duane, 140, 161
Allman Brothers Band, 9, 190
All Shook Up, 47
All Quiet on the Western Front, 45
allusion (use of), 7, 37, 39, 43, 69, 71–72, 77–78, 82, 88, 109, 118, 124, 137, 172
"Almost Grown," 154
Alpert, Richard, 108
Altschuler, Glenn C., 47
Amboy Dukes, The, 135, 137
American Academy of Arts and Letters, 6–7, 145, 194
American Bandstand, 47, 171
American Beauty, 127
American Hit Parade, 49
"American Prayer, An," 117
Another Side of Bob Dylan, 63, 68, 91–92
Anthology of American Folk Music, 57
Anxiety of Influence, The, 86
appropriation, 25, 86, 179, 195

Are You Experienced?, 81, 128–29
"Are You Experienced?," 128–29, 135
Ariel, 131
Armies of the Night, The, 130–31
Aronowitz, Al, 92
Artaud, Antonin, 108
Asphalt Jungle, The, 47
Astral Weeks, 81
Atlantic Records, 48–49
Au Coeur du fantastique, 121
authenticity, 32–44, 46, 56–57, 59–60, 62–63, 70, 85, 87, 90–92, 98, 103, 109, 150, 179
"Autumn Begins in Martins Ferry, Ohio," 41
Avalon, Frankie, 57, 160
"Avalon Blues," 62

"Baby Let Me Follow You Down," 64
"Back in the U.S.A.," 56, 154
backmasking, 128–29, 135
Badlands, 152
"Bad-Man Stagolee," 20
Baez, Joan, 9, 57, 66, 190
Baker, Houston A., Jr., 20
Baldwin, James, 167
"Ballad of a Thin Man," 77–78, 93
"Ballad of Hollis Brown," 66
Bangs, Lester, 174, 181
Baraka, Amiri, 19, 24–25, 37
Basketball Diaries, The, 172
"Battle of Evermore, The," 43
"Bayonne Turnpike to Tuscarora," 90
Beat Generation, The, 5

Beatles, 3, 6, 9, 11, 15, 43, 71, 81, 85, 86, 89, 90, 92–99, 115, 121, 123, 126, 128, 135, 147, 150, 161–63, 194
Beat poets, 3–5, 19, 21, 23–24, 37, 42–43, 45, 62, 64, 67–68, 70–72, 76–78, 81, 83, 85, 87–90, 92, 103, 105–6, 108, 115, 121, 123–25, 131, 139, 147, 150, 185
Beck, Jeff, 161
Beggar's Banquet, 100
Beggar's Opera, The, 3
"Beginning of a Poem of These States," 89
"Being for the Benefit of Mr. Kite," 95
"Bells of St. Mary, The," 178
Benét, Stephen Vincent, 20
Bergman, Ingmar, 105
Berry, Chuck, 12–13, 28, 46, 48, 50–57, 59, 68, 71–77, 85, 121, 146, 150, 154, 181, 189, 193–94
Bertrand, Michael T., 49
Betty Davis, 167
Between the Buttons, 100
Big Brother and the Holding Company, 127
Big Joe and Me, 62
"Big John Henry," 20
Big Heat, The, 47
Big Mama Thornton, 48
Billboard, 49
Bill Haley and the Comets, 28
Biograph, 57, 67
Black Arts Movement, 25, 81, 139
Blackboard Jungle, 47
"Black Crow Blues," 68
"Black Dust Blues," 42
"Black Magic Woman," 43
Black Noise, 185
Blackstar, 82
Blake, William, 81–82, 87–88, 107, 129
"Blessing, A," 42
"Blinded by the Light," 10
Blonde on Blonde, 72, 78, 89, 93
Bloom, Harold, 86
Bloomfield, Mike, 62
"Blowin' in the Wind," 13, 65, 155, 161
Blue Angel, The, 105
blue notes, 27–28, 31, 33, 63
Blues: An Anthology, 17
Blues and Haiku, 23
Bly, Robert, 42, 131–33, 142

Bob Dylan, 63, 91
Bob Dylan: Like a Complete Unknown, 15
"Bob Dylan's Blues," 65
"Bob Dylan's Dream," 65
"Bob Dylan's 115th Dream," 72
Bob Wills and His Texas Playboys, 52
"Bo Diddley," 25, 74
Bogan, Lucille, 35
Book of American Negro Poetry, The, 17
Book of Nightmares, The, 131
Book of Rhymes, 8–9, 185
Boone, Pat, 57, 121
"Boots of Spanish Leather," 65–66
Born in the U.S.A., 153
"Born in the U.S.A.," 153–54, 173
Born to Run, 148–52, 154, 175
"Born to Run," 13
"Both Sides Now," 80
Bound for Glory, 57, 59
Bowie, David, 81–82, 140, 147, 172, 178
Bradley, Adam, 5, 8–9, 185
"Break on Through (to the Other Side)," 43
Brecht, Bertolt, 3
Breton, André, 120
Bridenthal, Bryn, 118
Bringing It All Back Home, 46, 70, 72, 89, 91, 93, 121
Brown, Nappy, 35–37
Brown, Norman O., 107
Brown, Sterling, 17, 19–20
Browne, Jackson, 9, 147
Browne, Tara, 95
"Brown Eyed Handsome Man," 12–13, 55–56, 68
"Brown Sugar," 102–3
Brown v. Board of Education, 48
Buckdancer's Choice, 131
Build, 186
Bulgakov, Mikhail, 100
Burnett, T Bone, 55
Burns, Robert, 3
Burroughs, William S., 89, 149
Byrds, 9, 81, 89
Byron, Lord, 86, 140

Caen, Herb, 23
Caillois, Roger, 121

Cale, John, 81, 89, 147
Calt, Stephen, 62
Campbell, Glen, 163
Camus, Albert, 67
Cannon, Gus, 58, 62
Cannon's Jug Stompers, 58
"Can't Explain," 176
Can't Stop Won't Stop, 185
Carolina Tar Heels, 58
Carrier of Ladders, The, 131
Carroll, Jim, 172
Carroll, Lewis, 129
Carter, Asa, 48
Caruso, Enrico, 122
Carver, Raymond, 193
Car Wheels on a Gravel Road, 191
"Car Wheels on a Gravel Road," 191–92
Cash, Johnny, 5, 74, 162
Castaneda, Carlos, 108, 156
Cecil, Malcolm, 161
"Celebration of the Lizard," 116
Cellar Jazz Quintet, 23
Celler, Emanuel, 48–49
Chabon, Michael, 6–7, 192–93
Chang, Jeff, 185
"Change Is Gonna Come, A," 155
Charles, Ray, 32, 35, 119, 155, 162, 168
Charters, Samuel, 57, 62
Chess, Leonard, 52
Chess Records, 48, 52, 74, 83, 98
"Chimes of Freedom," 70
Chitlin' Circuit and the Road to Rock 'n' Roll, The, 50
civil rights, 56, 66, 88, 130, 151, 155
Clapton, Eric, 32, 38, 140, 161, 168, 173
Clash, 173–86
"Clash City Rockers," 176–78
clave beat, 25–27, 74, 125, 142
Clinton, Bill, 190
Close to the Edge, 185
Cobb, Henry N., 145–46
Cochran, Eddie, 180
"Cocksucker Blues," 103
Cohen, Leonard, 3–5, 9, 15, 71, 135–38, 141, 147, 193–94
Collins, Judy, 9, 136
Coltrane, John, 46, 128

Columbia Records, 63, 135
Combat Rock, 184
Commager, Henry Steele, 152
community, 26, 30–31, 36, 83, 90, 125, 128, 152, 170, 187
Concert for Bangladesh, 128
"Confessin' the Blues," 51
confessional, 19, 36–37, 43, 99, 147, 149
Confessional poetry, 42, 78, 88
"Consulting I Ching Smoking Pot Listening to the Fugs Sing Black," 89
conversational style, 36–39, 41, 63, 96, 147, 149, 156–57, 163, 191
Cooder, Ry, 62, 147
Cook, Bruce, 5
Cooke, John, 58
Cooke, Sam, 9, 155
"Corrina Corrina," 65
Corso, Gregory, 71
Costello, Elvis, 9, 147, 185
counterculture, 76–78, 83, 90, 92, 110, 123–32, 147, 165
Count M'Butu, 26
Country Blues, The, 57, 62
Coupe, Laurence, 71
Coursan, Pamela, 116
Cowley, Malcolm, 126
Crane, Hart, 17, 132
Crawford, Hank, 32
Cray, Robert, 25, 191
Cream, 9, 25, 135
Creedence Clearwater Revival, 182
Creeley, Robert, 21–23, 37
Crosby, David, 71, 80
"Crossroads," 40, 142
"Crow Jane," 34–35
Crowley, Aleister, 58, 139
Crudup, Arthur, 48
"Crystal Ship, The," 115
culture, 25, 32, 45–46, 49–50, 54, 56–57, 60, 63, 71, 77, 82, 86, 90, 93, 95, 98, 107, 121–23, 125–26, 131, 134, 139–40, 145, 148, 151, 165–67, 179, 181, 194–95
cummings, e. e., 17, 67

dance, 18–19, 51, 55, 107, 176, 186
Dannen, Fredric, 166

Darkness on the Edge of Town, 152
Davis, Betty, 167–68, 172
Davis, Miles, 21, 25, 46, 154, 167
"Day in the Life, A," 95–97
Days of Future Passed, 81
Dead Emcee Scrolls, The, 172
death, 20, 41, 64, 95–96, 100, 106–7, 114, 118, 135, 139, 141, 143, 163, 165, 172, 183, 192
DeBella, John, 104
Decca, 103
Deep Blues, 16
Deep Image poets, 42, 108, 132
Dejani, Virginia, 145
Densmore, John, 104, 108, 114, 117
DeSalvo, Albert, 101
"Desolation Row," 77
Devil Is a Woman, The, 105
Dharma Burns, The, 88
Dickey, James, 43, 86, 131, 190
Dickinson, Emily, 190, 192
Dickinson, Jim, 62, 147
Diddley, Bo, 25, 50–51, 72, 74–75, 125, 154
"Diddley Daddy," 74
Didion, Joan, 115, 131
Dietrich, Marlene, 105
"Dirt Road Blues," 83
Dixon, Willie, 43, 52, 60
"Do It Good," 168–69
Domino, Fats, 48, 50, 67
"Don't Call Her No Tramp," 167
Don't Knock the Rock, 47
Don't Look Back, 89, 121
Doors, The, 3, 5, 9, 15, 43, 85, 86, 92, 98, 103–18, 124, 129, 139, 147, 190, 194
Doors, The, 81, 109–10
Doors of Perception, The, 81, 107, 129
Dostoevsky, Fyodor, 77
"Double Image, The," 39
"Dover Beach," 130
"Down Hearted Blues," 29–30
"Down the Highway," 65
Dragstrip Riot, 47
"Dream Boogie," 19
drugs, 76, 90, 96, 99, 103, 107–8, 124–29, 131, 134–35, 148, 156, 173, 184, 188
Duke Bootee, 186–87
Dunn, Donald "Duck," 168

Dylan, Bob, 3–7, 9, 13, 15, 21, 24, 32, 36, 43–44, 45–46, 50–52, 54–57, 59–60, 62–72, 76–78, 81–83, 85, 87, 88–93, 98–99, 103–4, 115, 118, 120–24, 135–36, 139–40, 145–51, 155, 161, 173, 189–92, 194
Dylan's Visions of Sin, 15

East of Eden, 47
Ed Sullivan Show, The, 50, 114
Edwards, David "Honeyboy," 61
Einstein, Albert, 146–47
"Eleanor Rigby," 94
Electric Kool-Aid Acid Test, 97, 125
Electric Ladyland, 141–42
Electric Prunes, 135
Elektra Records, 104, 108, 110, 113, 115, 118
Eliot, T. S., 17, 19, 43, 67, 86, 88, 95, 148, 150–51
Ellison, Ralph, 24–25, 77
"Empty Bed Blues," 38–39
"End, The," 43, 109–13
Ertegun, Ahmet, 48
Estes, Sleepy John, 59–61, 65
Evans, Honeyboy, 17
Everly Brothers, 93
"Everybody's Down on Me," 27
Exile on Main St., 100, 103

Fahey, John, 62
fantastic, 6, 41–43, 63, 72, 75, 109, 111, 113, 119–43, 147–48
Fantastic, The, 120
Father Knows Best, 47
Fellini, Federico, 69
Ferlinghetti, Lawrence, 23
Fernandes, Sujatha, 185
Fields, Danny, 114
Filene, Benjamin, 60
film, 47, 50, 53, 57, 59, 69–71, 83, 89, 91, 96–97, 104–5, 114–15, 117, 121, 123, 127–28, 164–65, 180
"Fine and Mellow," 29
"Fingertips (Part 2)," 160
"First Party at Ken Kesey's with Hell's Angels," 89
"Fixing a Hole," 95
"Fixin' to Die," 63
Flack, Roberta, 166, 172

"Flyin' High (in the Friendly Sky)," 159
Ford, John, 152
For My People, 19, 20
"For Once in My Life," 160
Fowlie, Wallace, 15
Francis, Connie, 57, 121
"Frankie and Johnny," 34
Franklin, Aretha, 9, 62, 103, 166–67
Frazer, George, 147
Freed, Alan, 48
Freewheelin' Bob Dylan, The, 63–65, 91–92
Freud, Sigmund, 86, 113, 133, 146
Fricke, Jim, 185
Frost, Robert, 88, 105
Fugs, 89, 130
Fullfillingness' First Finale, 161
Funicello, Annette, 160
Funk Brothers, 156, 158, 160
"Furry's Blues," 38

Garcia, Jerry, 126
Gardiner, Diane, 117
Garvey, Marcus, 178
Gasoline, 15
Gates, Henry Louis, 32
Gathered Light, 16
Gay, John, 3
Gaye, Anna, 155
Gaye, Frankie, 156
Gaye, Marvin, 6, 7, 9, 15, 147–48, 154, 155–60, 162, 164, 186, 189, 194
gender, 34, 50, 51, 162, 166–67, 171, 178
Gentle on My Mind, 163
Gentry, Bobbie, 9, 147, 162–65, 168, 169, 171–72, 193
"Getting Better," 95
Gillespie, Dizzy, 21, 46, 67
"Gimme Shelter," 101
Ginsberg, Allen, 39, 48, 64, 67, 70, 71, 74, 87–90, 122–23, 128, 131–32, 139
Give 'Em Enough Rope, 181
Glen Campbell & Bobbie Gentry, 163
Glitter, Gary, 178
Glover, John, 160
Goat's Head Soup, 100
"God is my friend," 159
Goldbrook, Alvah, 88

Goldstein, Richard, 5, 114
"Good Morning Good Morning," 95
"Good Rockin' Tonight," 48
Gordy, Berry, 155–56, 160
"Got My Mojo Working," 118
"Got the Farmland Blues," 58
Graffiti Grrlz, 186
"Grandma's Hands," 169–71
Grandmaster Flash and the Furious Five, 186, 189
Grateful Dead, 9, 126–27
Gray, Michael, 15
"Great Balls of Fire," 68
Greetings from Asbury Park, N.J., 149
Gregory, Dick, 66, 70
Grohl, Dave, 185
Guthrie, Arlo, 62, 147
Guthrie, Woody, 20, 45–46, 56–57, 59–60, 63, 67, 83, 85, 87, 140, 152, 176

Hajdu, David, 58–59, 67
Hall, Donald, 105
Hamilton, Jack, 98
Hammond, John, 63
Handy, W. C., 16–18, 20, 25, 36
Hansberry, Lorraine, 167
"Hard Rain's a-Gonna Fall, A," 64
Harlan, Howard, 173
Harris, Wynonie, 48
Harrison, George, 128
Haskell, Jimmie, 164
"Have Some Fun," 33
Hawkins, Screaming Jay, 83
Hayes, Isaac, 156
Headon, Topper, 182
Heartbreakers, 174
Heilbut, Anthony, 169
"Hellhound on My Trail," 42
Hell's Angels, 125
Help!, 93
"Helplessly Hoping," 78–80
Henderson, Stephen, 19
Hendrix, Jimi, 3, 10, 32, 43, 71, 81, 85, 121, 127–29, 135, 140–43, 150, 172, 194
"Hey! Bo Diddley," 74
"Hey Good Lookin'," 52
"Higher Ground," 186

"High Water Everywhere," 40
"Highway 51," 63–64
Highway 61 Revisited, 72, 77–78, 93, 148, 190
Hip Hop Wars, The, 185
History of Rock 'n' Roll, The, 51
Hitchcock, Alfred, 69
"Hitch Hike," 155
Hit Men, 166
Hoffman, Abbie, 130
Hofmann, Albert, 125
Holden, Stephen, 172
Holiday, Billie, 25, 29, 46, 155, 166
"Holiday in the Sun," 182
Holly, Buddy, 45, 55, 93
Holzman, Jac, 108
Honeymooners, The, 47
Hooker, John Lee, 40, 190
Hopkins, Gerard Manley, 193
Hopkins, Jerry, 115, 118
Horton, Willie, 155
Hoskins, Tom, 62
Hot Buttered Soul, 156
"Hound Dog," 28, 48
House, Son, 61
HouseRockers, 33–34
How Bluegrass Music Destroyed My Life, 62
Howe, Gordie, 155
"Howl," 88–89
Howl and Other Poems, 15, 74, 87–88
Howlin' Wolf, 13, 40, 43, 49, 61, 72, 83
Hughes, Langston, 17–19, 21, 23–24, 37, 81, 185
Hummer, T. R., 5, 56
Hunky Dory, 81
Hunter, Alberta, 29, 38–39
Hunter, Robert, 126–27
Hurt, Mississippi John, 20, 59–62
Huxley, Aldous, 81, 107, 129
Hyde, Lewis, 122

I Am the Blues, 52
"I Am the Walrus," 43
"I Can't Give Everything Away," 82
"I Contain Multitudes," 82
"Ida Red Likes the Boogie," 52
I Do Not Play No Rock 'n' Roll Y'all, 27
I'd Rather Be the Devil, 62
"I Fought the Law," 180

Iggy and the Stooges, 174
Iglauer, Bruce, 34
"I Had Too Much to Dream Last Night," 135
"I Have a Terrible Fear…," 133–34, 136
"I Heard It through the Grapevine," 155
"I Know a Man," 22–23
I Love Lucy, 47
imagery, 11, 43, 64–65, 71–72, 80, 92, 97, 101, 105, 114, 135, 139, 147–48, 151, 156, 161, 169
"I'm a Loser," 93
improvisation, 21–22, 114, 127, 166, 186
In a Lonely Place, 47
Inevitable Rise and Liberation of Niggy Tardust, The, 172
"In My Time of Dying," 63–64
"Inner City Blues (Make Me Wanna Holler)," 159, 186
Innervisions, 161
In Search of the Lost Chord, 126
instruments and instrumentation, 3, 10, 12–13, 21, 26, 28, 37, 48–49, 68, 74, 81, 96–97, 110, 128, 135, 140, 142–43, 146, 149, 157, 160, 164, 177, 184–85
Invisible Republic, 58
I Put a Spell on You, 167
"It Ain't Me Babe," 70
It's Only Rock 'n' Roll, 100
I Want to Live, 47
"I Was Made to Love Her," 160

Jackson, Al, Jr., 168
Jagger, Mick, 7, 9, 32, 44, 46, 51, 54, 71, 85, 98–103, 115, 116, 118, 121, 147, 150, 172
James, Etta, 166
James, Skip, 31, 34–35, 62, 100
"Jazzonia," 18
Jefferson, Blind Lemon, 63
Jefferson Airplane, 43, 128–29, 135
Jennings, Waylon, 9, 55
Jiménez, Juan Ramón, 132
"Johnny B. Goode," 28, 50, 54
Johnson, James Weldon, 17, 19–20
Johnson, Johnnie, 52, 55
Johnson, Robert, 25, 31, 35, 38, 40, 42, 61, 98, 100, 138–39, 141–42, 190, 192
Jones, Booker T., 168–69
Jones, Brian, 103, 128

Jones, Mick, 175, 180, 182
Joplin, Janis, 9, 109, 127, 140–41
"Journey to the Center of Your Mind," 135, 137
Joyce, James, 81
Judkins, Calvin, 160
Just as I Am, 168–69
"Just the Two of Us," 171

"Kaddish," 39
Katz, Mark, 186
Keltner, Jim, 168
Kennedy, Caroline, 193–94
Kerouac, Jack, 23, 45, 48, 67, 71, 72, 74, 88–89
Kesey, Ken, 89, 97, 125–26
Khan, Hazrat Inayat, 13
King, Albert, 62, 81
King, B. B., 25, 32, 51, 61
King, Carole, 9, 15, 147, 166
King, Freddie, 143
Kinks, 15, 85
Kinnell, Galway, 131
Kipling, Rudyard, 130
Knights of Pythias, 16
Kooper, Al, 77
Krieger, Robby, 109, 117
Kubik, Gerhard, 37
Kupferberg, Tuli, 131

La dolce vita, 69
"Lady Lazarus," 42–43
Lait, Jack, 48, 55
Landau, Jon, 148, 150, 152
Land Where the Blues Began, The, 16
Lauterbach, Preston, 50
"L.A. Woman," 117–18
Lead Belly, 26, 45, 86
Leaping Poetry, 132–33
Leary, Timothy, 43, 89–90, 108
Leave It to Beaver, 47
Leaves of Grass, 194
Led Zeppelin, 9, 25, 35, 43, 139
"Legend of a Mind," 43
Leiber, Jerry, 48
"Lemon Song," 35
Lennon, John, 7, 9, 32, 44, 46, 54, 71, 88, 92–93, 95–97, 118, 147
Leone, Sergio, 152

Let It Bleed, 100–101, 116
Lewis, Furry, 20, 38, 59–60, 62
Lewis, Jerry Lee, 68, 85, 162
Lewis, John, 56
Life magazine, 57, 108, 114
Life Studies, 6, 37, 72
Light Around the Body, The, 131–32
Lightfoot, Gordon, 9, 147, 190
"Light My Fire," 109, 116
Light My Fire: My Life with The Doors, 105–6
"Like a Rolling Stone," 98–99, 123–24
"Lining Track," 26–27
Lipscomb, Mance, 60, 65
Lipstick Traces, 174
literature, 3–9, 14, 45, 64, 67, 115, 117, 125, 136, 145–46, 148, 165, 171–72, 190, 192–93
Little Richard, 48, 50–51, 59, 67, 85, 87, 121, 162
"Living for the City," 161–62, 186, 189
local music, 16, 36, 39, 41, 43, 55, 63, 65, 77, 147, 149, 163, 169, 182, 191
Lomax, Alan, 16, 26–27, 72
London Calling, 175, 181–84
"London Calling," 182–85
Lorca, Federico García, 132–33, 141, 143
"Lord Randal," 64, 71
Lords, The, 106
Lott, Eric, 49
Louie Bluie, 59
Love and Theft, 63, 83
"Love Me or Leave Me," 166
"Love Sick," 83
Lowell, Robert, 6, 37–38, 72, 88, 130–31
Luce, Clare, 108
Luce, Henry, 108
"Lucy in the Sky with Diamonds," 43, 95, 135
"Lunch Poems," 41

MacDonald, Dwight, 130–31
"Maggie's Farm," 72
Magical Mystery Tour, 97, 126
"Magic Bus, The," 125–26, 135
Mailer, Norman, 48, 57, 130–31, 135, 179
Malick, Terrence, 152
Malraux, André, 24
Mann, Manfred, 10
"Mannish Boy," 31
Manzarek, Ray, 98, 103–6, 110, 115

Ma Rainey, 20, 32, 35, 42
"Ma Rainey," 20
Marcus, Greil, 58, 151, 174
Margolin, Bob, 35
Margouleff, Bob, 161
Marley, Bob, 178
Marriage of Heaven and Hell, The, 107, 129
Masked and Anonymous, 83
Master and Margarita, The, 100
Matassa, Cosimo, 49
Mattison, Mike, 119, 163, 166
"Maybellene," 50, 52–55, 68
Mayfield, Curtis, 9, 147, 186
M'Butu, Count, 26
McCartney, Paul, 8, 9, 32, 44, 46, 71, 88, 89–90, 92–95, 118, 147
McClure, Michael, 106
McDowell, Mississippi Fred, 27
McLaren, Malcolm, 174
McLuhan, Marshall, 86
media, 57, 87, 89–90, 110, 122, 130, 147
Melle Mel, 186–89
"Memories of West Street and Lepke," 37–38
"Memphis Blues, The," 16–17
"Mercy Mercy Me (the Ecology)," 159
Merry Pranksters, 89, 97, 125–27
Merwin, W. S., 131
"Message, The," 186–89
meter, 9, 11–12, 21, 27, 37, 72, 78, 105
Mezzrow, Mezz, 36
"Midnight Rambler," 101–2
Miller, James, 49
Mingus, Charles, 23–24, 46
Miracles, 157, 160
Mitchell, Joni, 3, 7, 9, 15, 32, 43, 46, 54, 71, 78, 80–81, 91, 103, 109, 147, 166, 194
Moby Dick, 45
Modern Lovers, 174
Modern Times, 63, 83
"Mojo Hand," 142
"Molly Means," 20
Monk, Thelonious, 21, 46
"Monkey Man," 98
Monterey Pop, 127–28
Moody Blues, 9, 43, 81, 126
"Moondog House, The," 48
"Moonlight Drive," 106–7

Moore, Marianne, 19, 88
Morgan, Bill, 67
Morrison, Andy, 104
Morrison, Anne, 104
Morrison, Jim, 9, 44, 51, 71, 88, 103–18, 129, 139–41, 147
Morrison, Sterling, 81
Morrison Hotel, 117
Mortimer, Lee, 48, 55
"Mother's Little Helper," 99, 129
"Motorpsycho Nitemare," 68–70
Motown, 154–56, 159–60
Motown Revue, 154
"Move It On Over," 28
"Mr. Crowley," 139
"Mr. Tambourine Man," 72, 161
Muddy Waters, 31, 35, 49, 52, 60–61, 72, 83, 98, 118, 142
Murray, Albert, 24–25, 32
Murvin, Junior, 180
music: African traditions, 7, 25–28, 37, 55, 74, 81, 139, 142, 147, 161, 187; bebop, 21–22, 24, 48, 67, 185; bluegrass, 127; blues, 3–9, 13, 15–21, 24–25, 27–43, 45–46, 52–53, 56–58, 60–66, 68, 70–78, 81–83, 90–94, 97–98, 100–103, 106, 117–18, 119–21, 125, 127, 135, 140, 142–43, 146–48, 150, 160, 162, 164, 166, 172, 185, 191–92, 194–95; classical, 52, 81, 94, 106, 127, 166; country, 9, 52–53, 81–82, 120, 163, 165, 173, 175, 189, 191; dance, 8, 21, 140, 178; field hollers, 27, 29, 37–39; folk, 6, 20, 28, 46, 56–68, 70–71, 75, 78, 81, 83, 85, 87, 90–92, 94, 120–21, 135, 139, 148, 163, 166, 176, 190–92; funk, 161, 184–85; hip-hop, 8–9, 139, 172, 184–86; Indian, 93, 94, 128; jazz, 4, 6, 12, 15–25, 31, 36–37, 39, 46, 48, 55, 73, 81, 94, 120, 127–28, 139–40, 147, 160, 166, 185, 189; pop, 8, 52, 57, 68, 71, 78, 81–82, 100, 106, 121–22, 139, 155, 157, 163, 180, 194; popular, 3–4, 8–9, 12, 15, 63, 65, 70, 85, 94, 124, 127, 146–48, 151, 165, 176, 186, 194; punk, 9, 34, 172–86; rap, 8–9, 82, 172, 184–89; reggae, 178–80, 184; rhythm and blues, 48–49, 52, 54–55, 68, 82, 119, 155–57, 160, 168, 175, 189; rock, 3, 5–9, 15–16, 21, 24–25, 28, 34–35, 38, 43, 45–52, 54–57, 63, 65, 67, 70–74, 77–78,

81–83, 85, 87, 89–92, 94–95, 100–101, 103–6, 109, 114–18, 119–21, 124–29, 134–35, 138–42, 147–48, 150, 152, 163, 167, 172–75, 178, 180, 184, 187, 189, 191–95; soul, 160, 163, 166, 185; spirituals, 7, 29, 37–39, 154, 185; work songs, 7, 29, 37–38, 58
Music of My Mind, 161
"My Cherie Amour," 160
Myrow, Fred, 116
mysticism, 41, 81, 98, 120

Naked Lunch, 89
Nash, Graham, 80
Nebraska, 153
"Negro Dancers," 18–19
Negro Work Songs, 27
Neuwirth, Bob, 123
Nevin, Allan, 152
New American Poetry, 1945–1960, The, 105
New Creatures, The, 106
New Orleans, LA, 36–37, 40, 49, 77, 117, 140, 189
New Poets of England and America, 105
Newport Folk Festival, 72, 93
"New St. Louis Blues," 20
Newsweek, 66, 95, 151
New York City, NY, 17, 21, 32, 56, 67, 77, 91, 92, 98, 115, 135, 161–62, 174, 186
New York Dolls, 174
New York School, 41–42
New York Times, 115, 172
Nico, 115
Nietzsche, Friedrich, 104
Night and the City, 47
"Night Time Is the Right Time," 35
"19th Nervous Breakdown," 99
Nobel Prize, 3, 45, 145
No Direction Home, 60, 123
No Doubt, 185
No One Here Gets Out Alive, 115, 118
"North Country Blues," 66
"Norwegian Wood (This Bird Has Flown)," 11
"Not to Touch the Earth," 115
Now and Then, 185
"Nowhere Man," 93
Nugent, Ted, 135
Nyro, Laura, 9, 166

O'Connor, Flannery, 152
Ode to Billie Joe, 163
"Ode to Billie Joe," 163–65, 169, 193
Odetta, 66
Odyssey, The, 45
O'Hara, Frank, 37, 41, 193
Oldham, Andrew, 92, 98
O'Leno, Phil, 104
Olsen, Tillie, 171
Olson, Charles, 21–22
One Flew Over the Cuckoo's Nest, 126
On the Road, 15, 67, 74, 89
"On the Road Again," 72
On the Waterfront, 47
Orbison, Roy, 148
Orejuela, Fernando, 185
Orlovsky, Peter, 89

Pabón-Colón, Jessica Nydia, 186
Pack, Robert, 105
Paganini, Niccolò, 138–39
Page, Jimmy, 139
Palladino, Grace, 47, 50
Palmer, Robert, 16, 37
Parker, Charlie, 21, 46, 67
Parsons, Gram, 81, 100, 140
Patton, Charley, 40–41, 61, 100
Paul, Clarence, 160
Pearlman, Sandy, 181
Pegg, Bruce, 51
Pence, Charlotte, 5
Pennebaker, D. A., 121, 123, 127–28
"People Get Ready," 186
People's History of the United States, A, 153
performance, 4, 8, 11–13, 30, 32, 35, 45, 49, 50, 52, 59, 64, 66, 72–73, 78, 80, 85, 88, 91–93, 103–4, 107, 113, 115–17, 122, 126–27, 139, 153–54, 163, 166–67, 172, 176, 180
Perkins, Carl, 51, 162
Perkins, Pinetop, 35
Perr, Harvey, 115
personae, 6, 39, 46, 51–52, 59, 63, 70–71, 83, 85–87, 90–92, 94, 97, 100, 102–3, 118, 121–24, 140, 146
personal. *See* confessional
Phillips, "Daddy-O" Dewey, 48–49
Phillips, Sam, 48–49

Planet News, 131
Plant, Robert, 35
Plath, Sylvia, 37, 42–43, 88, 131
Pocket History of the United States, A, 153
Poe, Edgar Allen, 82, 193
Poetics of American Song Lyrics, The, 5
poetic song verse, 3–14, 24, 27–28, 33, 36, 38, 45, 62–63, 65, 67–68, 70, 72, 78, 82, 92, 101, 118, 119–20, 135, 139, 141, 145–46, 149, 156, 161, 163, 165–67, 169, 172–74, 176, 181, 186, 189, 191–95
poetry, 3–11, 14, 15–27, 31, 36, 38–43, 46, 52–54, 62–67, 70–72, 75–78, 80–81, 83, 85–90, 92–93, 100, 103–7, 109, 111, 114–18, 119–24, 127, 129, 131–36, 138–41, 145–49, 154, 165, 172, 185–87, 190–95
Poetry of Pop, The, 5, 8
Poetry of Rock, The, 5
Poetry Readings in the Cellar, 23
"Police and Thieves," 180
politics, 25, 32, 46, 52, 54, 66–67, 70, 90, 110, 114, 122, 129, 149, 151, 153, 157, 161, 167, 173, 175–76, 178–80, 183–85
"Portland Coliseum," 89
Pound, Ezra, 19, 67, 105
Presley, Elvis, 28, 47, 48–51, 54, 57, 67, 121, 123, 139, 150, 152, 180, 182
"Pretty Peggy-O," 63
"Pride and Joy," 155
Prime Green, 125
Prince, 9, 167
Prince Far I, 178
production, 3–4, 10, 12–13, 58, 65, 87, 121, 136, 146, 148, 168, 178, 181, 186
"Promised Land," 56
Prothero, Allan, 27
"Proverb of Hell," 107
psychedelia, 43, 89, 92–94, 96, 100, 109, 124, 126–29, 132, 134–36, 140, 148, 150
Psycho, 69

Quadrophenia, 148

race, 8, 12–13, 17–19, 24–27, 34–40, 46, 48–52, 55–58, 60–62, 66, 75, 98, 103, 121, 154–56, 160, 161–62, 167–68, 171, 173, 178–81, 186, 194–95

Rachell, Yank, 59–60
Rage to Survive, 166
"Rainy Day Women #12 & 35," 78
Raitt, Bonnie, 109, 147
Rampersad, Arnold, 19
Ramsey, Guthrie P., Jr., 21
Ransom, John Crowe, 43, 88
Rap and Hip Hop Culture, 185
"Rapper's Delight," 186
Reagan, Ronald, 153, 173
Really the Blues, 36
Rebel Without a Cause, 47
Rebennack, Mac, 140
Reckless Daughter, 15
Redding, Otis, 9, 103, 127
Red Hot and Blue, 49
Reed, Jimmy, 51
Reed, Lou, 9, 81, 147, 172, 194
Reeves, Martha, 160
religion, 34, 41, 81, 131, 135, 137–38, 152, 154, 160, 178, 180
"Revolution Will Not Be Televised, The," 139
Revolver, 81, 89, 93, 128
Rexroth, Kenneth, 17, 23, 71
rhyme, 5, 9, 11, 18, 20, 31, 53–54, 73, 79–81, 96, 99, 102, 123–24, 165, 186
rhythm, 5, 9, 18, 24–27, 33, 39, 44, 48–49, 52, 54–55, 68, 71, 74, 78, 80, 106, 112, 127–28, 139, 142, 154, 156, 158, 160, 164, 168–69, 182, 185, 189
Richards, Keith, 32, 46, 57, 98–99, 101–3, 118, 162
Ricks, Christopher, 15, 64
"Right On," 159
Rilke, Rainer Maria, 127, 133
Rimbaud, Arthur, 67, 72, 110, 114, 140
Rimbaud and Jim Morrison, 15
Rise and Fall of Ziggy Stardust and the Spiders from Mars, The, 172
River, The, 152
"Riverbank Blues," 20
Rivers, Johnny, 55
Robertson, Robbie, 78, 89
Robinson, E. A., 94
Robinson, Smokey, 9, 155, 160
Robinson, Sylvia, 186
"Rock and Roll Music," 54

"Rock Around the Clock," 28, 54
"Rocket 88," 48
Rock 'n' Roll High School, 151
"Rock 'n' Roll Party," 48
Rodgers, Jimmie, 52
Rogers, Bobby, 160
Rolling Stone, 106, 117, 118, 150, 157, 191
Rolling Stones, 3, 9, 15, 43, 62, 82, 85, 86, 92, 97–103, 115, 126, 129, 134–35, 147, 150–51, 174, 194
Rolling Stones Rock and Roll Circus, The, 126
Rolling Thunder Revue, 71, 91, 140
"Roll Over Beethoven," 51, 54, 194
Romantic poets, 81, 87–88, 106–7, 138–40
Romine, Scott, 32
Rose, Tricia, 185
Rothchild, Paul, 109, 116
Rotolo, Suze, 56–57, 59–60, 67, 91
Rough and Rowdy Ways, 63, 82–83
Rubber Soul, 93, 128
Rucker, Ursula, 172

"Sad Eyed Lady of the Lowlands," 78
"Safe European Home," 181
Salewicz, Chris, 175
Sanders, Ed, 131
Sandinista!, 184
San Francisco Renaissance, 21, 23–24, 71, 87–88, 105, 185
Santana, Carlos, 43, 167
"Satisfaction," 98–99
"Save the Children," 159
"School Days," 54–55
Scorsese, Martin, 60, 71, 91, 123, 140
Scott-Heron, Gil, 3–4, 8, 9, 15, 32, 81, 139, 147, 185–86, 189
Seeger, Pete, 72, 85, 110
"See that My Grave Is Kept Clean," 63
"Self as Agent, The," 86
Sex Pistols, 9, 175–76, 182
Sexton, Anne, 37, 39, 88, 99
sexuality and sexualization, 35, 49–51, 115, 118, 146, 167
sexual relations, 12, 35, 48, 55–56, 102–3, 106–7, 112, 126, 152, 154
Sgt. Pepper's Lonely Hearts Club Band, 81, 92, 94–97, 126, 156, 163, 165

"Sgt. Pepper's Lonely Hearts Club Band," 95
Shake, Rattle, and Rock, 47
Shakespeare, William, 45–46
Shall We Gather at the River, 131
"Shaman's Blues," 115
Shanghai Express, 105
Shankar, Ravi, 127–28
"Sheep Child, The," 43
"She Loves You," 11
Shelton, Robert, 66
"She's Leaving Home," 95
"Shoo-Be-Doo-Be-Doo," 160
"Should I Stay or Should I Go?," 184
Shout, Sister, Shout, 162
Simon, Paul, 7, 78, 147
Simone, Nina, 9, 55, 136, 166–67, 172
Simonon, Paul, 175–76, 182
Simpson, Louis, 105
Sinatra, Frank, 46–47, 155
Six Gallery, 87–88
slavery, 25–26, 28, 37, 60, 74, 103, 178
Slick, Grace, 129
Small Talk at 125th and Lenox, 81
Smith, Bessie, 20, 29, 35
Smith, Harry, 57–60
Smith, Howard, 115
Smith, Patti, 45, 140, 147, 172, 174
Smith, Willie "Big Eyes," 35
Snoop Dogg, 9, 185
Snyder, Gary, 132
Snyder, John, 166
social class, 49, 58, 66, 71, 73–74, 76, 165, 171, 173–75, 179
Soft Parade, The, 115
"Somebody To Love," 128
Sometimes a Great Notion, 125
Song and Dance Man III, 15
"Song for Bob Dylan," 81–82
"Song for Woody," 63
"Song of Myself," 82, 88
Songs of Leonard Cohen, 81, 135–36
sonics, 4, 13, 28, 43, 64, 71, 74, 78, 80–81, 85, 93, 121–23, 135–36, 161, 182, 184, 194
Sornberger, John, 16
Sornberger, Lisa, 16
Soulful Moods of Marvin Gaye, The, 155
"Sound of Silence," 78

Southern Road, 19–20
Spaniard in the Works, A, 88
Specialty, 48
Spector, Phil, 89, 148, 178
Spoelstra, Mark, 59
Spottswood, Dick, 62
Springsteen, Bruce, 5–7, 9, 10, 13, 121, 147–54, 173, 175, 180, 182, 184–85, 194
Starr, Edwin, 155
Stax, 48
"Steady Rollin'," 35
Stegner, Wallace, 126
Steinbeck, John, 152
Steiner, Rudolf, 58
"Step Away from Them, A," 41
Sternberg, Josef von, 105
Stevens, Guy, 184
Stevens, Wallace, 17, 19, 88
Stevenson, Mickey, 160
Stewart, Bill, 49
Stewart, Rod, 9, 147
Sticky Fingers, 100, 103
Stiff Records, 175
Still Bill, 168, 171
Stills, Stephen, 46, 71, 78–80, 103, 168
Stipe, Michael, 5
"St. Louis Blues," 17–18, 20
Stoller, Michael, 48
Stone, Jesse, 48–49
Stone, Robert, 125, 128
Stone, Sly, 161
Storz, Todd, 49
"Strange Brew," 135
Strange Days, 115
Strong, Barrett, 155
Strummer, Joe, 173–85
"Stuck Inside of Mobile with the Memphis Blues Again," 78
Suarez, Ernest, 192
"Subterranean Homesick Blues," 46, 54, 67, 72–73, 75–77, 122–23, 189
Suedeheads, 178–79
Sugar Hill Gang, 186
Sugar Hill Records, 186
Sugerman, Danny, 106, 109, 115, 118
Sundown, 160
"Sunflower Sutra," 88

Sun Ra, 140
Sun Records, 48, 74
Sunset Boulevard, 47
"Supermarket in California, A," 87
supernatural, the, 42, 57, 75–76, 118, 120, 136, 139–40, 142
"Superstition," 162
surrealism, 41–43, 64, 75, 77–78, 81, 87, 93, 95, 101, 105–6, 110, 117, 120, 123, 131–32, 136, 148
"Suzanne," 136–38
Sweetheart of the Rodeo, 81
"Sweet Little Sixteen," 54
Symbolist poets, 81, 87, 110, 140, 147, 150
"Sympathy for the Devil," 43, 100–101

Talking Book, 161
"Talking World War III Blues," 65
"Talkin' New York," 63
Tate, Allen, 6–7, 72
Taylor, Hound Dog, 33–34
Taylor, James, 147, 161
Teaching of Don Juan, The, 156
Tedeschi Trucks Band, 191
Tempest, The, 63, 83
Ten Days that Shook the World, 180
Terrell, Tammi, 155
Text and Drugs and Rock 'n' Roll, 5, 71
Tharpe, Rosetta, 162
"That's Alright," 48
Theatre and Its Double, The, 108
Their Satanic Majesties Request, 100, 126, 134–35
"34 Blues," 40
Thomas, Rufus, 48–49
Thompson, Hunter S., 125, 131
"Thunder Road," 151–52
Tibetan Book of the Dead, The, 93
Time magazine, 122, 130, 151
Time Out of Mind, 63, 83
Times They Are a-Changin', The, 63, 65–66, 91
Timperley, Clive, 175
"Tin Roof Blues," 20
"To Be Young, Gifted and Black," 167
Todorov, Tzvetan, 120
Together Through Life, 83

Tommy, 81, 126, 148
"Tomorrow Never Knows," 93–94
"2 Kool 2 B 4-Gotten," 192
"Too Much Monkey Business," 46, 55, 72–76, 189
Tosches, Nick, 46
Touch of Evil, A, 47
Townshend, Pete, 125, 173, 182
Tracy, Steven C., 18–19, 32
"Tradition and the Individual Talent," 86
transformation, 4, 63, 70, 77, 85, 88–92, 94, 97, 103, 106–7, 113, 118–19, 124, 128, 132, 135, 140–41, 186, 194
Tranströmer, Tomas, 133
"Traveling Riverside Blues," 35
Treanor, Vince, 116–17
Trickster Makes This World, The, 122
"Truckin'," 127
Tucker, Maureen, 81
Turner, Ike, 48
"Tutti Frutti," 50
Tuttle, Richard, 192

Ulysses, 81
"Unknown Soldier, The," 115
"Uptight (Everything Is Alright)," 160
USA Confidential, 48, 55

Vallejo, César, 133, 136–37
Van DePitte, David, 156
Van Morrison, 3, 9, 15, 43, 46, 71, 81, 147, 194
Van Ronk, Dave, 57–58
Van Zandt, Little Steven, 185
Velvet Underground, 89, 174
Velvet Underground and Nico, The, 81
verse practices, 8, 11, 18–21, 30, 37–38, 54, 64–65, 67, 72, 77–81, 87, 93–94, 96–97, 99, 102–3, 106, 146–47, 165
Vincent, Gene, 180
violence, 34–35, 52, 61, 102, 154, 179, 184
voice, 3–5, 13, 16–17, 20, 28, 34, 38, 43, 77, 83, 89, 91, 96, 99, 110, 146, 157–58, 162–68, 171
"Voodoo Chile (Slight Return)," 43, 141–43

"Wail," 88
Waiting for the Sun, 115–16
"Waking Early Sunday Morning," 130
"Waking from Sleep," 42
Wald, Elijah, 60
Wald, Gayle, 162
Walker, Margaret, 19, 20–21
"Walk on Water," 182
Walser, Robert, 48
"War," 155
Ward, Justin, 192
Warhol, Andy, 89, 115
Warner, Simon, 5, 71, 89
Waste Land, The, 43, 95, 148, 150
WCHB, 160
WDIA, 48–49
Weary Blues, The, 17–18, 23
Weill, Kurt, 3
Wells, Mary, 155
"Werewolves of London," 193
West, Vivienne, 174
Weston, Kim, 155
What Happened, Miss Simone?, 167
What's Going On, 154, 156–57, 160, 164
"What's Going On," 157–58, 186, 189
"What's Happening Brother," 158–59
WHBQ, 48
"When the Music's Over," 115
White, Bukka, 31, 63, 85
White, Josh, 66
White, Ronnie, 160
"(White Man) in Hammersmith Palais," 179–80
"White Man's Burden, The," 130
"White Negro, The," 48, 57, 179
"White Rabbit," 43, 129, 135
"Whitey's on the Moon," 186, 189
Whitfield, Norman, 155
Whitman, Walt, 82, 86–88, 146, 194–95
Who, The, 9, 15, 81, 85, 125–27, 135, 148, 150–51, 176
"Who Do You Love?," 72–76
"Wholy Holy," 159
Wild, the Innocent, and the E Street Shuffle, The, 149
Wild One, The, 47, 51
Will, George, 153, 173
Williams, Big Joe, 61–62
Williams, Hank, 28, 52
Williams, Lucinda, 78, 189–92

Williams, Miller, 78, 189–91
Williams, Saul, 172
Williams, William Carlos, 17, 39–40, 105
Wilson, Nancy, 26
Wind, The, 82
Winters, Terry, 192
"With a Little Help from My Friends," 95
"With God on Our Side," 65
Withers, Bill, 9, 147, 162, 168–72
Wolfe, Tom, 97, 125, 131
Wonder, Stevie, 6, 9, 147–48, 154, 159–62, 186, 189
Woolf, Virginia, 146
wordplay, 4, 9, 24, 70, 75–76, 80, 85, 93, 187
Workingman's Dead, 127
Wright, James, 37, 41–42, 131
"Wrong Turning in American Poetry, A," 132
Wyman, Bill, 101

Yaffe, David, 15, 17
Yeats, William Butler, 38
Yellow Submarine, 97
Yes Yes Y'all, 185
Young, Izzy, 60
Young, Kevin, 57
Young, Neil, 9, 71, 109, 147, 190
Your Hit Parade, 49
"You've Got to Hide Your Love Away," 93

Zapple, 90
Zero Time, 161
Zevon, Warren, 9, 78, 82, 147, 193
Zinn, Howard, 153
Zwigoff, Terry, 59

About the Authors

Credit: Alison Umminger

Mike Mattison is a native of Minneapolis and a graduate of Harvard University. As a touring blues singer and songwriter with the Derek Trucks Band and the Tedeschi Trucks Band he has won two Grammy awards for Best Blues Album, five Blues Music awards from the Blues Music Foundation, and two Canadian Maple Blues awards. He is also a founding member of the duo Scrapomatic. Mattison has published creative nonfiction and coedits, with Ernest Suarez, "Hot Rocks: Song and Verse," a regular feature in *Five Points: A Journal of Literature and Art* from 2013 to 2020 and in *Literary Matters*

Credit: Mia Ferris-Artiga

since 2021. He serves on the Council of the Association of Literary Scholars, Critics, and Writers.

Ernest Suarez is David M. O'Connell Professor of English at the Catholic University of America in Washington, DC, and the executive director of the Association of Literary Scholars, Critics, and Writers. His publications include *James Dickey and the Politics of Canon*, *Southbound: Interviews with Southern Poets*, an edition of bluesman Jim Dickinson's memoir *I'm Just Dead, I'm Not Gone*, and many essays. He was selected as the James E. Dornan Memorial Professor of the Year at Catholic University and the District of Columbia Professor of the Year by the Carnegie Foundation for the Advancement of Teaching, and was a Senior Fulbright Lecturer in Spain and China. He earned his PhD at the University of Wisconsin–Madison.

www.ingramcontent.com/pod-product-compliance
Lightning Source LLC
Chambersburg PA
CBHW030618230426
43661CB00053B/2053